Edith Head's HOLLYWOOD

Edith Head's

Edith Head & Paddy Calistro

With a Foreword by Bette Davis

HOLLYWOOD

E. P. DUTTON, INC. | NEW YORK

Published in the United States by
E. P. Dutton, Inc., 2 Park Avenue, New York, N.Y. 10016

Library of Congress Cataloging in Publication Data
Head, Edith.
Edith Head's Hollywood.
1. Head, Edith. 2. Costume designers—California—
Los Angeles—Biography. 3. Hollywood (Los Angeles, Calif.)—
Social life and customs.   I. Calistro, Paddy.   II. Title.
TT505.H4A33 1983   791.43′026′0924 [B]   83-5700

ISBN: 0-525-24200-7
Published simultaneously in Canada by
Fitzhenry & Whiteside Limited, Toronto

Designed by Nancy Etheredge

W

10 9 8 7 6 5 4 3 2 1

First Edition

To SNM

_____

FOREWORD

Edith Head was one of Hollywood's greatest designers. She was an amazing woman in a field that was dominated by men in the 1930s and 1940s. While other designers were busy starring their clothes in a film, Edith was making clothes to suit a character; for her, the character always came first.

Through the work of a fine costume designer, an actor or actress can *become* the character. We may rehearse our lines, our movements, and our expressions, but not until we finally slip into the costumes does everything come together so that we actually *become* the character. If we are not comfortable in those clothes, if they do not project the character, the costume designer has failed us.

Edith Head never failed.

She always took time to read the script and understand the character. She managed to make you look as good (or as bad!) as the script allowed. If the wardrobe was to be chic, it was chic. But if the director wanted a boozy old lady like Apple Annie to be wrapped in rags in *Pocketful of Miracles,* she dressed you perfectly in character.

Edith Head saw us through six decades of film fashion. The list of her films includes some of the best motion pictures ever made. For years the men and women who dressed the cast went unheralded; some didn't even get screen credit. Finally, in 1948, the Academy of Motion Picture Arts and Sciences recognized the costume designers for their contributions. For her work, Edith Head received thirty-five nominations and eight Oscars, more than any other costume designer.

My own memento of Edith's long career hangs on the wall of my home: a sketch of that fabulous brown cocktail dress Margo Channing wore in *All About Eve.* I bought the dress and I treasure the sketch. It's simply signed *To Bette, from Edith.*

In these pages you'll read her story the way she would have told it—and, indeed, *did* tell it in part, before her death. The tale is filled with humor, frustration, and above all, glamour. For you see, Edith Head's life was all about glamour—sixty-odd years of it —in the most glamorous place in the world, Hollywood.

Bette Davis

Hollywood, 1983

PREFACE AND ACKNOWLEDGMENTS

Edith Head was undoubtedly Hollywood's most famous costume designer as well as its most prolific. Her career spanned fifty-eight years of movie making. In those years she dressed almost every major star who shone in the industry, and she became as famous as most of them. Just a few weeks before she died, she was still waving at fans as the Universal City Studio Tour stopped at her bungalow.

Edith Head's story is as fascinating as the history of the film industry itself, for she helped shape the Hollywood we know today. At the time of her death, she was the last great costume designer to be under contract to a major studio. As her teacher and colleague Travis Banton once said, "She outlasted all of us."

I first met Edith Head in 1972. She was to be my first celebrity interview. Another shopping center was opening in the vast San Fernando Valley, and the bespectacled Miss Head, the very same woman I had watched so often on Art Linkletter's *House Party* as a child, was there to cut the ribbon. And I, the novice fashion reporter, was there to ask her the questions she had never been asked before. (Of course, I would find out years later, there were none.) She made me feel important that day, and she even called me to express her thanks when the article appeared in print. Her manners were impeccable.

Our paths crossed many times over the next nine years, but our relationship never went beyond the confines of business. She was, above all, the consummate professional. At social functions she could entertain and control any group with her witty anecdotes about the Hollywood she knew so well. People were fascinated by this wiry little fashion legend, who still wore the same suits that had become her trademark on the Linkletter show. The last time I encountered her, in the summer of 1981, she was dressed in a snappy red suit, signing autographs. She was vibrant.

Two weeks after Edith Head died, E. P. Dutton's senior editor, Bill Whitehead, called me to ask if I was interested in completing an autobiography that the costume designer had started in 1979. Hours of taped interviews, conducted by journalist Norma Lee Browning, would provide the foundation of the book, and my own study of Edith Head's contributions to the Hollywood costume design world would fill in the blanks. After accepting the project, I learned that very little has been written about the history of Hollywood costumes. Six books were helpful to me in my work. First is Susan Perez Prichard's exhaustively researched *Film Costume: An Annotated Bibliography* (Scarecrow Press, 1981), which proved to be invaluable. *Those Glorious Glamour Years* by Margaret J. Bailey (Citadel Press, 1982), *Hollywood Costume Design* by David Chierichetti (Harmony, 1976), *In a Glamorous Fashion* by the late W. Robert Lavine (Scribners, 1980), *Costume Design in the Movies* by Elizabeth Leese (BCW Publishing Ltd., 1976), and *Hollywood Costume* by Dale McConathy and Diana

Vreeland (Abrams, 1976) were all important tools in researching the history of Edith Head and her thousand-plus films.

While this book is in large measure autobiographical, with a major portion told in Edith's own words, it is still, in the strictest sense, a career biography. There were many things Edith was secretive about—her maiden name, for instance. It took much digging to discover that she was born Edith Claire Posener, on October 28, 1897. Although she had told interviewers many different, interesting stories about her birthplace, county records (which she said had been burned in a courthouse fire) showed that she was born in San Bernardino, California, to Max Posener and the former Anna Levy. When her parents divorced and her mother remarried, Edith assumed her stepfather's surname, Spare, which she used throughout her school years. She frequently told a story of spending her early years first in Mexico and then in Searchlight, Nevada, playing with and dressing burros, much as other little girls would play with dolls. She claimed she never went to grammar school, yet a yellowed diploma indicates that in 1911 little Edith Spare graduated from elementary school in Redding, California, a town in the northern region of the state, far from the Mexican border. When she came to Los Angeles, she had to be tutored in mathematics, but she graduated with honors and went on to the University of California and then to Stanford University. It was shortly after beginning a teaching career that she returned to Southern California and found her niche in Hollywood.

When confronted about why she kept the details of her past so secret, she told people that those facts were unimportant. To her, the years that preceded her film career were boring. In this book Edith doesn't comment on her early days. She remembers Hollywood.

My own research accompanies Edith's recollections. Where her memory proved to be mistaken, I have supplemented her account with factual material in my narrative. Edith's words appear in italic type, to separate her story from mine.

My research encompassed months of study at the Academy of Motion Picture Arts and Sciences Library in Beverly Hills, the

American Film Institute Libraries in Los Angeles and Washington, D.C., the Archives of the Wisconsin Center for Film and Theater Research at the University of Wisconsin in Madison, the Lincoln Center Library for the Performing Arts and the Museum of Modern Art in New York City, the Los Angeles County Museum of Art film department, and the libraries of the Fashion Institute of Technology in New York and the Fashion Institute of Design and Merchandising in Los Angeles. The staff members of each of these institutions were exceedingly generous with their time and knowledge, and they should consider themselves a part of this book.

What provided the most insight into the career of Edith Head were the interviews with the people who actually lived through that era with her. Her personal friends and co-workers, the stars, the Paramount and Universal executives, other designers—these are the people who know the Edith Head story and who shared so many of their memories with me. To all the following people I offer my heartfelt thanks for their unselfish contributions to this project. They are, in alphabetical order: Carol Burnett, Arda Clure, Renie Conley, Bette Davis, the late John Engstead, Robbie Fisher, Lily Fonda, Jean Tanner Full, Hubert de Givenchy, Cary Grant, Walter Hoffman, Richard Hopper, Elois Jenssen, Shirley Judge, Pauline Kessinger, Dorothy Lamour, Charles LeMaire, Art Linkletter, Bob Mackie, Steve Martin, Al Nickel, Donna Peterson, Marion Price, Carl Reiner, Helen Rose, Dennis Schoonderwoerd, Howard Shoup, Barbara Stanwyck, Myrtle Tyson, June Van Dyke, and Paul Zastupnevich. And without Norma Lee Browning's excellent and dedicated work, this book would be sadly lacking in any commentary from Miss Head.

There are other people to whom I owe a major debt of gratitude. Each of them knows the knowledge, expertise, support, and dedication they shared with me, but they should be recognized. They are, also in alphabetical order: Joan Cohen, Carol Cullen, Carol Epstein, Sam Gill, Betty Goodwin, Donnis Goodwin, Josephine Harper, Timothy Hawkins, Bertha Kelly, Ruth La Ferla, Christian and Joan Larsen, Maureen Lasher, Donna Lawson, Gloria Luckinbill, Michael Maron, David and Beatrice McAuley, Lisa Mosher, Paul Myers, James Rahman, Van-Martin Rowe, Anne

Schlosser, David Shepard, Sylvia Sheppard, Timothy Stansbury, Roy and Eleanor Stroup, Robert Vallier, Mark Wanamaker, Kathryn Welker, and Ruth Kramer Ziony.

My fondest thanks to Anne Bogart, Helen Corrigan, Stacy Endres, Barbara Friedman, Annette Samet, Bill Whitehead, and my mother, Ann Calistro, for their constant and invaluable assistance and encouragement. Each of them gave me the right push at the right time, and allowed me to go on.

There are no words to express my gratitude and love to my brother, Ronald Haver, for his enthusiasm, his ready wit, and his limitless knowledge of the Hollywood he treasures. Without him, there would be no book. Finally, to my husband, Scott Nelson McAuley, and my son, David George Calistro McAuley, my thanks for sharing so much of their lives with *Edith Head's Hollywood*.

PADDY CALISTRO MC AULEY
Santa Monica, California
1983

Edith Head's HOLLYWOOD

ONE

When the dress was zipped up, Edith Head burst out laughing. Yes, the costume fit perfectly, her star cut a rather sexy, shapely figure in it, and it was exactly what the script required. But the legendary costume designer could barely contain herself.

"I guess I've come full circle when I design the exact dress for Steve Martin that I did for Barbara Stanwyck. He looks very funny in it, doesn't he?" Edith said to Carl Reiner, director of *Dead Men Don't Wear Plaid* (1982).

She was delighted that almost forty years after she had dressed Stanwyck as the ill-fated heroine of *Double Indemnity* (1944), she'd be dressing the actor/comedian as her blond-wigged double. Reiner had been convinced that only Edith Head could give his spoof of 1940s private-eye films the period flair it needed. "When Edith Head said she'd take the assignment, I knew we had a good movie," he remembers. For Martin, working with Edith Head was a landmark in his film career. "I felt a sense of history working with her and I wanted to live up to what she represented. Going into her design salon for the first time was like entering some movie mogul's office. The Oscars were all around. The design sketches were on the walls. When we mentioned an old movie, like *Notorious,* she went to her file and pulled out the *original* sketch from the 1940s. Then she'd mull over how we could reproduce the costume today to make it look exactly like the original version. She was so unlike a lot of other people in the industry—she took a great deal of interest in what she was doing. And she did her thing, perfectly."

Reiner remembers that first meeting, too. "Her bungalow was filled with dozens of little machines. She asked if I liked her sewing machine collection and I told her I loved it, but that they weren't actually sewing machines. They were Willcox-Gibbs straw and hat machines. She was shocked and explained that she'd been collecting them for years. Barbara Stanwyck had given her the first one, in the 1940s. No one had ever told her they were meant for sewing hats, and she was delighted to know something new about her collection. We became instant friends."

As soon as the discussions began about costumes for the new film, Edith pulled out her sketch pad and began offering rough drawings of possible designs for the film. Reiner requested that Edith transform Martin into the quintessential private investigator —a touch of Sam Spade, a touch of Dick Tracy, plus a touch of Steve Martin. In other scenes, such as the Stanwyck segment, Edith would be called upon to duplicate costumes that were used in twenty-one films from the 1940s. Clips from these old movies would be integrated into the new motion picture, with Martin, his co-star Rachel Ward, and the rest of the cast seemingly stepping into some of the old footage.

Edith approached *Dead Men* with all the enthusiasm she could muster for what she claimed was her 1,131st film. When she couldn't exactly duplicate an old fabric with a new one, she had a modern version silk-screened to match the original. She supervised fittings, making sure that Martin's trousers had just enough bags and pleats to reflect the 1940s styles, but that the jackets had enough subtle shaping through the shoulders to give him a touch of 1980s sex appeal. "I loved the clothes," Martin says. "So much so, that I bought some of her wonderful linen suits for my personal wardrobe. When people ask about them I say, 'It's an Edith Head.' "

For one scene that was later cut from the movie, she made a satin gown for Rachel Ward, which Martin was supposed to borrow and then slip into. As she fitted the dress on the comedian, she probably reflected on the days when she had dressed Bob Hope and Bing Crosby in their famous series of *Road* pictures. Hope, in the true spirit of comedy, loved to dress up in women's clothes, but Crosby never agreed to be seen in drag. Martin, like Hope, had no inhibitions about wearing the satin gown and Stanwyck's dress—in fact, his humor blossomed in them.

On the set, Edith watched to make sure that every costume worked as she had planned it. Colleagues noticed that she would frequently become extremely fatigued. One day, virtually exhausted from the work, she fell asleep on a leather sofa, part of a set that had served as a private detective's office only a few hours before. Reiner peeked in on her and thought only "how sweet this dear little lady looked. If we had known how ill she was, we probably never would have let her take on the film. I'm glad we didn't know. She wanted to do the project. She was on the set the day we shot the last scenes. Two weeks later she was gone."

Edith Head went into the hospital almost immediately after completing the comedy. Two days before she would have turned eighty-four, she died of a progressive blood disease, clinically known as myeloid metaplasia. At her bedside was her housekeeper of thirty-six years, Myrtle Tyson. She left no relatives. A memorial service was attended by many of the people she had worked with in her Hollywood—the other costume designers, the cameramen, the guards from Paramount who still wore the uniforms she had designed so many years before, the directors, the moguls, the makeup artists, the commissary employees, the wardrobe employees, and several stars. Elizabeth Taylor was there, along with Loretta Young, Jane Wyman, Janet Leigh, Ann Sothern, George Peppard, and Roddy McDowall. The list of honorary pallbearers read like the cast of a Hollywood retrospective—Cary Grant, Charlton Heston, William Holden, Jack Lemmon, Paul Newman, Gregory Peck, Jimmy Stewart, Robert Wagner—yet none of them attended the church service.

It was Bette Davis, whom Edith had dressed in four films, who gave the eulogy. "A queen has left us, the queen of her profession. She will never be replaced. Her contribution to our industry in her field of design, her contribution to the taste of our town of Hollywood, her elegance as a person, her charms as a woman—none of us who worked with her will ever forget. . . . Goodbye, dear Edith. There will never be another you. Love from all of us, Bette."

TWO

Teaching French at Hollywood School for Girls in 1923 had its advantages: regular hours, summer vacations—and Cecilia and Katherine DeMille, daughters of Cecil B. Whenever DeMille was filming one of his more spectacular efforts at the studio, Hollywood School closed for a day while teachers and students headed for the lot to watch movies in the making.

Those treks to Famous Players–Lasky Studio at Sunset and Vine were French teacher Edith Head's first taste of the Hollywood she would come to know so well. Right there on the studio lot, the movieland fairy tale was all very real—the starlets cooing on command, the directors shouting into megaphones, the costumes dripping with glamour.

But for Edith it was just another day away from school. She wasn't especially star-struck. Impressed, yes. Overwhelmed, not at all. She rarely found time to go to the movies. Her concerns were far more this-worldly: how to run those art classes she was hired to teach along with the French. How to deal with a husband who drank too much. And how to pay the rent all summer—California teachers didn't get paid year-round in those days.

To keep pace with her precocious students, she enrolled in night classes at Otis Art Institute and later at Chouinard, a Los Angeles art school reputed to be one of the best in the States. Ever practical, she'd find five days' worth of lessons in what she learned at class one night a week. Her specialties were landscapes. If one of her girls wanted to draw the human body, Edith found a way to postpone the lesson until the next semester. At the time, she confided to friends that she didn't know the first thing about drawing lifelike silhouettes.

Her first husband, Charles Head, was the brother of one of her Chouinard cronies. A salesman for Super Refined Metals Company in Southern California, he and Edith had a relationship that was troubled from the start. They spent little time together. He traveled and worked; she continued to teach in Los Angeles. Their separations created an emotional distance far more destructive than the physical one. He began to drink, while Edith retreated into her own world. Charles's drinking clouded the times they could spend together and their lives became even more separate. Her staunch Catholic beliefs kept her married and perhaps, as she often reflected, helped her through an extremely trying period.

It was those art classes that eventually paved her way to the Paramount designers' studio. Howard Greer, chief designer at Famous Players–Lasky (which would eventually become Paramount), was looking for a sketch artist and placed a classified ad in the *Los Angeles Times*. Edith, in need of a summer job, applied and was called in for an interview, even though she knew nothing about drawing the human form and had no experience in costume design. Desperate but resourceful, she borrowed costume designs from a number of her classmates at Chouinard, signed her name to the sketches, and headed off to Paramount, her carpetbag portfolio bulging. Greer was noticeably impressed with her versatility (or her audacity—Edith was never sure which). She later reminisced about her borrowed portfolio:

I was studying seascape and all I could draw was oceans. I needed a portfolio, so I borrowed sketches—I didn't steal them. I asked everybody in the class for a few costume design sketches. And I had the most fantastic assortment you've ever seen in your life. When you get a class of forty to give you sketches, you get a nice selection.

It never occurred to me that it was quite dishonest. And all the students thought it was fun, too, just like a dare to see if I could get the job. I didn't say the work was mine. I said, "This is the sort of thing we do in our school."

Nobody really knows if Greer saw through her charade when he reviewed the portfolio, but in any event he hired her—at $50 a week, far more than double what a teacher made in those days. She could hardly believe it, and neither could her classmates.

The weeks that followed were a letdown. She had expected more glamour, more excitement. She rarely ever saw Howard Greer. He was locked in his spacious studio salon, designing for the important stars of the day—Pola Negri, Leatrice Joy, Gloria Swanson—actresses Edith would watch as they passed her tiny cubicle.

At first I just sat in the room with the other sketch artists and sketched. I never got down on the set to see the clothes. I never met the stars. But gradually this changed. Greer would bring me a little croquis, a thumbnail-size pencil sketch of a design, which I would enlarge in color for him. Then sometimes he would take me out in the workroom to watch him drape model figures with the garments made from these designs. It was like watching the drawings come to life.

Edith joined a pool of twelve Paramount artists, all trying to keep their jobs, all trying to fit the Hollywood artist's image.

Edith even dressed the part, complete with smock and beret. But her thick-lensed spectacles never fit her vision of herself as the young artist, so for years she took them off whenever she was photographed. She admitted that she hid behind them all through college, first at Berkeley, then when she earned her master's in Romance languages at Stanford.

She knew she wasn't half bad-looking. People had told her that her body was as alluring as any of the great stars Greer dressed, but she always focused on the minuses—the glasses, the broomstick-straight hair, and the flaw she tried so hard to hide, those teeth.

It wasn't long before she turned the glasses into a trademark and cropped her hair short with Dutch-boy bangs à la Louise Brooks. But she felt helpless about replacing her missing front incisors, so she carefully learned to smile without a trace of white. Her tight-lipped expressions were a reflection not so much of her temperament in those days as of her concern for those god-awful teeth. Twenty years later Barbara Stanwyck would cajole her into having them fixed:

I owe a great deal to Barbara for doing me a great favor that changed my life, or at least my personality. When we first began working on films together, she noticed a peculiar character quirk about me. I never smiled. She asked me why. Finally I told her. And showed her. Two of my front teeth had never grown in, not the ones smack in the middle but those on each side, the laterals, which left a conspicuous gap in my mouth. As a child I was teased and taunted for being toothless. I had two funny little pointed teeth in front. All the other kids made fun of me. They called me Beaver. So I grew up being self-conscious about my front teeth and not smiling. When I was old enough to have a career, I disciplined myself. I never smiled; I was very serious, horn-rimmed, dead-pan. Barbara would try anything to get me to smile. Finally she said, "Why don't you have your damn teeth fixed? People don't like people without teeth, so we're going to the dentist to get you some front teeth." She literally yanked me into her car and off we went.

8

Edith didn't meet Stanwyck until late in the 1930s. She had to live with her self-image of "Beaver" throughout her formative years in Hollywood. She often felt the urge to burst out flamboyantly and become the center of attention, but her vanity got in the way. It was easier to stay safely in the shadows, waiting her turn. She was still learning.

At Greer's request, Edith conjured a riding habit for an elegant woman in Central Park, a character in a DeMille film he was doing. When the designer saw the sketch, he complained that it was too ordinary for DeMille's outlandish taste. So she adapted it, as she would so often do in the years to come. Adaptation was an art she learned quickly and would prove to be a key to her whole career. She splashed gold paint on the boots, the hat, the whip. Flashy, yes; perfect DeMille fare.

I'd lived in California all my life. I knew who DeMille was. Everybody did. I knew he had horrible taste. He liked flashy things; he liked things that made people say, "What the hell is that?" He told us, "I never want anything shown to me as a design that you could possibly buy or wear. I want something original." I knew that the average person who rode horseback in Beverly Hills did not wear gold boots, so I assumed the average elegant lady in Central Park didn't either. DeMille loved it—no, he liked it. He never said he loved anything.

Since DeMille liked the sketch, Greer decided to give Edith more responsibility. It wasn't exactly the career she had dreamed of, but again she chalked it up to experience.

A young girl with no training who goes in on her first job as a sketch artist does not start off dressing a star. You go out in the workroom, you hand pins to a seamstress, you roll fabrics, you sharpen pencils, you do anything you're told. You do sketches if the designers have sketches to do, or you paint if you know how to paint. I could paint, so I was painting polka dots on six-foot butterfly wings for a fantasy scene in Herbert Brenon's Peter Pan *(1924). The next day I was taken off polka dots and given some small sketches to copy on silk. To break the monotony, I began adding my own creative touches. Nobody objected, so I became bolder and started throwing in my own original designs now and then.*

Edith was bored and ready to quit on numerous occasions, but she was making more money than she had as a teacher and felt a new sense of security. She continued to take night classes at Chouinard in an attempt to improve her sketching techniques. As always, she was a fast learner. To hide her dissatisfaction with the new job, she feigned enthusiasm, accepting every assignment willingly. She researched carefully and stayed away from anything that would bring her into the limelight. Painfully shy, she dreaded photographs. Even when her good friend, photographer John Engstead, asked her to pose for publicity shots in the design studio, she begged him to choose one of the wardrobe girls instead. At the time, she didn't want the attention.

Travis Banton came to Paramount to do *The Dressmaker from Paris* (1925) just a few months after Edith was hired. He had made a name for himself by designing Mary Pickford's gown for her secret wedding to Douglas Fairbanks and had become the number-two man in design at Paramount. Edith's $50 a week was a pittance compared with the $150 Banton had been hired for—not to mention the $200 per week Greer pulled in. But like most designers of the day, the men had come as highly experienced artists from custom design salons, and their talents and names were recognized by the public.

She learned very quickly from her two mentors. She may not have shared their design talent, but she knew she was smarter than either of them, *and* she wasn't a heavy drinker. Too much booze would eventually hamper both men's studio careers. Edith praised both of them publicly and would continue to do so until her dying day.

Though people in the industry expected them to be rivals, Banton and Greer became close friends. Both men liked Edith and knew she would eventually make something of herself.

Travis Banton and Howard Greer sort of adopted me, and I went with them to all their fittings. I was accepted as part of the team in the fitting room, which also included the head fitter and usually a wardrobe girl. Sometimes I just watched and took notes; I did whatever I was told. With both Howard and Travis there was never any feeling that I would be a threat to them, as is so often the case in boss-and-assistant relationships in any profession. They were secure in their own careers. Both went overboard in encouraging and helping me. I think I had the greatest break that any young designer ever had. Working for them was the kind of training you couldn't get any place else, in any school in the world.

At their bidding, Edith joined them in their afterhours revels. But as she piled into the back of Banton's chauffeur-driven Rolls-Royce with Banton, Greer, Engstead, and her husband, Charles, to hit the Hollywood parties and nightspots, she felt a little out of place. Though the designers treated her as an equal, she couldn't escape the fact that she was only an assistant.

As the months passed, she became more than just a sketch artist—she was given her own assignments. Her first major project came in 1924, when she was asked to design the candy ball sequence in DeMille's *The Golden Bed* (1925). Naturally, she was thrilled at the opportunity to work on one of DeMille's extravaganzas. The script called for life-size candy-cane and chocolate-bar women, and Edith took the script literally. She ordered lollipop beards, peppermint-stick fingernails, and chocolate-drop necklaces. She used real candy as often as possible, forgetting that those high-powered klieg lights would turn her sweet work—and the set —into a gooey, sticky mess. DeMille was outraged, Greer was embarrassed, and Edith was ready to call it quits again. But Greer and Claire West, DeMille's longtime designer, stepped in to save the scene, *and* Edith's first endeavor as a designer. After the film was released, critics cited costumes in the candy ball sequence as "colorful." Edith was, of course, delighted at the mere mention of her work.

On another early assignment, a scene in *The Wanderer*

(1926), she learned the hard way that pachyderms aren't as easy to dress as humans. Assigned to garb the leading elephant in a purely DeMille manner, Edith designed garlands of colorful wreaths to decorate the waist and ankles of the voluptuous beast. No sooner was the animal festooned than it devoured its fruit-and-floral ornaments. Filming was delayed for hours as the relentless elephant kept eating its finery. Edith finally solved the problem by opting for less-appetizing artificial flora.

Everyone laughed at me. How was I to know elephants eat fruits and flowers? I can still hear them laughing. I guess I would have laughed too, if I hadn't been so humiliated.

The incident, like the candy ball fiasco, remained implanted in her mind. In both instances she was determined never to leave herself open to such ridicule again.

By 1927 Greer's romance with gin had become a major problem. Edith sensed that things were beginning to go awry in the front design studio. Banton and Greer were still getting along well, but gossip was spreading that Greer was on his way out. She tried to stay on the sidelines, but it was difficult. People kept asking what was going on. Yes, she knew Greer had a drinking problem and, yes, he wasn't as organized as he had been.

Eventually Jesse Lasky, then president of Paramount, laid it on the line: Either Greer stopped drinking or he was out. Lasky was confident that Banton was more capable than Greer and that Edith could back him up. Rather than risk being fired, Greer let his contract lapse and left Paramount to open a custom design salon in Hollywood. He continued designing for the movies as a freelancer, never again as a studio designer. Banton became Paramount's chief designer and Edith was given the title of his assistant.

Edith accompanied Banton to the fittings of the most glamorous stars, absorbing every little detail of his creative process.

Travis was very slick and personable. He knew how to talk to the stars—how to make them feel absolutely beautiful in his clothes. I learned everything from him. Travis gave me more responsibility than I ever had. He let me do Westerns on my own. In the big pictures he'd do the leading lady—Marlene Dietrich, for instance—and I'd do the others. Actually, he was training me to be more than an assistant. He was training me to be a full-fledged designer.

So Edith dressed the grandmothers, the children, the eunuchs, the maids, and the extras, while her boss concentrated on the stars, giving them every chic new look he could dream up. Movie audiences weren't yet used to this kind of high fashion. Banton and his MGM counterpart, Adrian, represented a new concept in motion picture design.

Before 1920, costumes generally came from actresses' closets; only occasionally were they taken from the stockrooms of the studios or theatrical costume companies. Actresses often got their jobs on the basis of their wardrobes, so it wasn't surprising that thriving ladies-of-the-night spent their days making movies. Most production companies didn't even have costume designers on staff until about 1918, when Peggy Hamilton contracted with Triangle Studios in Culver City and DeMille secured Claire West as head of costume design for his films. By 1921 the chief costume designers at most of the major studios were women—Esther Chaffin at Lasky, Claire West at DeMille, and Sophie Wachner at Goldwyn— but by the time Edith came to Hollywood men were making headlines as the kings of costume design. Greer had come from the prestigious salon of Lady Duff Gordon in New York to work with West on *The Ten Commandments* (1923) and eventually replaced her.

Around the same time, Irving Berlin discovered an American designer in Paris whose talents were so incredible that he immediately shipped the young man, Gilbert Adrian Rosenberg, to New York to do costumes for his new *Music Box Revue* of 1923. Rudolph Valentino and his designer-wife, Natacha Rambova, convinced Adrian to come to Hollywood to design *The Hooded Cobra*, a film that was never released. By 1926 he was on his way to becoming the head of design at MGM.

Erté, the celebrated magazine cover illustrator, was brought to MGM at about the same time to dress up some of its upcoming films. Hollywood society was at once titillated and scandalized by the young artist's outrageous manner and blatantly homosexual repartee. As he recalled years later, "When I wore a silver lamé torero suit to a Hollywood party, everyone whispered, and the gossip columnists talked about it for days afterward. One paper even called me a freak!"

Edith watched Erté and Adrian carefully, noting how important it was to make the most of publicity and to get the fans to know your name. Somehow the studio appreciated you more. Travis Banton and Howard Greer kept fairly low public profiles and would live to regret it, but the whole world knew of Adrian and Erté.

Banton would have been content to dress only willowy glamour girls, but one of the biggest stars at Paramount at the time was the short, somewhat round Clara Bow. Banton detested dressing Clara, even though he was taken with her sexy, childlike manner. She was too short to look good in clothes and she had no concept of how to maintain a decent figure. When she finally ate one too many Hershey bars, even her baby-doll charms couldn't assuage Banton. How could he dress a sausage, he wanted to know? He turned her over to Edith.

Clara was Edith's first big star. She was the "It" girl—"It" being, of course, a not very profound but definitely uncensorable euphemism for sex appeal. With her flaming red hair, her bee-stung pout, and her hour-glass figure, she was everything "It" was about in the 1920s. The public adored her. Clara couldn't have been hotter than in 1927, when Edith was assigned to do the costumes for the now classic movie *Wings*. But with little Miss It's stubborn attitude and a script that was scarcely a costume designer's dream, Edith's first big chance turned into a battle of wills.

Clara played a flying wartime nurse and had to wear an Army uniform in most of the scenes. Armed-forces uniforms had to be authentic. But Clara didn't care about rules. She wanted a belt to cinch in the boxy uniform and flaunt her curves. Edith insisted there could be no belt and the producer and director backed her up.

But Edith was not about to let some little actress ruin her first big opportunity in Hollywood. They locked horns and Edith eventually won. No belt.

> *It was one of the first pictures I ever did and naturally I was very enthusiastic. Imagine how disappointed I was when I learned that I had to use regulation Army clothes and couldn't do something new for my motion picture debut. The United States Army was nothing to tangle with, especially not for me, on my first movie. Clara loathed the uniform and I couldn't blame her. She would sneak around and try to belt it. I'd have to be on the set every minute to snatch it off her. I think she thought I was out to get her, to make her look less sexy. Now, granted, it's pretty hard to look sexy in a U.S. Army uniform, but Clara managed.*
>
> *Putting Clara in a drab uniform was like bridling an untamed horse. She loved wild colors, the wilder the better. They reflected her true, vibrant personality. She was so happy go lucky that she made everyone around her happy. I still cherish an old photograph she gave me inscribed, "To Edith with love, but why don't you put your goddamn belts around your waist where they belong?"*

Edith and Clara eventually became friends, despite what Edith called Clara's "vulgarities"—her crude language and promiscuous habits. They'd go for wild rides with her twin chow dogs in the It Girl's Kissel convertible. (She had painted the car red and dyed the chows red, to match her hair.) At the time, Clara was having a passionate affair with Gary Cooper, then a stunt rider on the lot. She had even finagled a part for him in *Wings,* in which he played a secondary role to Buddy Rogers, the romantic lead. Edith would sit and listen as Clara went on and on spouting the delicious details of her love life.

Edith dressed Clara in *The Saturday Night Kid* (1929), Bow's second talkie. Unfortunately, Bow's voice and acting style and the advent of motion picture sound didn't mesh and her popularity started to slip. For Edith the film was memorable not because of Clara's clothes but because of the bias-cut satin dress she made for a slim brunette who had a bit part in the film. The girl would go on to become a major star in her own right, but Edith would never dress her again.

She was Jean Harlow, a second-stringer in those days, but once Howard Hughes convinced her to bleach her hair she became a star within a year. Of course, when I worked with her I just thought of her as another actress, but I was impressed with her sensuous body and I made the most of it with white satin, cut on the bias. I was afraid of how Clara would react, since Jean really upstaged her in that slinky white gown. Most stars would have resented sharing a big scene with such a sizzling, voluptuous creature as Harlow. Not Clara. She was simply fascinated by her. I won't take credit for Harlow's screen image, but I think I'm entitled to say that what she wore in those scenes inspired others to take a second look and realize her knockout potential.

The dress that Edith made for Harlow was actually an adaptation of French couturiere Madeleine Vionnet's latest design. No one had used the sexy bias cut in an entire gown before Vionnet, but it took Hollywood to turn the look into a classic—the slip dress. Harlow wore it, Lombard popularized Banton's version, and Dietrich slinked around in one. It became the uniform of the sex symbols. The gown, with its bodice styled exactly like the top of an underslip, complete with thin little straps, was especially alluring because it was worn with no undergarments. Since fabric cut on the bias—diagonally across the weave—has a gentle, inherent stretch quality, the slip dress clung to every curve and crevice of a woman's body.

Lupe Velez was Edith's second big star of the 1920s. A fiery Mexican beauty, Lupe wasn't at all pleased to have Edith, a mere assistant, dressing her. In *The Wolf Song* (1929), she starred as a rich Spanish señorita who fell in love with a handsome young cowboy, played by Gary Cooper. Lupe wanted lavish costumes and wasn't convinced that Edith could do the job, but the clever young costume designer relied on her facility in Spanish to woo Lupe into trusting her. Once the costumes were completed, the star was delighted. Determined to design memorable gowns, Edith had gone to extremes with lace and ruffles, creating an authentic but exaggerated hacienda look. Lupe had requested something very special for her love scene with Cooper, who was by then also her offscreen lover. Edith created a white lace gown with a skirt so full that Cooper couldn't get close enough for any real passion. Later critics would note that "if there hadn't been so much dress, there could have been more scene."

In covered-wagon days, ladies wore high collars. But Victor Fleming, the director, wanted Lupe to be so sexy that most of the time her bosom would be hanging out. I went to Mr. Fleming and said, "Don't you think it's a little inconsistent? Women did not uncover their bosom in those days." He told me, "Edith, if no woman had ever shown her bosom in those days, you wouldn't be here."

Period pictures like *The Wolf Song* posed few problems for Head. She had confidence in her research abilities and had little difficulty coming up with a dress that made the dark-skinned Velez look like a wealthy Spanish beauty. But contemporary pictures were a different story.

THREE

Throughout the flapper era dresses had been straight, with short skirts, and anything that showed up on the movie screen fit the fashion trends very well. Then suddenly, in 1929, when the stock market fell, so did hems, and Hollywood was literally caught with its skirts up. Daytime dresses fell to a point somewhere between mid-calf and ankle, the waist began to show up again, and shoulders were more defined. The world was giving all due credit to the likes of Chanel, Schiaparelli, and Lanvin, but Hollywood designers were cursing them.

The men who ran the studios knew that a sudden change in fashion meant that movies ready for release were going to look dated. They made feeble attempts to call the films current, but a discriminating public wasn't about to be bilked—not when moviegoers were paying 25 cents apiece to be entertained with "the latest."

The moguls resolved that the only way to avoid such an *haute* catastrophe in the future was to make a serious attempt to establish Hollywood, not Paris, as the fashion trendsetter. Official word went out to costume heads that they were to produce original designs. There was to be no more buying from French couture houses. Their goal was to make Hollywood the fashion capital of the world and to do it immediately. The studios were determined never again to be at the mercy of a small group of fey French designers.

The publicity departments went to work immediately, promoting every "A" picture as a fashion extravaganza. John Engstead, by then one of the best-known studio photographers in Hollywood, staged major fashion photo sessions with the big stars at Paramount. When the glossy pictures were supplied to major newspapers and magazines all over the States, press releases accompanied them, promoting the designers as "the most creative fashion minds in the world." Some gowns were used expressly for promotion and never ended up in films. If stars were hot on the social circuit, studio designers were asked to fashion personal wardrobes for them too. Courting the fashion editors and gossip columnists became a studio publicity department's major preoccupation. All to establish Hollywood's new chic image.

Within a very short time, the public relied on the movies for fashion guidance. The movie magazines supplanted *Vogue* and *Harper's Bazaar* as the major sources of trend news. Throughout the 1930s (and well into the 1950s), dressmakers, furriers, milliners, and beauty salons all kept a supply of the latest issues so their customers could pick out favorite styles and ask for a dress like Carole Lombard's, or a fur like Joan Crawford's, or a hairdo like Dietrich's.

The early motion pictures were pure escapism and quite unreal. Sometimes the clothes were pretty ridiculous. You know, the poor working girls going to work wearing sable, fan-

tastically dressed. People were rather sweet about it and said,
"Oh well, that's Hollywood." They liked it. In that period there
was something called the matinee audience. Women would
stand in line, come rain or come shine, to see what their favorite
stars were wearing. It was escapism from what they were doing
then and from the way they were dressed.

Paramount's new contract with Banton assured him two trips per year to Europe, a demand he had made through his agent, Myron Selznick. Banton insisted that the trips were important to his image, but Lasky viewed them as one more fringe benefit to keep Banton tied to the studio. While in Paris, he would view the French couture collections to make sure his styles were more progressive than anything the Europeans might be doing. He would contract with fabric mills in Lyon to provide luxurious silks, brocades, and laces for his creations. During his four- to six-week absences, Edith was at the Paramount design helm.

She loved the authority. At last, she was somewhat in control of what went on in the costume department, even if for just a temporary period. Usually no big pictures came up while Travis was away; careful scheduling took care of that. But in the spring of 1932 a woman who would become an international sex symbol was ready to make her first movie. There was no time to wait for Banton—it was up to Edith to dress Mae West.

Mae was already a legend by the time she came to Hollywood. She was forty years old, and the sexiest thing who ever wobbled on five-inch heels. She'd made a name for herself on Broadway, writing provocative plays like *Sex* and *The Drug*, even getting herself a stretch in jail for her efforts. Her notoriety prompted the powers at Paramount to sign her to a contract. She finally talked the executives into letting her film *She Done Him Wrong* (1933), an adaptation of her most famous play, *Diamond Lil.* She had expected Banton to dress her, but when she met Edith she wasn't disappointed. Neither was Edith.

I fell in love with Mae the first time I met her. It was ten
o'clock in the morning in her Hollywood apartment. She was the

sexiest thing anybody ever saw at that hour of the day. She was wearing a long, tight, white dress cut down to the navel, her bosom thrust out seductively. All her contours were splendidly outlined in a soft, clingy gown that looked like it belonged to a bordello queen. She turned around to me and before I could even introduce myself, she said, "This is the Mae West look."

Naturally, I was apprehensive, because Mae was my first truly big star since Clara Bow. But Mae couldn't have been nicer. She sat down with me and explained exactly what the Mae West image was. "Edith," she said, "I'm a lady but most of all I'm a sexy female—the black-velvet-and-diamonds type. I want my clothes loose enough to prove I'm a lady, but tight enough to show 'em I'm a woman."

She also gave me a bit of philosophy that I've never forgotten: "If you've found a magic that does something for you, honey, stick to it. Never change it."

Mae's magic had worked on the stage for about thirty years before she came to Hollywood. Her mother had put her on the vaudeville circuit when she was a child. Over the years she had honed her act perfectly, so there were no surprises. The audience knew exactly what to expect and that's why they adored her.

Edith had no intention of tampering with a proven success formula. She wasn't out to "improve" on Mae. Making the most beautiful costumes possible within the parameters of the script was Edith's early goal. Glorious Mae was the perfect vehicle for Edith to express herself.

Mae chose a handsome young actor on the lot as her leading man in *She Done Him Wrong*. He was about six feet one, with wavy dark hair, and had an appealing cleft in his chin. Born Archibald Leach in Bristol, England, his early training as an acrobat and music hall entertainer had brought him first to New York and then, in 1932, to Hollywood, where his agent advised him to change his name to something less grating—Cary Grant.

I doubt if the clothes I designed for Mae made as big an impact as Cary Grant did in his Salvation Army uniform.

Everyone on the lot fell in love with him, including me. He was by far the most handsome man I had ever seen. Since he wore a Salvation Army uniform from the wardrobe stock, I didn't get to dress him in She Done Him Wrong. *I was always very disappointed about that.*

Since Edith was to receive her first onscreen costume design credit for this film, she spent day and night planning, sketching, resketching, and evaluating. Knowing that Mae West was the best judge of her own costumes, Edith would consult with the star about every detail. She was striving for perfection and, in Mae's estimation, she achieved it. The curvaceous star said she felt "all woman" in the beaded black satin gown Edith designed. Mae and the designer had agreed that the skin-tight dress would reveal just enough bosom to captivate the men in the audience, but not enough to threaten the women—or irritate the censors. With her creativity soaring, Edith decided to appliqué a flock of glittering doves from shoulder to hip across the bodice of the gown. Mae's signature picture hat, this time in black, was laden with ostrich feathers to match the twelve-foot boa she slung over her shoulder.

Most of the film studios were suffering in 1931 and 1932. The Depression had finally come to Hollywood, and Paramount was among the worst hit. But Mae changed all that. *She Done Him Wrong* provided audiences with just the diversion they needed. When it opened at the Paramount Theater in New York with a scheduled appearance by the stars, Times Square was bulging with people waiting for a glimpse of Mae. The film broke all attendance records at the theater, and when it opened in theaters across the country, it grossed $2 million in less than three months, going on to become a Mae West classic. She and Grant followed up with *I'm No Angel* (1933), and Paramount was back on its feet.

Mae-mania swept the country, with fan clubs cropping up all over. Movie magazines carried "Dear Mae" columns with questions like "Is it true you wore padded dresses in *She Done Him Wrong?* If so, why? Was it to conceal your beautiful form?" "Yes, I wore pads," she said, penning her own answers for the magazine. "Stage experience, not modesty, dictated the use of padded dresses."

"And," her fans pursued, "do you think the revealing garments you wear in pictures are decent?" Mae replied with a jab at the film censors, "There's a saying, you know, 'The evil's in the eye of him who sees it.'"

Censors were seeing a great deal of "evil" in the early 1930s, even more than they'd seen in the 1920s, the decade notorious for its blatant decadence. What better target than that sexy, suggestive temptress Mae West? The Hays Office* set the standards of decency for the motion picture industry and laid down the law about exactly what could be said and shown on the screen, leaving very little about Mae that was beyond reproach.

Despite the Hays Office's careful censorship of new films, Alice Ames Winter, the Carry Nation of the National Catholic Legion of Decency, went after Mae with a vengeance. She approached the California legislature, demanding action against West's "vile" films. Speaking to women's organizations and church groups all over Southern California, Mrs. Winter attacked Mae as a threat to "the happiness and the onward movement of our children and our homes. Children represent 40 percent of the movie-going public, and we want the forces that play on them to be of the best and most inspiring kind. They don't need Mae West as a teacher."

But Mae wasn't about to let some Pasadena prude get in her way. She very sweetly went about her business, conforming to rules only when the studios forced her to abide by them. But nobody was going to tell her how to be Mae West. Writing her own stories, as she had done in vaudeville and on Broadway, Mae had control of her roles. When producers or directors brought in their writers, she battled with them over every line. And when the press questioned her about censorship, she didn't, as the studios had requested, beg off. She bluntly told the world that her freedom of choice was being thwarted and that morals should not be legislated except by criminal law. As she noted in her biography, *Goodness*

---

*Set up and paid for by the industry itself, the Hays Office acted as a morals watchdog. It was administered by Will Hays, a former Postmaster General and a man of impeccable virtue.

Had Nothing To Do with It, "Every person who is not a moron or a mental defective of some sort carries a very effective censor and supercritic of his actions in his cerebral cortex—and in his heart. If that doesn't work, no amount of censorship from the outside will do anybody any good."

Mae continued to wear her version of Victorian-style gowns. Her legs were covered and her breasts were covered, so she dared the censors to complain. And if the covering fit like a second skin, so be it. There weren't any rules about how tight a costume could be. The gowns were usually made in duplicate, with one slightly larger than the other for use in scenes where she was seated or reclining. The tighter version was reserved for standing and walking.

She didn't wear corsets or brassieres under the gowns; they were so tight they shaped her without foundations. The dresses had bones so they would stay up, but that was it. Whenever she'd come for a fitting—and she was one of the few stars who understood how important fittings were—she would act out the scene in the dress to make sure it was right. If she was supposed to sing a song, she'd belt it out right in the fitting room. She never once said, "Let's do something different." She knew what she had.

The look didn't work for anybody else. Never in my entire career did I make a Mae West dress for anyone but Mae. Mostly, other people wanted to look like Garbo or Dietrich or Crawford.

Even though Mae was determined not to change her act, she couldn't prevent the censors from cutting scenes once a movie was finished. She so carefully worded the provocative dialogue in *Every Day's a Holiday* (1938) that only two lines had to be cut. Even though other typical West double entendres had slipped through, Hays Office censors took out "I wouldn't let him touch me with a ten-foot pole" and "I wouldn't even lift my veil for that guy," lines Mae felt were perfectly innocent.

Once censors began to tame Mae's product, her box-office appeal started to dwindle. In an attempt to increase her audience,

Paramount reversed its anti-Paris policy and signed famed French couturiere Elsa Schiaparelli to design costumes for *Every Day's a Holiday*. The designer and Mae had conferred in Paris about the costumes, but when it came time for fittings they were on different continents. Paramount shipped a life-size plaster replica of Mae's form to the Schiaparelli salon. Overwhelmed by the figure, the designer reportedly called the silhouette "shocking" and named her signature perfume "Shocking" in Mae's honor. But when the costumes arrived in Hollywood they were all too small and had to be virtually remade. Since Schiaparelli's designs weren't particularly better than those Travis Banton had done for eight of Mae's films (or, for that matter, than Edith's work in *She Done Him Wrong*), the studio decided it was too expensive to make trans-Atlantic costumes. It was years before any Parisian designers would work for Paramount again.

The censors kept a watchful eye on Banton's designs after he costumed Claudette Colbert in DeMille's *Cleopatra* (1934). The designer had thrown caution to the wind when Colbert requested that he bare as much of her bosom as possible, focusing attention above her waist, which she thought was too thick, and deemphasizing her neck, which she thought was too short. Banton indulged her. But just as the shooting was about to commence, Colbert refused to be photographed in any of the costumes she had already approved. Banton was forced to redesign, creating costumes one day to be shot the next. Colbert was obsessed with how she looked on screen. Her most famous costume in the film was a metallic slink of a dress that revealed as much cleavage as Colbert had to offer, as well as her beautiful legs, via a slit that stopped vampishly at mid-thigh. Although Edith assisted Banton on Colbert's costumes, she was not given credit for her work on the film.

The vagaries of the censors made them more of an irritation than an enemy to the costume designers. Banton and his crew tried to follow the rules as closely as possible, but when the rules changed mid-film, critical time was lost remaking costumes.

Censorship was kind of crazy in that period because we could show a girl in the shortest little abbreviated underclothes as long as they looked like sportswear. But if they had lace on them we couldn't show them because they were then considered underwear. Lace was sexier than no lace. The navel was something you never showed. We used to stuff pearls in navels with glue. Sometimes we'd have a whole row of dancers with jewels in their navels. Even that kind of camouflage wouldn't always pass, so we finally had to put a band of gold or jewels around the waistline to hide the navel. I don't know why navels were so censorable, but they were. And why only women's navels? Male bellybuttons seemed to be okay. I could never understand the discrimination.

Even censorship couldn't get in the way of the glamour that epitomized films of the 1930s. The public was hungry for some form of escape and going to the movies provided it. The fans wanted big stars, romance, riches, magic. Dreams had to be coming true somewhere.

It was truly the Golden Era, the prettiest period in motion pictures, with some of the most beautiful, talented, and glamorous stars that have ever been seen on the silver screen. The movie scripts were pure escapism. The stories were about people who lived glamorously. They had money, prestige, all the luxuries that so few people in the Depression years had. All the men were rich and handsome, the women beautiful and glamorous; everybody had swimming pools, butlers, Rolls-Royces; they wore beautiful and elegant clothes, drank champagne, and lived happily ever after. There was little realism in the movies of the Golden Era. The fantasies and myths of motion pictures do not always coincide with the state of the world.

While the movies of the 1930s provided the rest of the world with escape, they established Edith firmly in a profession that she was to honor for the next fifty years. By 1933, when she first saw "Costumes by Edith Head" flash on the screen in the credits for *She Done Him Wrong*, the five-foot designer knew she was on her way. This was her career. She was still assisting Banton on many of the major films, but her status had improved. She was now a full-fledged designer. She designed almost every "B" picture Paramount produced, always in the Banton style.

I learned more from Travis Banton by watching him dress Carole Lombard than anything I've ever done—before or since. I learned more by watching him dress Marlene Dietrich and Claudette Colbert than I could have learned in years of formal study in a design school. When I wasn't racing between my "B" pictures and horse operas, I spent every possible moment staying glued to Travis, trailing him everywhere like a puppy. After all, he was the best designer, bar none, in the world. And he taught me everything I knew about designing.

Occasionally Edith received a good assignment, such as *Little Miss Marker* (1934) with Shirley Temple, the first of the nine features the six-year-old would make that year. Edith dressed her like a doll with all the ribbons, ruffles, and bows befitting America's first little princess. From Temple she moved on to Betty Grable and Mary Martin, both starlets whose names would later become important. But in those days, like Edith, they were merely on the road to fame.

By 1936, Edith was a veteran at Paramount. She had been there for thirteen years and had helped fit every major star on the lot. She had more friends than she'd ever had in her life. She felt confident designing for anyone, and most of the stars accepted her as the next best thing to Banton.

She had learned to mimic his sketching style. On days when he inexplicably didn't show up for work she'd fill in for him, supervising the seamstresses, taking over his fittings—everything Banton would do. If he went on a drinking binge for three or four days at a time, she could even originate a design, sketch it, and sign Banton's name with nobody knowing the difference. She and Travis were such close friends that she was glad to cover for him.

What he taught her best was how to dress the glamour girls. As far as Edith was concerned, Carole Lombard and Marlene Dietrich *were* the 1930s. Travis gave their clothes all his love and attention, and the women were very loyal in return. Every year Carole sent extravagant Christmas presents to Banton and his crew. Dietrich showed her affection in other ways, such as sending him samples of fabric from faraway places or putting in hours, even weeks, at fittings when other stars might have tired or stormed out in a rage.

Dietrich had come to Hollywood with director Josef von Sternberg. She was intended to be Paramount's answer to Greta Garbo. Since the highly acclaimed designer Adrian dressed Garbo at MGM, Banton would of course dress Marlene. Between 1930 and 1935 Banton created her image in six of her most important von Sternberg films: *Morocco* (1930), *Dishonored* (1931), *Shanghai Express* (1932), *Blonde Venus* (1932), *The Scarlet Empress* (1934), and *The Devil Is a Woman* (1935).

Banton spared nothing in dressing Marlene—not money, not time, not creative energy. She was the *femme fatale,* and he used his couturier flair to define her character. He accentuated her long, lean body and even put her on a diet to slim her into greyhound lines. Her trim silhouette allowed him to use thick, luxurious fabrics that would make most actresses, even the slim ones, look plump on screen. But not Dietrich. He could pile on ruffles, furs, and feathers and she always projected her svelte image.

Banton consulted with von Sternberg on every Dietrich costume. The Svengali director would spend hours choosing the right hat or handbag, or take pains to adjust a wisp of hair on her cheek. He expected the same devotion to detail from Banton and from his star.

Dietrich was not difficult; she was a perfectionist. She had incredible discipline and energy. She could work all day to the point of exhaustion, then catch a second breath and work all night just to get something right. Once we worked thirty-six hours straight—from early Monday to late Tuesday—preparing a costume for her to wear on the set Wednesday night. I thought it was all settled. I was still working at midnight on Tuesday when Marlene came in and said, "Edith, I'm not happy with this hat. What can we do about it?" We sat up for hours trying on dozens of different hats, changing them, tilting them, taking the feathers off this one and trying them on that one, snipping off a veil or a brim, switching ribbons and bows. Marlene was clever with her fingers. She helped. We worked on the hats far into the night and finally got what she wanted. I was amazed at her stamina and determination.

Edith studied Banton's artful mix of textures in Dietrich's costumes. She watched as he mixed chiffon and feathers with tapestry; velvet with satin, lace, and appliquéd crepe de chine. His work was a collage of drama and fantasy, shaped to his vision of the perfect creature.

Lombard was Banton's other passion. Likening her to a sleek Arabian horse, the designer often told people that he could just throw a length of fabric at her and she would wear it well. He created radiant, slithering, memorable gowns for her that became the focal point of all her movies. Fans paid to see Lombard fashion fare. Hers was the body that best displayed the definitive Banton look: solid beading draped on the bias sliding over her braless breasts, falling gracefully over her delicate hips, caressing her thighs, casting barely a shadow of shape at the knee, and finally cascading into a train that rippled with every step. Banton considered hers to be the perfect body, and Edith agreed. But Lombard was more than a mannequin for his latest creations. She was a comedienne, a very important star, and, what Edith remembered best, a compassionate friend.

Carole would come to Travis' studio at lunchtime, and she and I would just sit and talk and laugh until Travis got there. Sometimes he'd be hours late and Carole would be furious, but just as he walked in she'd soften up and tell him how much she loved the newest costumes. She never asked to approve sketches as so many other stars did. Whatever Travis did was good enough for her.

While Banton dressed his clotheshorses Dietrich and Lombard, Edith continued to practice on the rest. When Banton sent

Dorothy Lamour to Edith, the young designer had no idea that this starlet who had just been cast in her first film would become one of Hollywood's brightest stars in less than a year.

For months, Adolph Zukor, who was then head of Paramount, had been trying to cast the lead of a movie called Girl of the Jungle. *He had already tested more than two hundred girls, so it had gotten to be somewhat of a beauty contest. Girls filed in and out of the executive offices, some still with a hibiscus behind one ear, but he rejected all of them. During her screen test, Dorothy let down her waist-length hair, stuck a flower in it, and got the part—Zukor was that impressed. He also knew that he could hire her for $200 a week, which was peanuts for good actresses in those days.*

Dottie was overjoyed to get the role until she found out that the only costume she'd be wearing was a sarong. I wasn't extremely sympathetic until I realized that she was a very young, sweet girl who had envisioned coming to Hollywood and wearing beautiful gowns like so many of the other big stars did. She wasn't confident at all—in fact, she was constantly degrading her figure. She thought her hips were too big and her shoulders too narrow. The only thing I thought she suffered from was a waist that was too small, and that was hardly a problem. She was so self-conscious about her feet that she told her director, William Thiele, that she wouldn't appear in the film unless something was done to make her feet look prettier. The makeup department concocted some rubber feet which were flawless, and she attempted to wear those with her sarong, but they were so delicate that "new feet" had to be made every day. At $300 a pair, her vanity was getting expensive. In any case, the rubber feet were so slippery that she eventually kicked them off, accepting the fact that even if her feet weren't as gorgeous as the rest of her, they were functional—and function does have its own rewards.

The first sarong I made for Dottie was of a very authentic Malaysian cotton, accurate right down to its uneven weave and its island print. It was also extremely ugly. The fabric didn't drape well, making Dottie look like she was wearing a flower-print sack. If I tied it tight she was uncomfortable, and if I didn't she looked awful. I decided to use satin crepe instead of cotton, so I had it screened in exactly the native print I wanted. It draped beautifully and created the voluptuous look I wanted for the star of The Jungle Princess. *(When Mr. Zukor saw how beautiful Dorothy looked in her full makeup and costume, he changed the name from* Girl of the Jungle *to* Jungle Girl *and finally to* Jungle Princess, *with highest compliments to Miss Lamour.)*

The new fabric achieved exactly the form I wanted, but function was again suffering. You couldn't count on knots staying tied in this slippery cloth, especially if it got wet.

The cameras were on one day as Dorothy set out for her first scene in a tropical stream—actually it was a wooden pool on one of the smaller sound stages. Her co-star, Ray Milland, was to join our lovely water lily when all of a sudden Dorothy screamed and the sarong floated to the surface, along with the bust pads we had stuffed into the suit to make her look chesty. Milland was laughing himself silly. Dorothy grabbed for the cloth, wrapped herself up as best she could and we sewed her (and the pads) into the sarong, forgetting all the authentic sarong wrapping techniques I had learned. From then on, I sewed her into every sarong she wore.

When Dorothy Lamour reflects on those days, she sighs and admits that after almost fifty years she finds it a bit boring to talk about the sarong. "I wore sarongs in only eight of my films and I made more than fifty. Edith made some other beautiful costumes for me, such as the ones in *Masquerade in Mexico* (1945) and *Road to Morocco* (1942), but nobody remembers those. Just about every costume she ever made for me was gorgeous. In those days, the studio designers often made personal wardrobes too—which, of course, we had to pay for—and I always asked Edith to make mine. She even made the dress I wore to my wedding. It was blue with a sweetheart neckline and long sleeves, and she had shoes and a hat dyed to match. I still have the shoes in my closet. Edith was always very good to me and dressed me well. I don't know why she told those stories about using pads in my sarongs. I guess it made a good interview. I didn't ever wear pads. I *did* wear panties that exactly matched the sarong. Edith thought of those. That way I could run, get caught in windstorms or whatever else I had to do, and not have to worry about getting past the censors."

Despite Edith's passion for authenticity, the sarong Lamour wore in *The Jungle Princess* was far from accurate. True sarongs were made of cotton and tied at the waist, leaving the breasts bare. After experimenting with assorted ways of covering Lamour's chest with strategically placed flowers and her long hair, Edith and Thiele decided that it would be impossible to clear the censors in an authentic version and opted for the breast-covering model.

Edith's adaptation of the tropical coverup uncovered enough of Lamour to establish her as one of the world's most popular pinup girls. By the middle of World War II, 1,325,000 U.S. soldiers in 202 Army posts chose her as their favorite pinup, and she eventually became Paramount's biggest female box-office draw of all time.

I would never say that the sarong made Dorothy Lamour a star. If someone else had worn it, chances are that neither the girl nor the sarong would have been heard of again. But when Dottie filled out that piece of cloth, it was magic. All of a sudden she was Ulah, Marama, Tura, Manuela, Dea, Mima, Arla, Tama, Shalimar, and Aloma—all the South Sea island beauties she was supposed to be.

And just as suddenly as Dorothy became a star, so did the sarong. I was getting calls from newspapers all over the world to ask about this "new fashion innovation." Swimsuit companies were calling every day to ask me to design sarongs for them, and the ones that didn't call were putting sarongs into their collections. *

*Hollywood had such a major impact on the swimsuit business that by 1947 California's largest swimwear house, Catalina, contracted Edith and several other film designers, including Travis Banton and Warner Brothers' Milo Anderson and Howard Shoup, to lend their names to a collection of "Hollywood swimsuits" that were promoted in fashion and fan magazines all over the country.

Barbara Stanwyck was another Travis Banton castoff when Edith first met in her in 1937. She was to play a young doctor in *Internes Can't Take Money* (1937), a film based on a Max Brand hospital novel.* That she dressed Stanwyck in a white satin uniform and pumps amused Edith years after the fact.

It was so very typical of the 1930s. Imagine, an intern wearing tight white satin! At the time, that's what audiences wanted—escapist glamour. So we gave it to them. Barbara had been a little insulted that Travis didn't want to dress her, but she and I hit it off immediately and it was the beginning of a long and important friendship.

Barbara and I went on to do more than twenty-five pictures together, a major portion of her sixty-plus films. I designed the costumes for the three motion pictures she always said were her favorites: The Lady Eve *(1941),* Double Indemnity *(1944), and* Sorry, Wrong Number *(1948). But those films come later in the story.*

In 1937, while Banton was in Europe, Edith designed what was to be her only picture for Carole Lombard.

Lombard put as much trust in me as in Travis. I designed her clothes all by myself for True Confession *(1937), her last film for Paramount. Lombard was one of the top stars of the 1930s; by 1937, in fact, she had become the highest-paid film star in the world, earning just under a half-million dollars per year. She could have well afforded any designer in the world. But she gave me a warm, friendly welcome and the same free rein she had always given Travis. She loved the clothes I designed for her. Lombard went from Paramount to RKO, but she told friends, "If I ever make another picture at Paramount I want Edie to do all my clothes."*

*When Paramount didn't take an option on the main character of the script, Dr. Kildare, MGM did. *Internes Can't Take Money* was the first installment of what went on to become a thirty-five-year saga, eventually ending in a TV series.

In 1938 Travis Banton left Paramount to join Howard Greer in his custom salon business. Edith Head was immediately named chief designer at Paramount. Hedda Hopper, the former actress and then-powerful syndicated gossip columnist, quickly spread the word that Edith had conspired to force him out. Word had it that Hopper got the story straight from Banton. Rumors spread on the lot and Edith's good fortune was met with mixed emotions, for none of the stars wanted to see Banton out.

The truth was that Banton was a lush. Edith had covered for him loyally when he was out on drunken binges. Sometimes he'd inexplicably call in from another town, hundreds of miles from Hollywood. He'd miss appointments. He'd forget about a gown or two that was needed on the set. Edith had spoken confidentially to a few friends about his problems, but was publicly stoical about having to handle the design department by herself while Banton was off guzzling.

When the rumors about Edith started to fly, Carole Lombard came to her defense. "Edie wouldn't try to get Travis. She loves him like we all do." Lombard confided to one of her best friends that she knew what really happened. Carole and Travis had the same agent, Myron Selznick, who had told her the whole story. "Travis had asked Paramount for a raise from $1,750 to $2,000 a week," she related. "They said it was too much and complained that he wasn't very dependable lately. Myron told him to hold out and figured Paramount would come through with the money. Instead, Travis got fired. *That's* what really happened."

Edith never commented publicly on the episode, except to say that she was offered the job when Banton left.

When Travis left Paramount in March of 1938, I suddenly became the head of the department. There was no fanfare, no dramatic transition, no popping of champagne corks, no raise in salary. I had been working six days a week, fifteen hours a day, and I continued this routine. Since I had been Banton's chief assistant, it was just assumed that now I was chief designer. No formal announcement was made by the studio until the fall of 1938. Meanwhile, I inherited Banton's beautiful, big, superelegant office and his most popular and most difficult star, La Belle Colbert.

Edith's first experience with Colbert was her last. In *Zaza* (1939), Colbert was cast in a role she didn't like and was asked to wear bustled and bowed costumes circa 1894. Unhappy in period clothes, Colbert complained throughout the fittings, claiming that she was too small to carry all the gewgaws on the costumes. When she finally told Edith that Banton would have approached the costumes differently, the designer told her that she could certainly have another designer finish the costumes if she wanted. Colbert brought in someone from New York who merely refitted the costumes, assuaging the star's fears that she looked too much like a sweet version of Mae West. After that experience, Colbert requested her personal couturiere, Irene, who was soon to become the supervising designer at MGM, to design her wardrobes, while Edith costumed everyone else in any Colbert films.

I don't blame Colbert. She was a big star. And she still thought of me as a second, as Travis' assistant. Everybody can't like everybody—and Colbert didn't like me. I tried my best for her. I saw a very different side of her from what her fans saw, and I used to get irritated when everyone thought she was so sweet. But I'm much more philosophical now.

Losing Colbert to Irene was a blow to Edith's ego, but she rationalized that she didn't need one more prima donna constantly complaining that she wasn't doing things "the way Travis would."

I had the job of head designer, but after the episode with Colbert, I realized that I had my work cut out for me. I had to gain a great deal of respect from a number of stars to get me to the point of being "Edith Head" instead of being "Travis Banton's replacement." Taking over didn't seem like such a big deal to me, because I was still dressing all the stars of the horse operas (as we called the Westerns in those days) as well as the leading stars and feature players of the "B" pictures. Dorothy Lamour,

Martha Raye, Frances Farmer, Heather Angel, and Gail Patrick were the girls who were under contract and did so many of the "B's." I got so I could make dresses for them without any initial fittings; I knew their likes, their dislikes, their measurements.

The "B" pictures and Westerns kept me very busy toward the end of the 1930s. I worked on thirty or forty films a year, but most of them had titles I don't even remember. When I look through my list of credits for those years I wonder how I ever did it. I was responsible for dressing all the stars, male as well as female. Sometimes we had four or five films going at once. I would be preparing the costume sketches for some while working on the advanced design stages for others. Eventually I began hiring more sketch artists, assistants, wardrobe girls, and wardrobe men who would help me to keep up with the hectic schedule.

The pace was ridiculous, but it was such a great training ground. I would never be the designer I am today, if it hadn't been for the 1930s.

The decade ended with the release of David O. Selznick's *Gone with the Wind* (1939), the most famous period picture in history. Walter Plunkett's costumes set a trend for the 1940s that had women all over the world wearing Melanie's snoods and Scarlett's ballgowns from the Civil War period. Petticoats were back and so were corsets. The film captured eight Academy Awards, but because there were no Oscars for costume design in 1939, Walter Plunkett was not officially honored for his fine work. When Edith spoke with the MGM designer after the award ceremony, she consoled him and added, "Maybe in another ten years we'll be getting our due."

FOUR

Very few people knew about the Charles Head in Edith's life. He was part of her private world and she maintained a rather strict silence about anything she did afterhours. Her friend, photographer John Engstead, had met Charles and called him extremely quiet. "He didn't really want to be a part of Edith's life in Hollywood—he just didn't fit in," recalled Engstead, whose Hollywood portraiture has become almost as famous as Edith's costumes. The Heads lived very separate lives: He retreated to booze and Edith to work. When she socialized, she socialized without Charles. That was easier than trying to ignore or explain away his drunken stupors. It was easier than driving him home and trying to roll his dead weight up the stairs of their Doheny Drive apartment.

Observers couldn't understand why she stuck it out with Charles. She didn't seem to love him—maybe it was merely a matter of being duty-bound. Finally, in 1938, put off by one too many of his drunken binges, she gave up and divorced him. Duty never let her forget the man whose name she would carry forever, and even years later, as he lay dying, she would be at his bedside.

Edith's longtime friend Wiard Boppo Ihnen soon became the "other man" in her life, during the last years of her marriage to Head. Ihnen, whom everyone called Bill, was a highly acclaimed art director on staff at Paramount. The two had met while working together on *Cradle Song* (1933) and had developed a strong platonic friendship. Bill left Paramount soon after *Cradle Song*, working first at RKO and then at Twentieth Century-Fox, where his set designs earned two Academy Awards. He and Edith stayed in close touch. Bill would consult her when he needed advice about his latest love affair or his personal wardrobe. He respected her taste and intellect and she liked his gentleness. They'd launch into long discussions about art and Mexico, where she had spent time as a child and where he longed to live. For hours they'd contemplate the psychology of film, the importance of subtle visuals, the lack of intelligence in scripts of the day. He'd make her laugh occasionally with his jokes about foreigners and his feigned European accents. She liked to laugh, but it was hard to loosen up in the evenings when she was spending eighty hours a week being the corporate woman.

Bill's name was not linked to Edith's in the gossip columns until September 9, 1940, when Hedda Hopper announced that they had married in Las Vegas the day before. She misspelled "Wiard" and mentioned Edith's latest movie, neglecting the fact that Bill's latest projects, *The Return of Frank James* (1940) and *Youth Will Be Served* (1940), had been released and would put him in the running for an Academy Award for art direction. The couple had flown to Las Vegas in a friend's private plane. Edith recalls wearing a bright red and yellow frock and a straw hat.

I really didn't know that we were getting married until the night before we did it. Our friend Victor Calderon unwit-

tingly challenged us to get married simply by asking why we hadn't. I told him that Bill had never proposed. The next thing I knew, Bill said, "Let's get married tomorrow." Victor had the plane chartered, and we were on our way to Las Vegas the next morning. Until Bill picked me up at the door I really didn't believe we were getting married. I remember losing $35 in the slots at the Golden Nugget that day.

The new couple set up housekeeping in a rambling California-style hacienda in Encino, then the hinterlands of the San Fernando Valley, half an hour's drive from their respective studios. Decorating was Bill's forte. A slave to detail, he created a little Mexico within the walls of their adobe. The grounds even had the same type of burros Edith had played with when she was eight. Every room reflected Bill's love for Mexican culture—every room, that is, but Edith's bedroom. Her sanctuary was French provincial, steeped in lace and Louis XIV. The decor in Bill's bedroom was bold, oversized, and powerful; authentic cannons and Mexican artillery flanked pictures of his relatives and his dear little wife, "Edo." Each spent hours in their respective haunts, Bill dabbling with oil paints and formulating architectural plans, Edith plotting wardrobes for her next movie. They met on common ground, the living room or cantina or garden, to laugh, to exchange ideas, to build a foundation that was to last for the next forty years.

Bill was an exceedingly sentimental man. He had a strong sense of being the man of the house. It was important to him to be in charge and I liked that very much. It was always very important to me to be taken care of. And Bill did that so well. But Bill's greatest contribution to our marriage was his strength of character and his ability to accept my career. There were not many men like him in 1940. It was never easy being married to Edith Head, Costume Designer.

The 1930s had given Hollywood costume designers a powerful name in the world of fashion. From their exclusive *haute couture* salons, designers such as Chanel, Schiaparelli, Patou, Molyneux, Mainbocher, Charles James, and Hattie Carnegie hesitantly admitted that film fashion was having an impact on what real women wore. And why not, when Paris and New York designs were limited to society women and the pages of *Harper's Bazaar* and *Vogue*? But a fashion show of Hollywood's glamorous chic, modeled by the world's most beautiful and well-known women, was available to every American woman at every neighborhood theater.

In the same way that Lamour's sarong had turned U.S. beaches and swimming pools into a sea of mass-produced tropical-print body wraps in 1936, the broad-shouldered look that MGM's Adrian gave Joan Crawford in the 1930s began to show up on department store racks everywhere. Adrian had broadened the shoulder line of almost every contemporary suit he designed in the late 1920s and throughout the 1930s. And by 1935 many adventurous American women—the ones who spent $55 for an entire year's wardrobe instead of $100 on just one suit—were stitching Woolworth's shoulder pads into their favorite outfits and adopting a chic Crawford posture. Yet it wasn't until 1937 that Schiaparelli gave the French nod to the look and added shoulder pads to some of her couture designs.

Realizing the financial potential of hookups between costume designers and the garment industry, studio executives had negotiated contracts with garment makers, fiber producers, and retail stores. Now the already overworked costume designers began meeting with New York- and California-based companies to approve designs for retail production. They were making personal appearances in department stores all over the country and were even endorsing new brands of yarn. Labels on ruffled dresses for twelve-year-olds carried the Edith Head signature, and ads for the latest rayonlike yarn noted that the Paramount designer thought "Clairanesse taffeta" was every bit as good as silk (yet Edith never used the synthetic in her Hollywood costumes).

For Edith this was the beginning of what was to be one of the most important aspects of her career: publicity. By 1940, when she was entrenched as costume head at Paramount, Edith was well aware that MGM wasn't about to get rid of Adrian. Women went to the movies as much to see his creations as they did to see Garbo and Crawford. The fans knew his name; Adrian was a star. There was absolutely no reason Edith couldn't develop that same kind of stronghold, so she set out to do it. And she determined that she would do it by showing women clothes they could really wear, not the outrageous fantasies that had made Adrian famous.

Edith's greatest career anxieties came when she viewed Adrian's latest film costumes. To those closest to her, she admitted feeling pangs of inadequacy when she watched his whimsical Munchkins emerge in *The Wizard of Oz* (1939) or when she saw Garbo slink across the screen in one of his perfectly engineered gowns of sequinned silk or simple satin. Adrian had been exposed to fashion even as a child, since his parents were couture milliners. The years he spent at the New York School of Fine and Applied Art (now Parsons School of Design) had taught him the essentials of artistic design, and his exquisite flair had been nurtured by working with fashion masters. When she compared their backgrounds, Edith was constantly reminded that she had attained her position at Paramount as a result of a number of fortunate coincidences, not by building a reputation as a great designer.

If Edith felt inadequate, the executives at Paramount didn't know it. She kept within her budgets and produced costumes that perfectly suited the stars and the scripts. She was a producer's and director's dream. In the 1930s critics and stars alike had compared Banton to Adrian. Many thought Banton to be as talented, as capable, as productive. But when Banton left Paramount and joined Howard Greer in a couture salon, Adrian stood alone as the film costume master. Edith was in a different league.

Adrian had worked with virtually no budgetary limitations at MGM. His extravagant costumes for the studio's lavish musicals were the reason he was drawing $75,000 a year, the same as the President of the United States was making in 1940. He used the world's most expensive fabrics and demanded intricate labor on every gown, causing costs to skyrocket. Restraint wasn't his style. Adrian was an artist for art's sake, sometimes forsaking his living mannequins. In one of his last films at MGM, *Ziegfeld Girl* (1941), his costumes for one humorous segment transformed Lana Turner, Judy Garland, and Hedy Lamarr into comical varieties of South

American flora, with no regard to their figures. His concern appeared to be only that his costumes come to life on the screen—not that his stars look their best. With his svelte clotheshorse, Greta Garbo, he didn't have to worry; she provided the perfect canvas for his creations.

In 1940, however, directors started putting demands on Adrian. He was told to dress Garbo more like the ordinary American woman, to make her less aloof. At the same time, he was presented with budgets and ordered to adhere to them. The cutbacks didn't allow for the all-out glamour that had become his trademark. The corporation was making itself known, and Adrian saw his power being taken away, quickly. He lost no time in leaving MGM to open his own couture salon, a business he would maintain until 1952. Irene, the famed couture designer at prestigious Bullock's-Wilshire in downtown Los Angeles, was brought in as supervising designer at MGM. Edith could now proceed, free from Adrian's shadow.

Her first opportunity for a fashion picture came in 1940 when Barbara Stanwyck was cast in the lead of Preston Sturges' *The Lady Eve.* Dubbed in Paramount ads as "the vexiest picture of the year" (released 1941), *The Lady Eve* coupled Stanwyck, as a gutsy female gambler, with Henry Fonda, the handsome-but-shy herpetologist and heir to a multimillion-dollar ale business.

Stanwyck's wardrobe was Edith's greatest achievement to date. The designer helped turn the actress into an instant sex symbol and a trendsetter. Each of twenty-five changes was a statement of advanced 1941 fashion. And Edith had created every piece in early 1940.

"I was never a clotheshorse," admits Stanwyck, "but suddenly I felt like one in that picture. For *The Lady Eve* Edith made the most beautiful clothes I had ever worn. Every change was spectacular."

Lady Eve *changed both our lives. It was Barbara's first high-fashion picture and her biggest transition in costuming. She was already a top star and she had an image long before I got to her. She was always playing plain Janes, women to whom clothes meant nothing. Yet Barbara was quite trim and had a better shape than most of the other actresses around. She possessed what some designers considered to be a figure "problem" —a long waist and a comparatively low rear end. By widening the waistbands on the front of her gowns and narrowing them slightly in back, I could still put her in straight skirts, something other designers were afraid to do, because they thought she might look too heavy in the seat. Since she wasn't the least bit heavy, I just took advantage of her long waist to create an optical illusion that her derrière was just as pertly placed as any other star's.*

The Lady Eve brought Edith the kind of acclaim that had eluded her since taking over from Banton in 1938. The script had demanded that she transform Stanwyck from a tarty gambler into a British noblewoman—from sex kitten to Windsoresque beauty.

If you hadn't seen the first part of the picture you probably wouldn't know who the elegant lady was. It was a complete metamorphosis; in the first half of the film she was one person and in the other half, another. It wasn't merely a change of costume. The way she stood and walked was different. Her makeup and hair became much more elegant to suit her character.

For her gambler character, I had used sharp contrasts— black on white, all black, all white—to make her appear a tad coarse. Naturally I chose much richer, more luxurious fabrics when she was supposed to be of noble birth. I also used different colorations that would show up more subtly in black and white. I left the sequins and glitter to the lady gambler in the beginning.

Barbara made the great transition beautifully, but she told me after we saw the completed film that she wasn't aware of changing as she was playing the role. It was a natural evolution.

43

Director Preston Sturges was delighted with the progression of the costumes and congratulated Edith on her "coming of age." Stanwyck, charmed with the idea of being a screen-fashion sensation, credited the designer with changing her image. "From then on I had Edith Head's name written into every contract, no matter what studio I was working for," Stanwyck recalls, noting that in the 1940s she was a freelance actress who worked for several studios. Edith was elated at the success of the film and the praise from her colleagues, but she was most excited by the public's response to her designs.

I had used Spanish motifs on much of the Lady Eve *wardrobe, and luckily anything with a Latin American touch was extremely topical in the months before America entered the war. The story was set on board a ship from South America, so that was enough excuse for me to inject some ethnic styles into the wardrobe.*

Barbara looked sensational in poncho and serape styles, and she was so sexy in the clothes that suddenly Latin American fashions swept the country. Of course it was really Barbara Stanwyck who started the trend, not me—just as it was Dottie Lamour who launched the trend toward tropical prints and sarong drapings. Over the next few years I was loaned to other studios to design the clothes for Barbara's pictures. The prestige of dressing her naturally led to requests from other important stars and assignments on their films.

Barbara Stanwyck's wasn't the only character she had to dress in *The Lady Eve*. Sturges had introduced a snake into the script to reinforce the allusion to Eve in the title. He wanted Edith to come up with an outfit for the critter, Emma, to add a little humor. With her early experience costuming elephants, Edith considered dressing a snake to be a minor challenge. At least it wouldn't eat its finery as the pachyderm had done so many years before.

I made Emma a nice diamond necklace from a jeweled buckle, hoping it would fit when it came time to shoot the scenes.

Emma was a tiny king snake, harmless as a kitten. The only problem was that it was the hibernating season for snakes and Emma just wanted to sleep, so she proceeded to shed her skin in the middle of production. She was sleepy, lethargic, and uncooperative. I wasn't the least bit afraid of this harmless snake, since I grew up with snakes on the desert, and I didn't mind handling Emma to try to get the elegant necklace on her. But each time I tried, she slithered out of it. We finally had to let her do scenes without the necklace, one of my few costuming failures. I was also supposed to engineer a hat that Emma could wear during the opening credits so she could wriggle across the screen and squeeze through the "O" in Preston's name. That didn't work either. Preston finally ended up using an animated snake in the credits—even he *couldn't make everything work. He tried, though, and that's what I loved about working with Preston Sturges. His wit came across in his visuals as well as in his writing and direction.*

It was shortly after *The Lady Eve* that Stanwyck dragged Edith off to the dentist to replace those missing front teeth. As the actress recalls, "Edith always covered her mouth when she laughed and I didn't understand why. Finally she showed me her teeth and I understood. They were awful—not diseased, but some were missing and she felt self-conscious. She told me that she had been to dentists and they had said nothing could be done. I informed her that my dentist could fix anything. He had fixed my smile, so I was sure he could help Edith." Within a few days, the spaces were gone. Smiling still didn't come easily to Edith. She remained "Beaver" inside. Gradually she did learn to grin, but only among her closest friends. Few photographs exist of a smiling Edith Head.

By the end of 1940 there was little to smile about. The country was less than a year away from a world war. The fall of France had already had its immediate effect on the costume departments. No more lush French fabrics—those fabulous silks and glamorous glitter cloths would have to come from wardrobe stock or be produced domestically.

Costumes from earlier films were changed—a collar added or removed, sleeves shortened, skirts narrowed, an entire dress dyed—and used over again to dress second leads and extras in new films. The technique had been in practice for years as a means of cutting costs, but never because dramatic fabrics were impossible to locate or in short supply.

Despite the shortages, Edith's workload was heavy. Directors and producers didn't want to hear excuses. They wanted costumes, and they wanted them on time. She turned out wardrobes for forty-seven films in 1940 and forty-five in 1941. While other studios with similar schedules had several designers working simultaneously, Edith told Frank Richardson, who headed up the wardrobe department, that she didn't need anyone else; she could handle it all. And she often did, occasionally with the help of only one sketch artist, sometimes with as many as three. But against Edith's wishes, Richardson brought in Natalie Visart to work as primary designer on DeMille's films.

It took a true executive to dress Paulette Goddard, Dorothy Lamour, Olivia de Havilland, Joan Blondell, Veronica Lake, Mary Martin, Madeleine Carroll, Constance Moore, and Ellen Drew and still have time for Barbara Stanwyck, Loretta Young, Frances Farmer, Anne Baxter, Betty Hutton, Ginger Rogers, and Ingrid Bergman. Edith kept everything exceedingly well organized. If things did get out of hand at times, no one outside the sewing room knew about it. When the seamstresses called her a tyrant behind her back, the wardrobe mistress, Billye Fritz, shushed them and told them to be happy they weren't working in the sweatshops in downtown Los Angeles.

Occasionally Billye would complain to Edith and they'd argue behind closed doors in the designer's salon. Billye rarely won the arguments, but Edith listened to what the wardrobe mistress had to say. The day after a disagreement Billye would find a bottle of cologne or an embroidered hanky on her desk—a peace offering of sorts.

If she was a taskmaster, she was often a sensitive one. She recalled the days when Paulette Goddard, newly married to Charlie Chaplin, would parade through the sewing room flaunting her newfound riches in front of the seamstresses, who worked from early morning till dusk to earn their $32 a week.

Paulette often carried cigar boxes filled with jewels, precious jewels that Chaplin had given her. She would open the cigar box, pass it around temptingly for all the seamstresses to see—but no, don't touch, they're not cigars, they're precious gems, jerks. That was her attitude. I think she was actually much better known for her jewels than her acting, at least at Paramount. I designed her wardrobe for The Cat and the Canary *(1939) and* The Ghost Breakers *(1940), both with Bob Hope, but I don't remember her clothes at all. I just remember her tormenting my staff with that damn cigar box full of jewels.*

Edith liked to describe the 1940s as her transitional years. She quickly developed from Banton's replacement into a costume design professional in her own right. She was rid of Colbert and Goddard early on, and the rest of the Paramount stars and starlets sincerely liked working with her. They liked her style, her good taste, and her spirit. They liked the fact that she really tried to make them look their best and not just showcase some fabulous costume.

For the first time since she came to Paramount in 1923, Edith felt important, needed, appreciated. Having earned her share of acclaim for her *Lady Eve* costumes, she could experiment and be respected for it. Since she knew more about clothes than anyone at the studio, even her "failures" would be disasters only in her eyes. To the rest of the world they were "artistic endeavors." That was freedom.

The fun began when Bob Hope, Bing Crosby, and Dorothy Lamour teamed up for the *Road* pictures. The three had been around for several years at Paramount. Edith met Crosby when he had his first starring role in *The Big Broadcast* (1932), and Hope when he made his film debut in *The Big Broadcast of 1938* (1937). And she had dressed Lamour several times since *The Jungle Princess* (1936).

We all grew up together at Paramount, but Hope was the baby. My most vivid memory of his first film is Hope singing a duet of "Thanks for the Memory" with Shirley Ross, who was dressed in a silly black hat and leopard-skin vest and muff I designed for her. By then Bing was a well-established star and Dorothy Lamour was one of the top pinup girls and box-office attractions.

What a team! It was a masterpiece of casting. Audiences went mad for them as they chased one another from Singapore to Zanzibar to Morocco, to Utopia and Rio and wherever. They always went to exotic places in exotic costumes. The story didn't matter; everybody came to see the latest gags.

I didn't have to worry about authenticity. If somebody wrote and said, "Edith, in Morocco they don't wear headdresses like that," I didn't give a damn. If Bob Hope wanted to wear it because it was funny, he wore it.

At the start of every Road *picture I would do two things. First, I'd read the script to see where they were going, then call the research people and ask them to find out whatever they could about the locale. If Dottie was playing the princess or queen of some obscure country, I would ask research to find pictures of that special brand of royalty. I could tell from the pictures whether they wore veils, turbans, crowns, or pompoms. I tried to differentiate between the rich people and the peasants, between the lords of the land and their slaves.*

Then I would have the wardrobe people go down to West-ern Costume, the largest-stock costume house in Hollywood, and bring back samples of anything they had that might be a reason-able facsimile of costumes worn in the country. Keep in mind that the settings weren't restricted to the name of the film. In Road to Singapore, *for instance, they landed on a South Seas island where they encountered the beautiful sarong-clad Mima (we* had *to get Dorothy into a sarong somehow, remember!), and from then on the hilarity began. My job was to make sure that the costumes matched the frivolity.*

I would base my sketches, rather loosely, on the samples from Western Costume. From my sketches, we'd dress the princi-

In one of her earliest publicity
photographs for Paramount, Edith wore
a gown of her own design; 1928.

As assistant to Travis Banton,
sketch artist Edith Head put
the finishing touches on his sketches
and also designed for supporting
cast members; 1930.

Looking very much like Paramount
star Louise Brooks, Edith posed for a
publicity shot; 1936.

Edith tried out a new
rolled hairdo to replace her
severe chignon; 1938.

On her first trip to Europe
as Paramount's head designer,
Edith bought this Schiaparelli
suit; 1938.

Having wrapped
Dorothy Lamour in a
"sarongown" with
its colossal hibiscus
pattern, Edith
debates the finished
product; 1938.

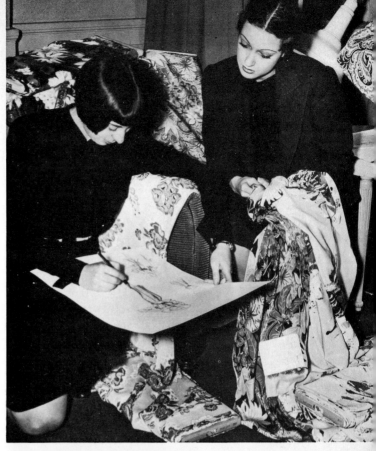

After Dorothy Lamour
became one of the
most important stars
in Hollywood,
Edith included her in
initial costume meetings
and discussed fabric
selections with
the Paramount headliner;
1939.

Looking quite glamorous,
the five-foot designer
posed for a portrait; 1939.

Edith examines
one of Mary
Martin's costumes
for *The Great
Victor Herbert*
(1939); 1938.

(OPPOSITE TOP)
Mary Martin
and Edith relax
on the set of
*The Great Victor
Herbert* (1939); 1938.

(OPPOSITE
BOTTOM) Edith and
Wiard (Bill) Ihnen
shortly after
their marriage in
September 1940.

Edith often used dolls as models before
completing her stars' wardrobes.
Here she shows Ginger Rogers a model of
one of her costumes for
The Major and the Minor (1942).

Frequently quoted in newspapers and
magazines during World War II, Edith told
women how to economize by sewing their
own clothes. Modeling one of her
own designs, Edith suggested that women
hand-paint a safety-pin motif on
blouses or dresses and actually use
safety pins as buttons. Note the safety
pin earrings; 1944–45.

(FAR LEFT)
At forty-six, Edith enjoyed
adding a ribbon to her braids and dressing
in Mexican garb afterhours; 1944.

(LEFT) Edith and Loretta Young inspect
a gown for *The Perfect Marriage* (1946); 1945.

Wearing a signature blouse, Edith reviews
one of her sketches; 1946.

Edith poses at the door of her
Paramount salon; 1946.

Edith and hairstylist
LeVaughn Speer put
the final touches
on Joan Fontaine in
The Emperor Waltz
(1948); 1946.

Edith okays sketches for
The Emperor Waltz (1948); 1946.

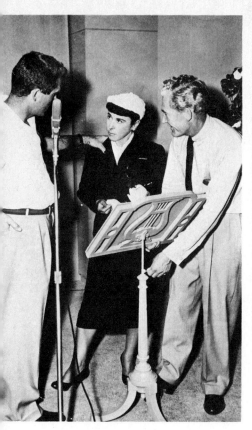

(ABOVE, LEFT)
Just before winning her sixth Academy Award, for *A Place in the Sun* (1951),
Edith posed for a publicity photo; 1952.

(LEFT)
While vacationing on the northern California coast, Edith let her husband,
Wiard Ihnen, photograph her with her hair down and her skirt blowing
in the Pacific ocean breezes; early 1950s.

(ABOVE, CENTER)
On the set of *Lucy Gallant* (1955), director Robert Parrish tries to help
Edith relax as she prepares for her first speaking part in a film.
Since the director requested that she not wear her spectacles, Edith had a
difficult time seeing what was going on. Playing herself, she was to
read fashion-show commentary from the podium that assistant director
William McGarry adjusts here.

(ABOVE, RIGHT)
On the set of *Lucy Gallant* (1955), Edith slipped out of her size-5 pumps
and sipped some coffee; 1955.

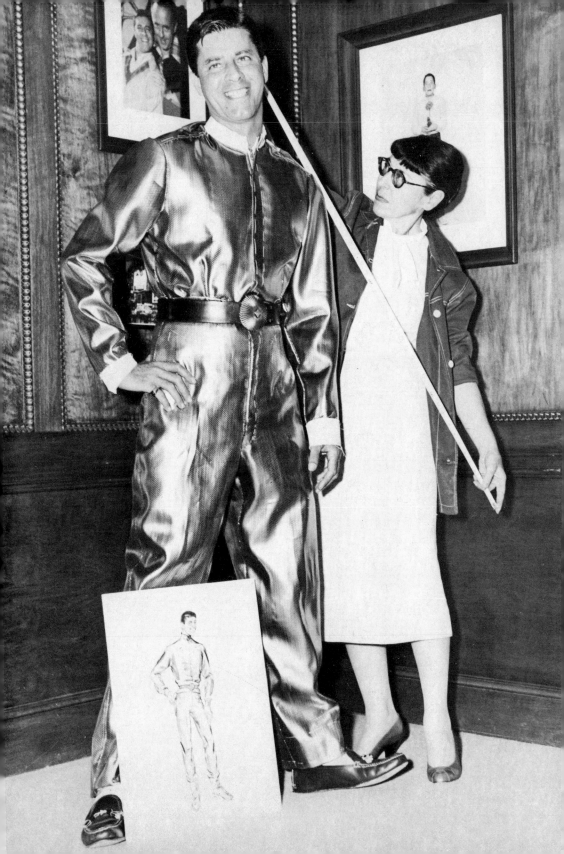

(OPPOSITE)
In a rare chance to experiment with outer-space garb,
Edith had fun dressing Jerry Lewis for *Visit to
a Small Planet* (1960). "I used fabric that was the
closest thing to aluminum foil I could find,
and I made Jerry trade his Italian moccasins for
more alien boots," she recalled.

After winning her seventh Academy Award, for
The Facts of Life (1960), Edith agreed to another publicity
shot; 1961. (© AMPAS®)

During one of her frequent appearances on Art Linkletter's *House Party* in the early 1960s, Edith showed Linkletter how to dress for the rain, not for secret-agent work as it might appear here.

In a rare photograph of a smiling Edith Head, the designer joked with sketch artist Richard Hopper; 1967. (Yvonne Mozée)

On the set of *The Last Married Couple in America* (1979), Edith confers with a roller-skating Natalie Wood; 1978.

Edith had frequently designed airline uniforms for major companies. In 1980, when United Airlines celebrated its fiftieth anniversary, the company asked a number of fashion designers to predict what flight attendants would be wearing in the year 2030. Edith's practical fantasy included a computerized communication belt and sleek helmet.

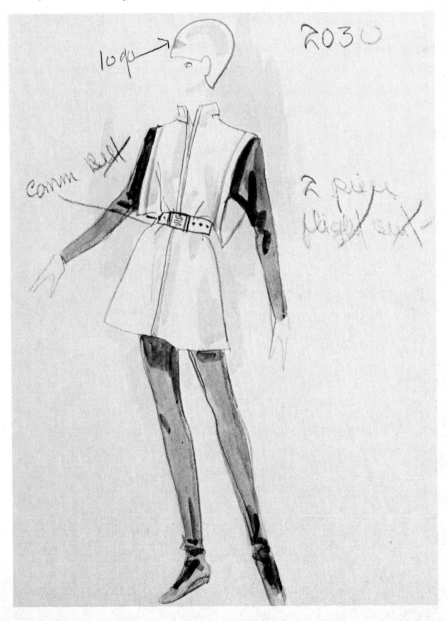

At a posthumous tribute to Mae West at the Academy of Motion Picture
Arts and Sciences, Edith appeared in a vibrant red suit; 1981.

(OPPOSITE, TOP)
Edith earned her first onscreen credit dressing Mae West in *She Done
Him Wrong* (1933). West originated her own look, and Edith interpreted it,
here with sequinned doves flocking bosom-ward. (Ronald Haver Collection)

(OPPOSITE, BOTTOM)
For Mae's daytime wear, Edith eschewed sequins for a braided décolletage and traded
walking stick for parasol. Mae used some form of staff to keep
her balance when she wore high platform shoes. (Ronald Haver Collection)

The sarong worn by Dorothy Lamour in *Jungle Princess* (1936) set
a fashion trend. Here, as Ray Milland casts a passionate glance at Ulah,
a safety pin near Lamour's right elbow helps hold her sarong in place.

As assistant to Travis Banton, Edith often helped the Paramount designer dress Carole Lombard. But her only official screen credit for dressing the blond star came in 1937, for *True Confession*, above. The spectacled fellow is Porter Hall.

(LEFT, ABOVE)
In one of her first major assignments as head designer at Paramount,
The Big Broadcast of 1938 (1937), Edith's designs dripped with fantasy,
as in this tiered tulle gown with enormous sequinned bow trim.

(LEFT, BELOW)
Shirley Ross, star of *The Big Broadcast of 1938*, posed for publicity photos
in Edith's sequinned midriff-baring top and bias-cut skirt, so
reminiscent of the work of the designer's former mentor, Travis Banton.

(LEFT, CENTER)
Edith rarely did her own sketching after she became Paramount's
chief designer. This original Head sketch for Dorothy Lamour in *Tropic
Holiday* (1938) shows the Mexican influence that was beginning to
appear in the designer's work. The sketch called for bright embroidery
to enhance the wide leather belt, which picked up the red, blue, and
yellow color scheme of the handwoven *rebosa* or shawl.

(ABOVE)
For *The Great Victor Herbert* (1939), Edith dressed Mary Martin in a frilly,
sheer blouse of pink *mousseline* with ribbon-and-lace trim.
Note that only the belt buckle and the position of the neckline
decoration changed from sketch to finished garment.

(ABOVE)

Mary Martin models a panne velvet gown that Edith designed for
her personal wardrobe (the chunky bracelet is made of Mexican silver
beads and bells). On the dress form is the suit Martin wore in *The Great
Victor Herbert*. The drape of the skirt was changed from sketch to garment
to create the illusion of a slim, waspish waistline. The added
kolinsky-fur (Russian weasel) trim on the finished version also
helped accentuate the waist.

(OPPOSITE)

After working with Edith on several films in the late 1930s and
early 1940s, Mary Martin asked the designer to do her personal wardrobe
as well. The ballooning pants and bare midriff top were reportedly
worn for daytime shipboard parties; the pink *souffle* gown with
black floral appliqués was reserved for more formal occasions. Martin chose
satin Persian pajamas and a floral satin negligee for her boudoir.

Edith used yards of ivory bridal satin to fashion Barbara Stanwyck's gown.

Director Preston Sturges, with his de rigueur ascot, helps Henry Fonda, in matching shoes and jacket, escort Barbara Stanwyck to the set of *The Lady Eve* (1941). Stanwyck was camera-ready in Edith's shipboard trouser outfit.

To create a flattering line for Stanwyck's figure, Edith frequently raised the waistline in front. In this cocktail dress for *The Lady Eve*, the designer combined black chiffon and crepe with a delicate French lace camisole.

As the Lady Eve, in the film of the same name, Stanwyck woos Fonda in a white apron-front gown emblazoned with brilliants and rhinestones. In back the gown is bare to the waist, except for the glittering caped-shoulder treatment.

On the set of *The Lady Eve*, Fonda and Stanwyck are tested for proper lighting. Stanwyck's two-piece black ensemble featured the sweetheart neckline that Edith would use so often in future films. Though the split skirt did not appear in the sketch, the finished product allowed for plenty of leg, especially in this chaise longue scene.

pals, but there were still seventy-five to one hundred extras to costume. I supervised all the costumers who dressed the extras, and I had to make sure that all the clothes would fit with the outfits worn by Bing, Bob, and Dottie. We rented many of these from Western, so at least we didn't have to do individual designs for all the extras.

Bob loved dressing up for the films. He didn't mind wearing a burnoose or a turban or whatever I wanted to put him in. The funnier and more bizarre it was, the better he liked it. Bing was the opposite. He loathed dressing up. I don't think Bing really cared about playing any character but himself. His movie roles were usually variations of Crosby the Crooner. With his singing voice, that was enough. Sartorially he preferred simple clothes: a sport shirt and slacks. It pained him to put on any headgear more exotic than a Panama hat or a golf cap. He wasn't unpleasant about it, just unhappy. He couldn't really have the fun with his getups that Bob had. I doubt if anyone was ever conscious of the fact that Bob was always more amusingly dressed than Bing. I always noticed because I knew of Bing's aversion to costumes.

Bob was always enthusiastic about Dottie's costumes, too. I thought they were pretty fantastic myself, even if I did design them. She had put on a few curves since The Jungle Princess *and had a more mature, sexy image in the* Road *roles. In some scenes she was breathtakingly beautiful and in others her costumes were as ridiculous as Bob's. But she carried them off perfectly. Bob was wide-eyed over her costumes and always made her feel beautiful.*

Bob has a special place in my heart for what he did for my costumes in the Road *pictures. It was his enthusiasm that really inspired everyone else to get into the spirit of the* Roads. *There were chaotic plots and gags and lavish sets and great music, but Bob Hope pulled it all together.*

Road to Singapore, released in March 1940, was not only Paramount's biggest film that year but the top money-making film in Hollywood to date. It was followed by *Road to Zanzibar* (1941),

Road to Morocco (1942), *Road to Utopia* (1945), and so on into the 1950s. All were considered to be financial successes. But when Crosby and Hope teamed up in 1962 to produce *Road to Hong Kong,* with Lamour in a bit part and without Edith, the series had passed its prime and the *Roads* came to an end.

I hated to see the Road *pictures end. They represented such a happy time to me. That period could never be duplicated. We all laughed despite—or maybe in spite, at—the world situation.*

Road to Morocco (1942) was the first of the series made while the United States was at war. I was faced with the challenges of wartime shortages and restrictions: no more silk, not even the domestic variety, could be used, because the country's silk production was going to the war effort. In 1942 a directive that we referred to as L-85 had come from Washington, which drastically limited the amount of fabric that could be used in any garment construction—including Hollywood costumes. It meant no pleats, no cuffs, no ruffles, no long jackets, no extra frills.

This austerity campaign was meant to set an example for the public. Despite these limitations, I was supposed to give Dorothy Lamour exotic Moroccan costumes. I made every possible concession. When I wanted her to wear silk pantaloons, I substituted sheer cotton. When I wanted gold metallic trim, we used kidskin and painted it gold. It all worked, thanks to some ingenuity and clever lighting effects.

FIVE

While Edith's husband Bill was off at war, serving as a camouflage expert for the Army, Edith took it upon herself to do her patriotic part. Whenever her name was in print, it was attached to a declaration of a woman's responsibility in time of war. In February 1942, she told a reporter, "This year a woman has a new duty, as her wardrobe must reflect the spirit of sacrifice through its adaptability. It must reflect the spirit of enthusiasm through its brightness. It must reflect the spirit of determination through its lack of ostentation. This sacrifice, enthusiasm, and determination will make the woman behind the man in the defense lines a willing and inspirational factor in winning the war."

In another message to American women she tried to make

sacrifice sound desirable: "All designers are turning to cotton. Silk is out of style for 1942. Synthetic materials will be used more than ever before, and we are fortunate because they have been perfected to such a degree that it is almost impossible to detect that they are not pure fibers. Imported furs are a thing of the past. Double-duty clothes will cut down on budgets. Coats with zip-in, changeable linings and suits with reversible jackets are the fashion news."

The reality, of course, was that there *was* no silk, since it was all going to the national cause, but saying it was out of style seemed to help make the shortage more tolerable. As late as 1944 Edith continued to make patriotic pitches to fans: "Remember, there isn't anyone who can't look better. . . . Just because we are at war doesn't mean we have to go around looking grim and drab. Drabness has no place in our modern life, in our national scene. Taking the time and trouble to choose the right clothes and have them fitted properly to your figure is vital not only to your personal improvement but to improvement in home-front morale."

Directive L-85 limited Edith's explorations into the world of fantasy. What she did for Lamour in the *Roads* was about as far as she strayed into never-never land. Most of her other wartime films were strictly realistic, with touches of glamour here and there. In Mitchell Leisen's *Masquerade in Mexico* (1945), Head surprised everyone by having Lamour come out in a sexy black lace dress over a nude-colored *souffle* slip. Used under lace or rhinestones, a sheer fabric like *souffle* becomes totally transparent, creating the illusion of lace worn over bare skin. Irene was renowned for her *souffle* creations, but Edith's gown for Lamour was as spectacular as anything Irene had shown.

It was a beautifully elegant dress, which totally changed the Dorothy Lamour screen image into something very chic. There wasn't a single sarong in the script, nor a flower over her ear. She looked like an entirely different person. You'd never believe that the little girl with no bosom and that silly flower back of her ear could look like a fashion model.

I worked with Dottie in so many pictures, with so many

*makeups and hairdresses, that she became one of my main ex-
hibits for my fashion magic. I could transform her into anybody. In a sarong she slithered and looked sexy; in* Masquerade
in Mexico *she looked elegant and alluring. In* Caught in the Draft
*(1941) with Bob Hope she was a colonel's daughter and I designed
twenty-two outfits, all in black and white, and not a single sarong! She was delighted.*

Veronica Lake came to Paramount in the same way that
Lamour had: a child-woman cut out to be a star. Her slight stature
and baby face made her an unlikely pinup candidate until Wally
Westmore, supervisor of Paramount's makeup and hair department, discovered her gorgeous hair (she had kept it hidden under
a beret). He shaped it, parted it on the side, and let it fall, vampishly
covering one eye. Edith set out to turn Lake's size-3 body into
something that at least looked voluptuous enough to live up to that
hairstyle.

*Her figure problems seemed insurmountable. She was
short, like me, and very tiny—possibly the smallest normal
adult I had ever seen. Her waist was the smallest in Hollywood,
20 3/4". That was 5 1/2" smaller than the average waist. Far
from a designer's dream like Dietrich or Lombard. Yet everyone
was telling me to make her into a sex symbol. She had a good
bust, but I couldn't show it because of the Hays Office's anticleav-
age rules. I was forced to be extremely careful in every costume
she wore. The fabrics I used in Veronica's clothes always had
some type of vertical interest; horizontal lines would shorten
her. I devised necklines that called attention to her bust without
actually exposing it. I always played up the fact that she had big
breasts, which made her seem like a larger woman.*

In her first film, Sullivan's Travels *(1941), I dressed her in
gold lamé and beaded gowns. She was sultry and an immediate
hit. Veronica was married and was, unfortunately for me, very
pregnant at the time we were making that film. The important
question was: How do you photograph a girl so she does not
appear pregnant? She can stand behind a piano. She can carry*

a large muff and you can assume it's a winter picture. Or, what was most successful for Veronica, she can carry a huge fan. Sullivan's Travels was full of these devices, but looking back, there are still times when she looks like a pudgy, short girl—you can't do a whole movie behind a muff, fan, or piano. But by the end of the film I was an expert at concealing pregnancy. She became a sex symbol, so I must have done something right.

Next I wardrobed her for I Married a Witch *(1942), with Fredric March, and she finally worked with Alan Ladd in his first starring role, in* This Gun for Hire *(1942). They became one of the most famous teams of the 1940s, ranking right up there with Bogart and Bacall.*

We did Ramrod *(1947), with Joel McCrea. Costuming the film was very funny because, according to the script, the story was supposed to be set in the 1890s. I didn't feel the clothes from that period would be attractive on Veronica. After I researched the gowns of the 1880s, I realized they wouldn't be right for her either. She was more of an 1870s girl if we had to place her somewhere in history. She looked adorable in the tiny-waisted looks of those days. So* Ramrod *was suddenly set in the 1870s and Veronica was beautiful.*

But for some reason Veronica didn't have the staying power of other stars. By 1949 she was finished.

Though Lake's fashion styles never became a trend, her hairdo swept the country. Women everywhere were peeking out from behind a shock of mane that fell seductively over one eye. Brushing it back in the Lake manner was a mark of sex appeal. The war years had created a bevy of sex symbols. The soldiers needed pinup girls, and the women at home needed something to keep their minds and money occupied. Women went to the movies every chance they had, and tried the latest hairdos or makeup or clothes that might turn them into the next Lamour or Turner or Grable lookalike. They wanted to be gorgeous when their guys came home. They read movie magazines to find out every beauty secret the stars had to offer. Paulette Goddard spoke woman-to-woman with fans in a Woodbury soap advertisement—"To be his guiding star, try my W.B.N.C. (Woodbury beauty night cap)"—and soon many screen beauties joined the endorsement bandwagon.

Photoplay kept women vicariously occupied with stories titled "The Ten Most Attractive Men in Hollywood" and "The Truth About Stars' Dates" and "New, Exciting Whispers About Ann Sothern and Bob Sterling—Goodbye to Marriage, Hello to Romance." Newspapers carried fashion hints from the Hollywood designers, and few weeks went by without an article about Stanwyck's new clothes in this film or Lake's new look in that one. Since manufactured clothing was in short supply, women spent most of their money on makeup and hairdos. Those who sewed at home tried to copy the Hollywood styles, but they soon realized that all the glamour wasn't going to do much good until the men returned.

It was late in August of 1942 when Ingrid Bergman came to Paramount, two days after she finished *Casablanca* (1942) at Warner Brothers. She was to begin the film version of Ernest Hemingway's *For Whom the Bell Tolls* (1943), with Gary Cooper. Until a few days before, the part of Maria had belonged to a Norwegian ballerina, Vera Zorina. But after director Sam Wood saw the first few dailies, he demanded that Bergman replace Zorina.

Bergman was under contract to David O. Selznick's studio at the time, but he had recommended her for the part of Maria from the beginning. Cooper and Hemingway himself had also suggested her.

Ingrid told me that she had wanted the part ever since she read the book, and that Selznick had promised it to her. It took him a while, but he finally made good the promise, apparently after much wheeling and dealing at Paramount.

I had never met her before. At first sight, Ingrid was an imposing woman. In those days she weighed about 135 pounds and wore a size 14. She might have taken a smaller size, but her height—almost six feet—demanded a larger cut. I remember thinking that her feet were small, a 7B, considering her overall presence.

Selznick was extemely possessive of Bergman, even

though he had loaned her to Paramount for $150,000. He demanded that he be present when her hair was cut for the role, and that Sydney Guilaroff, MGM's chief hairstylist, do the work. It was Selznick's opinion that Paramount's stylists had botched Zorina's hair, so he wasn't about to let them touch Bergman. He spent several days supervising her makeup tests, too, so I was mentally prepared when I heard that he wanted to talk to me about her costumes.

For Whom the Bell Tolls was not a fashion picture by any means. In fact, her scenes called for nothing but dirty old pants and shirts. Ingrid had told me that she wasn't interested in clothes, and suggested that we just use something from wardrobe stock. Together we rummaged around in the men's wardrobe and found things that fit her. She was very happy, but when Selznick found out, he was furious. He told me in no uncertain terms that he wanted brand-new pants and shirts for Ingrid. So I ordered new clothes which were then bleached and redyed to look as old and worn as the original costumes had.

Rumors began to circulate that Ingrid and Coop were having more than just a screen love affair as the film was being made. Coop was always falling in love with his leading ladies, as I had learned so early on Wolf Song (1929) with Lupe Velez. I never knew if the rumors were really true, but I guessed they were. Many years later Bergman was extremely diplomatic when she said, "Every woman who knew him fell in love with Gary." The rumors may have been a press agent's invention, but when For Whom the Bell Tolls was released in the summer of 1943, it was an instant box-office hit. Their love scenes in the sleeping bag were hot enough to excite the public. Ingrid was nominated for an Academy Award, but lost to Selznick's other protégée, Jennifer Jones, in The Song of Bernadette (1943), the film that really launched that actress's career, as well.

My next film with Ingrid was another totally nonfashion movie, The Bells of St. Mary's (1945), with Bing Crosby. Imagine how frustrated I was after I had seen how chic she could look in Orry-Kelly's costumes in Casablanca (1942) and I realized I had to dress her in a habit.

Since Bergman played a nun, there wasn't much Edith could do with her costume. The Catholic Church was very particular when it came to fictionalized accounts of its clergy, so Edith was, by necessity, painstakingly accurate when dressing Bergman, Crosby, and Barry Fitzgerald.

In this period of motion pictures, accuracy was becoming a prime concern—unless, of course, you were working on a silly comedy like the Road *films. When I first started in films, we might have redesigned a nun's costume just to be amusing. But in this period we had discovered that the public was more interested in details. If you did something wrong, you got letters, especially from students.*

Since I wasn't about to trifle with the Catholic Church, I went to my parish and the priest gave me a book on habits. Ingrid's particular order was very rigid. I copied the drawings of the robes line for line and reproduced them for her role. That was the least fashion I've ever done in a film.

Crosby and Bergman both won Oscars in 1944, he for *Going My Way* and she for *Gaslight*. The day after the awards, they were both on the set filming *Bells*, which was a sequel to *Going My Way*. Selznick had tried to discourage her from taking the part, claiming that sequels were rarely successful, but she begged to do it and Selznick finally capitulated. Even dressed in ecclesiastical garb, Bergman was a huge success. So was the film, and poor Edith just waited to see what kind of boring uniform she'd have to put Bergman in next. Her chance to dress Bergman properly at last came when she and the star were loaned* to RKO for Alfred Hitchcock's *Notorious* (1946) with Cary Grant. This was to be Edith's first Hitchcock film, and it marked the beginning of a director/designer relationship that would last for more than thirty years. Bergman

---

*If a producer or director wanted to use a star who was under contract to a competitor, he could pay the other studio to borrow the talent. Stars "on loan" were paid only their usual salary, not a percentage of the loan fee. Because they were in demand, the actors and actresses could stipulate whom their costume designers would be.

was cast as a secret agent who had to use her body as a lure; Grant was her jealous director of operations and the man she loved.

Notorious was my first opportunity to dress Ingrid the way she should be. For such a big woman, she was a joy to dress. I was able to do evening clothes, sports clothes, street clothes— the whole gamut. I just had to be sure that what I did pleased Hitch. He was very specific about costumes for his leading ladies. He spoke a designer's language, even though he didn't know the first thing about clothes. He specified colors in the script if they were important. If he wanted a skirt that brushed a desk as a woman walked by, he spelled that out too. For Notorious, he repeated many times that the clothes must not be a focal point, that Bergman was to be a believable secret agent.

The job was tricky. Her clothes couldn't be smart in the ordinary sense. They had to avoid the fussy and extreme. And they had to be right for her.

In the first scene at the party where she met Cary Grant, I dressed her in a zebra-skin print blouse with her midriff exposed. In a black-and-white film the eye is immediately attracted to the stark contrast of black and white, since other colors become various shades of gray. Visually, she became the most important woman in the room. In other dramatic scenes she was dressed either in pure white or solid black, and true to Hitchcock's form, these colors reflected her mood.

Throughout the film she wore demure, covered-up costumes and very little jewelry. To be glamorous, some women need accessories galore—jewels, furs, feathers, silly hats—all the things Ingrid hates. She looks marvelous in plain things, a smock or a blouse and skirt or a tailored dressing gown. She must have simplicity, skillful design, and practically no ornamentation. Hers is elegance in the subtlest sense. For a costume designer, an Ingrid Bergman picture is an education in restraint.

I learned my restraint lessons very well. In what was one of the sexiest love scenes ever on screen, Bergman and Grant were totally dressed, but who remembers what they wore?

When Edith heard that Ginger Rogers had been cast as Liza Elliott in *Lady in the Dark* (1944), the part Gertrude Lawrence had played on Broadway, she shook her head. Ginger could handle the singing, the dancing, the lighthearted aspects of the character, but could she act? Edith wasn't sure. She had seen the play in New York and realized that the part called for an actress with great depth and experience. It seemed that it would be easier to teach Bette Davis to sing and dance.

Rogers had recently won an Oscar for *Kitty Foyle* (1942), which had pushed her into the ranks of "actress," rather than merely being Fred Astaire's partner in those extravagant RKO musicals. Some directors weren't convinced of her acting talent. Still, Rogers was in constant demand for starring roles, and she became increasingly particular about the parts she accepted, making sure that each one reinforced her new image as a serious actress.

Shortly before she was chosen for *Lady in the Dark*, Rogers had completed *The Major and the Minor* (1942), part of a multifilm pact with Paramount she had carefully arranged. Edith was assigned to both films. In *The Major and the Minor*, Edith was asked to design costumes that would allow Rogers to transform herself first into a twelve-year-old girl and then back into a middle-class working woman, all on screen. Then, in *Lady in the Dark*, the designer worked with director Mitchell Leisen and Broadway designer Raoul Pène du Bois to create Ginger Rogers' extraordinary clothes in one of the most talked-about costume pictures of the 1940s.

Both films depended enormously on the clothes to tell the story and, as the costume designer on both of them, I must say the job was a test of fortitude rather than talent.

In The Major and the Minor, *it would have been easier to turn a thirty-one-year-old Ginger Rogers into a twelve-year-old if we could have done it behind the scenes. But the plot hinged on Ginger doing it herself, with the audience watching. Wally Westmore was doing the makeup and hair for the film and his problems were as complex as mine. We conferred for weeks on*

*just what to do, and we finally decided what the working-girl
look had to be so that we could ease into the little-girl look. Then
we presented our ideas to Billy Wilder, who was making his
directing debut. Naturally, Billy had his own thoughts so I had
to sketch and resketch until I had finally pleased everyone.*

*Ginger appeared first in a simple belted blouse that could
be quickly unbelted into a low-slung middy blouse, a knee-length
plaid skirt that could be hiked up above her knees easily, stock-
ings that could be crumpled down to look like anklets, and a
wide-brimmed hat that looked extremely* ingenue *with two blond
pigtails hanging out. Ginger made the transformation perfectly, and the movie received raves from the critics. After that
film she asked me to do her next films at RKO, before she returned to Paramount for* Lady in the Dark.

*Mitch Leisen and I had been working together off and on
for years. I had done the costumes for the first film he ever
directed,* Cradle Song *(1932), and since then we had done* The Big
Broadcast of 1938 *(1937),* Artists and Models Abroad *(1938),* Remember the Night *(1940),* Hold Back the Dawn *(1941), and* No
Time for Love *(1943). So I was very aware of his idiosyncrasies
and his perfectionism. Mitch was extremely knowledgeable
about costumes and even fancied himself a costume designer, so
on every film I did with him Mitch and I would first discuss the
costumes. Then I'd prepare sketches, he'd redo them, I'd redo
them. Finally we'd come up with something very much like what
was done in the beginning. Then when we'd get to the set, something wouldn't work and we'd be back to square one.*

As Liza Elliott in Lady in the Dark, *Ginger was the fashion editor of the world's greatest fashion magazine. Her costumes were superlative. She was constantly having daydreams
that she was a glamorous sexpot instead of a tailored-editor
type, and the dreams created a perfect plot excuse for fabulous
gowns. One of these sequences involved the circus, and Ginger
wore one of the most expensive costumes in Hollywood history.
It has come to be known as the mink dress, but actually it was
a mink overskirt which was lined with sequins, worn over a*

*matching sequinned bodysuit. There was also a mink bolero and
muff. It cost about $35,000 to make in those days, and couldn't
be made today without a limitless wardrobe budget.*

*Over the years there has been a great deal of controversy
over who designed that costume. Some people have even said
that I had nothing to do with it, which is ridiculous. Mitchell told
me exactly what he wanted, I interpreted what he had to say, as
I would with any director, and my staff made the gown. Mitch
had originally requested that the mink skirt be lined with* faux
*rubies and emeralds, but when that huge expanse of mink was
backed with stones, Ginger couldn't even lift it, let alone dance
in it. We relined the skirt with sequins in a paisley pattern and
it moved beautifully. Since the skirt was open down the front it
bared her beautiful legs, which was always a goal when you
worked with Ginger Rogers.*

That film cost $2 million to make, and many people thought
that was a terribly extravagant amount of money to spend on
frivolity at the height of a war. But Paramount was making so
much money from the *Road* pictures that *Lady in the Dark* was
an affordable extravagance.

In 1944 there were still no Oscars awarded for costume
design (costume designers were first recognized by the Academy
in 1948), but Edith often speculated that *Lady in the Dark* would
surely have won the award for its lavish wardrobe, had designers
been so honored. Despite the minor disputes that arose over who
designed what in the film, Edith and Leisen went on to do several
films together. Du Bois, whose extravagant gowns in *Lady in the
Dark* were highly touted for their opulence, did two more films in
Hollywood and returned to Broadway. He later became one of
Edith's few detractors, one who publicly questioned her originality.

Shortly after *Lady in the Dark* was released, Hollywood's
much-read gossip columnist Hedda Hopper, who still held a grudge
against Edith for taking Banton's spot as chief designer at Paramount, named the designer to her list of Hollywood's worst-
dressed women. She also included Dorothy Lamour on her illustri-

ous list, but Lamour took it in stride with a "You can't win 'em all" attitude. For Edith, it was shattering.

Hopper publicly chided Head for always wearing tailored jackets and boring shirts teamed with equally boring skirts. The columnist wasn't impressed that Edith rarely wore the same outfit twice, since to her every ensemble looked the same. Hopper was outraged that the same woman who was constantly giving fashion advice in newspapers and on the radio to the nation's women was always dressed in ultraclassic designs that might have come from the pages of the Sears Roebuck catalog rather than from the sewing rooms of exclusive tailors. It was a greater insult, insinuated Hopper, that this fashion ingrate should be dressing the world's most glamorous women. The fact that everything she wore had at least two sets of pockets (even her nightgowns, she admitted) and that she never wore hats, except in New York, made her clothes seem all too practical for the fantasy capital. In Edith Head's personal fashion world, function was foremost.

The designer made no secret of the fact that she purposely wore a nondescript uniform to work—tasteful suits in forgettable shades.

I never use color in the room in which I work or my offices or my fitting rooms. And I never wear color myself. I mean never. I wear beige, occasionally gray (my favorite shade is a beigy-gray) or white or black. When I stand behind a glamorous star who's fitting a glamorous dress, I don't want to be an eye-catcher. I want the actors to concentrate on themselves. Any distraction such as pictures on the wall or the reflection of me in a very fashionable or brightly colored dress would only take their eye away from their image. I play down how chic I can look. An actor must be totally absorbed with how he or she appears.

Many of the studio's stable of stars stopped by to console Edith—it was one thing for Hedda Hopper to pick on them, but not their Edith. Even Bing Crosby, who wasn't one to show his emotion at the studio, brought the designer a selection of embroidered workshirts from Mexico, with a message that she'd be beautifully dressed no matter what she wore. And in her column, Louella Parsons, Hopper's rival, stated that only a fashion moron would discredit Edith's fine taste and subtle sense of style.

For a short period, Edith began to be more experimental with her appearance. She tried wearing more jewelry—the charm bracelet Barbara Stanwyck gave her became a frequent accessory. When she went to New York she bought some elegant new dresses from couture houses and began wearing them to the studio. Most people around the lot who noticed Edith's new look credited Hopper's slur with giving her the jolt she needed to try to make the most of herself, but some of those who worked with her more closely surmised that Edith's new self-improvement drive was in reaction to Mary Kay Dodson, a new designer under contract at Paramount. The pace at Paramount had become so frantic that the well-known and strikingly beautiful couturiere from Beverly Hills was hired to design some of the films Edith couldn't handle. Dodson occupied an office down the hall from Edith's salon, distance enough to prevent too much interaction between them. But it wasn't long before the two were assigned to work on two films together, *Duffy's Tavern* (1945) and *Miss Susie Slagle's* (1945).

Working on the same films meant presenting sketches to the same director at the same time; it meant attending meetings in tandem and occasionally consulting with each other. Dodson was getting a good reception from the men on the lot, especially the men in power. Though she was extremely professional in her approach to the job, Dodson was also at ease with men and knew how to return a flirtatious greeting. In those days Edith was extremely uncomfortable with men in any but the most businesslike situations. Though she later became quite a flirt, her early image of herself as the corporate executive didn't leave room for even innocent verbal play. But it was obvious to everyone, especially Edith, that Dodson seemed to be making important career strides with her likable, easy manner. The new designer also struck up an office friendship with Edith's sketch artist, Donna Kline, and with her secretary, Jean Tanner.

After the two films she did with Edith, Dodson was assigned to such prestigious films as *Monsieur Beaucaire* (1946), *Golden Earrings* (1947), with Dietrich, and *A Connecticut Yankee in King Arthur's Court* (1949), all films Edith would have liked to have had to her credit. But it was wardrobe head Frank Richardson who made the assignments. If he deemed that Edith was too busy to handle eight or nine films simultaneously, he assigned some to Dodson. Edith complained, but rarely changed Richardson's mind. His major goal was to make sure all the films were costumed well, not to please Edith by putting her name on all of them.

Dodson's presence forced Edith to work harder, both on assignments and in the creation of a public image that would ensure her presence at Paramount. She made the most of every assignment, trying to get as much publicity as possible for each new costume. She struck it big in 1945 when her costumes for director Hal Walker's *The Stork Club* (1945), with Betty Hutton, were so well received that the owner of that New York nightspot, Sherman Billingsley, made one of Edith's designs the official uniform for his hat-check girls. When *The Bells of St. Mary's* (1945), with Bergman and Crosby, came out a month after *The Stork Club* was released, the Paramount publicity department planted stories in every major paper about Edith doing months of research to come up with exactly the right habit for Bergman.

At about the same time, a man named Arthur Gordon Linkletter was planning a new radio show, *House Party,* for CBS network affiliates, and Edith's name was to make its biggest splash ever. *House Party* soon became the number-one daytime radio show in the country. Linkletter, who functioned as both host and talent coordinator, booked guests who would appeal to his predominantly female audience. With speakers ranging from doctors, chefs, and makeup artists to movie stars, teachers, and authors, he needed a fashion expert to round out his general-interest format. A shrewd analyst of his audience, Linkletter felt that rather than opt for a New York ready-to-wear designer, he should give his listeners a Hollywood fashion personality. In 1945 Edith Head's name was the best known. Linkletter contacted Paramount's publicity department and offered her a slot on his show once a month.

Quick to accept free air time to plug a new film or just mention the studio name, Paramount accepted for Edith.

Her first appearance on *House Party* came just as *Notorious* (1946) was in its final production stages. Edith was prepared to talk about dressing Bergman and the other big stars of the day. But Linkletter urged her to talk about how average women could make the most of themselves and suggested she merely spice their conversation with tidbits about the stars. So rather than telling her audience how to be glamorous like Bergman or Stanwyck or Loretta Young, Edith offered tips and advice. She'd suggest sprucing up a plain white blouse by painting safety-pin motifs on it and then using safety pins as buttons. Or she'd note that large women should stay away from large prints—in her words, "Ingrid should never wear golf-ball-size polka dots. I give her pin dots and save the large ones for Veronica."

Edith had given the same type of information in frequent articles that appeared in popular fan magazines. At one point she even offered to write letters to readers who sent in full-length pictures of themselves, telling them how to look smarter by changing their manner of dress. Thousands of pictures were sent to *Photoplay*'s editorial offices on Sunset Boulevard, then forwarded to Paramount. Her direct approach was one more way to ingratiate herself with a public whose power she understood. In print, her advice was succinct and witty, qualities Linkletter knew would be even more effective on radio. As she told her readers in *Photoplay* in 1944:

If you have a large bust, do not wear your clothes so tight that you suggest a sausage. The larger a bust, the lower it will fall. This means that your waistline should be lowered, that you should favor a V-neckline rather than a round or oval cut, that you should invest in a good brassiere, and that you should avoid fabrics that catch the light or cling too tightly.

If you are flatter than you wish you were, raise your waistline and nip in your clothes at this point. Wear soft fullness at the bust. And remember, there is nothing wrong with bust pads. It is very stupid to pretend there are no such things.

That sort of straightforwardness was exactly what Linkletter wanted—but he would have to coach her to get it. Writing for a magazine where there were editors to smooth out the rough edges was one thing; speaking before a live audience on radio was another. Before every appearance on the show, Edith would be extremely nervous, and would pace in and out of her office, asking her secretary which subjects sounded the most interesting.

When she arrived at the CBS studios at the intersection of Fairfax and Beverly boulevards, Linkletter would spend thirty minutes helping her relax, building her confidence, and giving her pointers on how to speak clearly and forcefully. He recalls, "She was painfully shy. It was fortunate that she started with me on the radio, because that way at least she didn't have to worry about the camera. As long as she knew what she was going to talk about, she felt safe behind the microphone. If she was giving pointers to a member of the studio audience, I would describe what the person was wearing and Edith would suggest changes. As her confidence grew, she became more and more blunt with the ladies, but they never took offense."

Fan mail started to pour in. Mrs. America loved hearing what the world's most famous costume designer had to say, and wanted to hear her more often. Soon she was appearing every three weeks rather than every four. Edith adjusted quickly to her new celebrity role. She liked it and she liked the fact that the people in the front office at Paramount were commenting favorably about her appearances.

A number of important movies opened in 1946, and Edith dressed an impressive group of films: *The Blue Dahlia*, with Lake and Ladd; *The Bride Wore Boots, California,* and *The Strange Love of Martha Ivers,* all with Stanwyck; *To Each His Own* and *The Well-Groomed Bride,* with Olivia de Havilland; *The Perfect Marriage,* with Loretta Young and David Niven; *Notorious,* with Grant and Bergman; *Blue Skies,* with Joan Caulfield and Bing Crosby; *Our Hearts Were Growing Up,* with Gail Russell; and *The Virginian,* with Joel McCrea and Barbara Britton. She was also on loan to Warner Brothers to dress Barbara Stanwyck for *My Reputation,* so it hadn't been a quiet year for Edith.

Edith's bids for publicity proved to be extremely effective. Her newfound public began to respond. Six months or a year after she would finish a film she'd get a flurry of letters from fans. If she had put Stanwyck in a cinched-waist gown with a décolletage, at least one fan would write in and ask how to adapt that look for the office. In addition, she had to be well versed on the films that were ready for release, so she could talk to the magazine editors who worked two months in advance of publication and wanted to be right up to date with their Hollywood fashion reports. Talking to the press meant keeping pace with what all the other designers in the world were doing, and finding a new way to say that Hollywood was the world's fashion center. The war was over and Paris was starting to get back on its feet, so if Edith and the rest of the Hollywood design force were to keep their leadership positions, they had to be more verbal and get their names in the news. And, of course, they had to design costumes too.

Edith had embarked on a new series of films with Bob Hope in the 1940s, beginning with *My Favorite Blonde* (1942), with Madeleine Carroll, and followed by *My Favorite Brunette* (1947), with Dorothy Lamour.

The difference between 1942 and 1946 was more than just years. Madeleine Carroll's clothes were stiff, formal, and elegant. Dorothy Lamour's were as comfortable as what Hope wore in the film. I felt that in the future clothes would get more and more comfortable, and I tried to employ that theory in the film. Once people began to wear easy clothes I knew it would be impossible to get them into restrictive garments again. And besides, the new generation had better bodies than I'd ever seen before. There was less reason for camouflage. The stars had better taste, as well, and they wanted to look like human beings.

Dorothy had given the studio an ultimatum on My Favorite Brunette: *She wasn't going to wear a sarong. There was even a publicity stunt where she burned a sarong to make her point. I was elated, because I was tired of having to come up with new sarong ideas. The closest we came to a sarong was when she wore a white slip with a bare midriff. She had a beautiful figure, so* *we could put her in anything and she looked gorgeous. We spent $2,500 on one gold lamé gown she wore, but it was worth the expense. The glimmer highlighted her every curve.*

While she was working on Lamour's film, several other big pictures had begun costume production: *Cross My Heart,* with Betty Hutton (1947); *Arch of Triumph* (1948), with Ingrid Bergman and Charles Boyer; and *The Emperor Waltz* (1948), with Joan Fontaine and Crosby. And Bette Davis, who had been dressed for years by Orry-Kelly, was going to wear Edith's designs in *June Bride* (1948).

Along with Stanwyck and Crawford, Bette Davis was one of the reigning queens of Hollywood. She had made her name in the prewar and war years in such films as *Of Human Bondage (1934), Dangerous* (1935), *Jezebel* (1938), *Dark Victory* (1939), *The Letter* (1940), and *Now Voyager* (1942). She had won an Oscar for *Dangerous,* and had been nominated for several Oscars after that. Davis had depended on Orry-Kelly and the Warner makeup team to transform her physically into each role, while she made the necessary mental transition.

By 1947, I had dressed most of the great stars in the industry. There were few thrills left for me—most of my leading ladies were just bodies to hang clothes on. Then I met Bette Davis. There was no greater star, in my eyes, and now I finally had the opportunity to dress her. I was slightly disappointed that the script was just mediocre. I wasn't going to have a scene like Orry-Kelly had had in Jezebel, *where Bette walked into a ballroom full of women dressed in white wearing a blazing scarlet dress—which, incidentally, was really made of brown satin, the only color which Kelly could get to look like red in a black-and-white film.*

No, costumes were not integral to her role as a magazine editor in June Bride. *But that didn't stop Bette from coming in and working long hours with me, discussing the costumes, fitting them, and moving around in them to make sure they worked well for her. We became good friends on the initial fittings for this movie because she realized that I was as profes-*

sional as she was, and that we had a mutual goal—to dress her to suit her part and to make her comfortable in what she was wearing. She has an especially long stride, so it was always important that her skirt did not inhibit the way she walked. You would never put her in a tight straight skirt without adding a slit to make it maneuverable.

Though Hollywood designers had slowly drifted away from the rigid fabric-conservation stipulations of Washington's L-85 edict, the straight skirt and other streamlined, often skimpy, fashions were still the most popular look on screen. Then, in 1947, Christian Dior reintroduced the 1890s corset and petticoat, and called this rigid hour-glass architecture his New Look.

Suddenly the sight of a slim skirt on film was a self-inflicted slap in the face to Hollywood. Every movie that was made in 1946 and held on the shelf until 1947 looked miserably dated from a fashion point of view. Women who were going to the movies for a fresh look at clothes scoffed at Hollywood's meager offerings when Paris was presenting a return to the ultimate in femininity—a wasp waist shaped with a boned corset called a *guêpiere*, and yards of romantic skirt brushing just above a provocative ankle. Anything less than the New Look was depressing, a reflection of a war gone by, and nobody wanted it. Paris had regained its stronghold on fashion—and Hollywood was in trouble again. It was as if the film industry had forgotten everything it had learned in 1929, when Paris caused the first screen-fashion catastrophe.

Costumes had to be hastily remade for a number of films in production; nothing, of course, could be done about films in the can. Producers and directors who didn't understand the ins and outs of fashion wanted to know why their films looked so austere. When they became educated about the whims of *la mode*, they wanted to know how to avoid future costume catastrophes.

I learned my lesson the hard way. Just after Dior brought out the New Look, every film that I had done in the past few months looked like something from the bread lines. With each screening, I was reminded. I vowed that I would never get caught by a fashion trend again, and became a confirmed fence-sitter. When skirts became full, I widened mine gradually. If lengths were at the ankle, mine were mid-calf. The result has been that if you look at my films it is very difficult to date them. Some of my designs are as wearable today as they were in 1949. I realize now that that's what I should have been doing throughout the 1940s.

I hated the fashions of the 1940s; those huge shoulders were ugly. I call that style the lady-football-player look. There is no reason why a woman's shoulders should be extended; she has a bustline to balance her hipline, and shoulders to offset a slender neckline. It is a natural proportion. But that was the 1940s look and I felt that I was stuck with it. If I'd had the wisdom then that I have now, I never would have put a star in those horrid big shoulders. It took the New Look to teach me that moderation is important in the motion picture business.

The same year that Edith dressed Bette Davis for the first time, she put Barbara Stanwyck in a glamorous bed jacket and nightgown in *Sorry, Wrong Number,* a Hal Wallis film so terrifying that the *Christian Herald* called it unethical and immoral, "a vicious and torturous film for its presentation of unrelieved terror." The film had been adapted from a script originally used on a spine-tingling episode of CBS radio's Mystery Theater. On radio, the entire story was played from the lead's bed as she overheard a telephone conversation plotting her murder. In the film version, Stanwyck begins as a healthy and wealthy heir to a fortune who then becomes bedridden, so Edith had ample opportunity to dress her leading lady before she was limited to a negligee. Early in the film, Stanwyck marries Burt Lancaster, and is gowned in twenty-five yards of silver brocade with a matching cathedral-length veil. Rather than wearing traditional orange blossoms in her hair, Stanwyck dazzled her audience with diamonds. Throughout the film she wore more than $250,000 worth of diamonds and assorted jewels, including a sparkling necklace and earring set that her then-husband, Robert Taylor, had given her for Christmas. A 40-carat diamond made the story's point—that this intended murder victim was richer than the average millionaire. As Stanwyck noted, "I simply reeked of rocks, but I didn't wear them for ostentatious display. They advanced the plot. I was the heiress to a drug fortune, the Cough Drop Queen, they called me. I imagine anybody called that would go in for diamonds."

During this period, Edith also continued to dress Bergman, giving her her first pinup girl look in *Arch of Triumph* (1948). She wore a tight V-neck sweater that started gossip columnists talking about more than Bergman's eyebrows and imposing carriage. After losing Marlene Dietrich to Mary Kay Dodson in *Golden Earrings* (1947), Edith seemed to feel a sense of personal triumph when she was assigned to dress the star in *A Foreign Affair* (1948). Although she had slaved for hours with Dietrich, selecting fabrics and accessories in the 1920s and early 1930s, the films had been credited to Travis Banton. With an older but still statuesque Dietrich, Edith added one more great name to her accredited list of "Women I've Dressed." Dietrich played a bargirl in a nightclub, hardly a glamour queen, and wore battered old suits, dressing gowns, and raincoats, but those who worked with Edith said she relished the assignment and imitated Banton's method of dressing the now-aging star.

The Emperor Waltz (1948) had taken months of Edith's time, but when the film was released she called it her finest work to date. The story, set in turn-of-the-century Austria, finds a lederhosen-clad Bing Crosby as a traveling phonograph salesman from America trying to sell a talking machine to Emperor Franz Josef, while wooing a gorgeous countess (Joan Fontaine), whose poodle has fallen in love with his mutt. If the plot was ridiculous, Edith's costumes were sublime. She had exceeded her costume budget, but director Billy Wilder had urged her not to be inhibited by cost. So while Gile Steele, the noted men's designer, dressed Bing and the other male players, Edith draped the women in late-nineteenth-century finery. Since the romance of the dogs was a major part of the script, Wilder asked Edith to costume the poodle as well as the rest of the women.

We knew from the beginning that this was to be an extravagant period picture, and a rarity, since it was also to be a comedy. But Billy wanted it to be perfect. He sent a crew of two hundred to Jasper National Park in Canada, two thousand miles away from Hollywood, for the filming. That was one of the first times a film had been shot on a faraway location, and it was certainly the first time I had traveled long distance with the crew. We had heard stories that the park was inhabited with nine-foot grizzly bears weighing more than one thousand pounds. (I had trouble envisioning Bing coming up against one of those, and fortunately he never did.) We had a special train that took us all up to Jasper, the largest national park in North America. The dogs had a special car all their own, and first-class food. We had even taken a hairdresser for the poodle.

I wondered what it would be like to try to shoot a film in the wilds, but to my surprise everything went much quicker than it did in Hollywood. There were no distractions. Everyone had planned so carefully that every detail was covered. I had every color of thread that we needed to make adjustments to costumes; the wardrobe mistress had sent every pin, needle, and piece of fabric she could think of. Virtually nothing went wrong. It was the last time I remember such a trouble-free location shooting.

The film was not shot entirely on location, of course, so we returned to Hollywood to finish filming. One scene was shot on Bing's own tennis court at his home in Beverly Hills. In another that called for a field of daisies, four thousand daisy plants had to be painted blue and planted in a field. Technicolor was so temperamental in those days that the white daisies were too brilliant to be photographed as they were. With the blue tint, they appeared white on the film.

During one sequence, 250 couples were required to curtsy for more than a minute. It would be difficult to maintain balance for that long dressed in today's clothes, let alone in the heavy hoopskirts and ornate dresses the female extras were wearing. We did take after take, but at least one or two women would start to wobble or fall. So Billy Wilder stopped filming while we had tiny stools fitted under each skirt so the women could actually sit while they were curtsying. There was only one take after that and the scene was complete.

In that same sequence, Joan Fontaine wore a very low neckline, something she had rarely done on screen before. I laughed out loud when she told a newspaper reporter that "it was the only way I could steal a scene from those dratted dogs."

The year after it was released, *The Emperor Waltz* was nominated for a number of Academy Awards, including one for the first award in costume design. Edith and several other designers had been instrumental in establishing the award in the first place. Too many pictures in which clothes were recognized as imperative to the story line had been recognized for everything but their costumes. Edith made it well known that she expected to win the Oscar for her Austrian period clothes.

It was Oscar night, March 24, 1949. I'll never forget it. It was snowing in Hollywood, a totally unexpected act of nature during the first week of spring. I should have taken that snow as an omen, but I was too busy going over my acceptance speech as Bill and I walked into the Academy Awards Theater, which then was located on Melrose Avenue in Hollywood. After we sat down, I asked Bill if I looked all right. "Should I take off my glasses?" I asked. He told me to leave them on so I wouldn't fall on my face. "Besides, you wouldn't be Edith Head without them."

There was no doubt in my mind that I would win that Oscar. I deserved it—for longevity if nothing else. I had been doing motion pictures before the Oscars even existed. And besides, my picture had the best costumes of any nominated picture. The serious competition was Joan of Arc, designed by Madame Karinska and Dorothy Jeakins. To my mind there was no way Ingrid Bergman's sackcloths and suits of armor could win over my Viennese finery.

I dressed in a pencil-slim, high-necked black faille gown embroidered in tiny gold and silver elephants with their trunks up for good luck. It was a conversation piece, as I had intended it to be. My hair was pulled back as high and tight as I could get it and my bangs were perfect. My makeup was camera-ready.

Elizabeth Taylor was only seventeen when she presented

that first award for best costuming, and she was as beautiful as everyone had ever imagined her to be. She was dressed in a full-length gown with a six-foot hoopskirt wreathed in forget-me-nots. As she flounced up to the podium, I could feel my whole body get tense. She announced the nominees, then opened the envelope and named the winners.

Karinska and Jeakins for Joan of Arc.

It took a moment for me to realize that I had lost. Since I am not very emotional, no one knew that I was in shock. Bill squeezed my hand and we watched the remaining presentations, but I do not remember the rest of the evening.

The next few days were very quiet in the wardrobe department at Paramount Studios. Edith continued to come in by 10:00 at the latest and to leave by 4:30 at the earliest. There was no small talk, and her patience was short. Sketch artist Donna Kline remembers that Edith admitted her disappointment over the awards but made no further allusion to the event. Her secretary, Jean Tanner, recalls, "We had all been hoping, for our own sakes, that she would win. But after she lost that first one she was surprisingly quiet. She would just sit in her office behind closed doors and do her work. She came out when she needed me or Donna to do something, and that was it." The reclusive mood lasted only a few days and it was back to business as usual. There would be plenty of time for Oscars.

Two of Edith's most important films opened within a few months after she lost her first bid for an Academy Award. They were William Wyler's *The Heiress* (1949), with Olivia de Havilland, and *Samson and Delilah* (1949), a Cecil B. DeMille film starring Hedy Lamarr and Victor Mature. Both films would go on to become Academy Award-winning pictures, but not in the same year. Although *Samson and Delilah* was released in December 1949, it didn't open in Los Angeles until February 1950, making it ineligible for the 1949 Academy Awards.* Its name was not placed in nomination until the year after *The Heiress*.

*To be eligible for a given year's Academy Award, a picture must play in the Los Angeles area for at least two weeks during that year.

Olivia de Havilland and Edith had worked together on several films before William Wyler brought them together for *The Heiress*. In both *Hold Back the Dawn* (1941) and *To Each His Own* (1946), director Mitchell Leisen handed Edith scripts that called for de Havilland to play first a naïve and rather prudish schoolteacher and then an old maid who reflects on her painful past. Neither was a costume picture, but both presented challenges. In the earlier film, the designer was asked to help de Havilland maintain the stodgy, almost sexless spirit of Emmy Brown until she meets the debonair Charles Boyer and realizes that there is more to life than the three Rs. With very subtle changes in textures, tones, and silhouettes, Edith's designs for the lovestruck Emmy symbolized her newfound sexuality. In *To Each His Own*, the script required that de Havilland age from an innocent teenager to a young woman in her twenties and, finally, to a weary middle-aged woman.

It was extremely difficult to make Olivia de Havilland look plain or old, but it seemed that that's what I was always asked to do. For To Each His Own, *the makeup man, Bill Woods, and I studied old photographs of Sir Winston Churchill, to observe how everything about him aged over a similar time span. I paid special attention to how his clothes fit him differently as he got older—how a shoulder line drooped or a hat fit lower, the little details that the untrained eye misses. Bill watched the chin line, the jowls, the lines in the forehead.*

Olivia gained fifteen pounds as the film was in progress, up to 120 from her normal weight of 105. She kept her head tilted down to accentuate the double chins and I padded her in all the right places. Then we added a tightly laced corset to create the illusion of a well-dressed woman who had lost the bloom of youth but who had gained a beauty that comes with maturity. The cameramen arranged the light so her shoulders and arms appeared to be heavier than they actually were. It was a marvelous transformation.

De Havilland won an Oscar for her role in *To Each His Own* (1946) and she won another as the lead in *The Heiress* (1949), the film that also brought Edith her first Academy Award for costume design.

The Heiress is possibly the most perfect picture I have ever done. I have never seen anybody else do a better period film. The reason is that Willy Wyler was so adamant about accuracy that he sent me east to do research in the different costume institutes, particularly the Brooklyn Museum, to make sure that even the underwear was correct to the smallest detail.

The film took place in two distinct costume periods: first in the Victorian period, when women wore crinolines and then, the Edwardian, when they wore bustles. I was forced to study two fashion eras and for each I had to have the right kind of buttons, buttonholes, fabric, and so on. Everything was as perfectly executed as it could be. There might have been certain things that I overlooked, but I doubt it.

My directive from Willy was to be absolutely correct. I remember his exact words, "I don't want anything that you make up or imagine or substitute," so my only real work was to make the clothes complement Olivia's character. Being a former schoolteacher, it was a great pleasure to put so much emphasis on historical accuracy.

After I did my extensive research, The Heiress *became one of the easiest pictures I had ever designed, because I had a blueprint. In other words, I knew exactly what I was doing. I knew exactly how many ruffles were in the petticoats, how many stays in a corset.*

Willy was trying to get across the fact that Olivia's character, Catherine Sloper, was slightly clumsy and awkward. You had the feeling she wasn't quite put together. She dropped things. She had a terrible inferiority complex, which her father helped to bring about. He tormented her by telling her how beautiful her mother was, how "immaculate" Catherine looked. She went to the ball in a scarlet dress and said, "This was my mother's favorite color," to which her father cruelly replied, "Your mother dominated the color," implying that she looked horrible in it.

I had to get across how uncomfortable she was with herself in whatever image she projected. I could not do it by giving her inexpensive or ugly clothes, because her father was a wealthy man and everything she wore was of the finest quality. No matter how much money she had, she never looked soignée *because she was insecure.*

Rather than give Olivia a perfect fit, I made things purposely gap or wrinkle in the wrong place. I would cut a collar too high, or a sleeve a bit too short. When Olivia wore a shawl we discussed how she should carry it to imply her subtle fears. She rarely let a shawl sit comfortably on her shoulders; instead, she grasped it or fiddled with it. If her dress had ruffles, it had a few too many ruffles combined with too much ribbon and a bit too much lace, reflecting her unsophisticated taste. All these details remained precisely accurate to their period, but it was up to me to interpret them for Catherine Sloper and Olivia's figure. That's why I call this my finest period piece.

This film was the first time that I had worked with a director who was so acutely aware of the way clothes can advance a story line and help to change a character. Willy and I discussed the character's personality changes and how best to indicate these changes through her clothes. In the beginning, she is a rather dowdy spinster. Her clothes are simple, befitting her lot in life. She isn't the kind of woman who appeals to men; even her meticulous hairdo reflects how uptight she is. Then, when she meets Montgomery Clift, she chooses a ballgown which is too overdone and makes her look foolish. When her new love leaves her, she becomes embittered, and her clothes are dark, severely tailored, and matronly. At the end, as her suitor returns and she is ready to get revenge, she becomes a seemingly confident, exciting woman wearing a gown totally unlike the costumes she wore earlier. For the first time, her clothes make her look breathtaking.

If The Heiress *had been a silent picture, anyone could have told the story simply by watching the transition of costumes. I realize now that this is why I was awarded the Oscar. The Academy Award is given to the costume designs that best advance a story, not necessarily for the most beautiful clothes. My costumes in this film were not the most beautiful costumes I had ever done, but they were the best suited to the script.*

As prepared as she was for an Oscar for *The Emperor Waltz,* Edith was unprepared to win for Wyler's film. It had been exactly one year since she had lost, but she hadn't forgotten the anguish she suffered after that defeat.

I wasn't at all ready to bounce up on the stage when my name was called. I had no prepared speech. I wasn't expecting to win at all. I was vying with Vittorio Nino Novarese, one of the finest costume designers in the industry. I had been nominated for a period film whose leading lady was not cast as a glamorous beauty. I suppose I still didn't understand what it took to win.

Bob Hope was master of ceremonies the night I won my first award. He led me up on stage and then, when he realized I was totally speechless, he covered for me by saying, "Edith says thank you." The next day people called me to tell me that my response was "charming." I didn't let on that I felt totally ridiculous.

Edith ended the 1940s designing a spate of films that would be released in 1950. Except for their sheer numbers, films such as *Copper Canyon* (1950), *Mr. Music* (1950), *My Friend Irma Goes West* (1950), *Riding High* (1950), *Dark City* (1950), *Let's Dance* (1950), and even *The Furies* (1950), with Barbara Stanwyck, would do little to establish Edith as Hollywood's most acclaimed designer. But her other releases, *Samson and Delilah, Sunset Boulevard,* and *All About Eve* would become the first important films of her career's most important decade.

SIX

On October 28, 1950, Edith Head would be fifty-three years old. She had worked in Hollywood for twenty-seven years; she had been involved with more than five hundred films, many of them carrying her name as the designer. She had spent the 1940s pleasing her stars, her directors, her producers—everyone she needed to please to succeed. She was finally ready to satisfy her own artistic needs, to design clothes that would put her indelible mark in the motion picture history books.

The 1950s would be good to costume designers in the film industry—that is, to the ones who had jobs. As the industry entered an era of high-fashion clothes on screen, designers who were under long-term contracts to a studio, as Edith was to Paramount, had an opportunity to express their creative fashion talents. Those who didn't have established spots were faced with an industry that was cutting production, and jobs with major studios were at a premium.

Paramount failed to renew a number of contracts, and even the well-liked Mary Kay Dodson's was let go. Once again Edith was the sole designer at Paramount, competing only with intermittent freelancers. She faced no imminent threat to her position, so she could relax and concentrate on her two passions: design and self-promotion.

With Dodson gone, it wasn't long before Edith replaced her secretary, Jean Tanner Full, who had become a close friend of the other designer. It was at approximately the same time that Edith's reliable sketch artist, the talented Donna Kline, resigned to become a full-time designer for the children's TV show *Beany and Cecil*. Edith was forced to assemble a new support team, of which the most important member was sketch artist Grace Sprague. In years to come, this artist would help Edith design some of her most famous costumes.

By 1950 it was clear to studio executives that television represented a major threat to the future of motion pictures. If the films in theaters weren't superior to TV fare, why would people pay to go to the Bijou, the money men were asking. More appealing than a mediocre movie was curling up on the sofa with a bowl of homemade popcorn and watching a thirty-minute escapade with Lucy and Ricky Ricardo.

The money men provided their own answer in the form of a demand: It was time for the film industry to start putting more energy into each film, making fewer but better movies, the kinds that would bring people back to the theaters. It was only fitting that Cecil B. DeMille's *Samson and Delilah* be released in December of 1949, to become the first blockbuster of the 1950s.

With *Samson and Delilah*, DeMille delivered everything he had promised: a Bible story with sex appeal. He had cast the brawny, wavy-haired Victor Mature as Samson and Hedy Lamarr, whom columnist Ed Sullivan had called "the most beautiful woman of the century," as Delilah. DeMille slated five costume designers to dress his cast, but the glamour assignment, dressing Delilah and her sister (played by Angela Lansbury), went to Edith.

I won an Oscar for dressing Hedy Lamarr in Samson and Delilah, *but it is not a film of which I'm proud. I don't even have fond memories of it.*

I never thought I did good work for DeMille. I was always part of a team; he never let me do a film on my own for him. I always had to do what that conceited old goat wanted, whether it was correct or not. He never did an authentic costume picture in his entire career, and in my opinion that made him a damn liar as well as an egotist. The people I knew hated to work with him. He made us all uncomfortable. I thought of him as a freak, trying to play God. He never treated us as if we were talented —we were supposed to feel honored, and know *that we were good, simply because we were working for him.*

I will never forget the day I mustered up the strength to complain that he never complimented my sketches. He snapped back at me, "If I didn't like them, I wouldn't let you work for me." Another time he looked at my sketches and calmly told me, "Edith, I think my four-year-old daughter could do better than these. Try again." Tact had little meaning to him, at least where his staff was concerned.

There were easier stars to work with than Hedy Lamarr, too. Beautiful, yes. A great actress? I had my doubts. But De-Mille wanted her, so she was Delilah. Dressing her wasn't easy. It took a while for her to get a sense of the character she would be playing (I'm not sure she had acquired that sense before the cameras started rolling, either), so she didn't give me much trouble with regard to the costumes. She did, however, have very specific demands about how things should fit. DeMille wanted her to look voluptuous, but she was small-busted and she wouldn't wear padding. She told me she couldn't act if she felt she had unnatural proportions. So I draped her and shaped her until I finally achieved DeMille's required sensuousness and Hedy's requested natural look.

Often when she would come into my salon for fittings,

she'd float past my secretary, one hand dramatically placed on her forehead, and immediately plop down on the floor, complaining that her back gave her constant pain, that she had never been the same since she had had children. She'd get up to fit a dress but in between pinnings she'd plop down on the floor again, which gave me the impression that her back wasn't really aching; she was just lazy. We fitted a multitude of rather bare bras and skirts for her role as Delilah, but the real work came from helping her get up off the carpet.

She never registered any enthusiasm at her fittings. Since I was fitting Olivia de Havilland for The Heiress, *Bette Davis for* All About Eve, *Gloria Swanson for* Sunset Boulevard, *and that sweet, young Elizabeth Taylor for* A Place in the Sun *during the same months, the contrasts made it all the more difficult to enjoy working with Hedy Lamarr.*

DeMille had originally sold Adolph Zukor on making the film by telling him that Samson and Delilah *would be a sexy biblical story, and he was depending on me and the other designers (Gile Steele, Dorothy Jeakins, Gwen Wakeling, and Elois Jenssen) to leave as little as possible to the imagination, yet still get past the censors.*

We ran into constant sexual discrimination with the censors—the very problem I thought I had left behind in the 1930s. It was okay, for instance, to put Victor Mature in a brief tunic or to wrap him in a loincloth with his navel showing, but if Hedy's navel was exposed, it was censored. If I stuffed it with a pearl, we got by. I designed jeweled belts to cover her bellybutton, but when I really wanted a sexy look, I used a jewel of some sort. Naturally we could bare men's chests and thighs as much as we wanted, but if I showed too much of Hedy's cleavage or any protruding pelvic bones, the morals watchdogs were after us.

Since I was frequently called to the set during filming to make sure that Hedy was uncensorable, I wasn't finished with the film until the last day of shooting. The studio had a specialist on what was censorable and what wasn't, so I would have long discussions with him about Hedy's costumes. By working with Hedy very carefully from 1946 to 1948, when we finally finished shooting, we ended up with a very sexy, but "morally acceptable" Delilah.

DeMille never made things easy for Edith. Although other directors treated her with the respect she had earned in her almost thirty years in the industry, he still demanded that she formally present all her sketches, with fabric swatches attached, for his approval. Three or four sketches of each costume were plenty for most directors, but for DeMille, Edith showed twenty, sometimes thirty. Each was thumbtacked to the wall so he could walk past and evaluate it. If he approved, he'd give a slight nod. Often none was approved. To keep his designers honest—that is, to make sure that finished costumes looked like the renderings he had approved— DeMille had photostats made of each finalized sketch and kept them on file in his office. He began this procedure when he realized that Edith would occasionally try to slip in some unauthorized costumes. His action was a slap on the hands as well as an insult to Paramount's head of design. She would often return from De- Mille's office in tears, close the door to her salon, and remain inside for hours. Sometimes she would go straight to wardrobe head Frank Richardson's office for a shoulder to cry on. On many occa- sions she declared that she hated working with DeMille.

The meetings that preceded the creation of Delilah's famous peacock-feather cape were held at DeMille's convenience, often in the office at his home. Edith likened DeMille's office to a minor palace, with its stained-glass windows, vaulted ceilings, bear rugs, and enormous oak desk. At first his elaborate lighting setup in- timidated Edith. He would flick a switch and shine a bright beam directly into her eyes, creating a blinding glare. When she realized that taking off her glasses would reduce the effect, she removed them before entering his inner sanctum. Then, as she recalled, he would talk at length about the importance of a particular costume in a particular scene—in this case, the peacock cape.

I had barely sat down opposite his mammoth desk when he flashed the light on me and started to talk. By this time I had been subjected to the light treatment so often that I found his dramatics somewhat amusing as well as irritating, but far from intimidating. I knew exactly what he was going to say: He wanted something special for the scene where Delilah sits on the throne just before Samson tears down the walls of the temple.

Her costume was to be nothing like the scant things she had worn in the more erotic scenes. Here she was to demonstrate the power of her position; she was to be beautiful, but not a seductress. It took C.B. a very long time to communicate what he wanted. In this particular case, we did not brainstorm as we had on so many other occasions. He said he wanted a costume with feathers—for what reason, I don't know. He never gave reasons. But beyond that, he was leaving the rest up to me. That was a surprise.

I had no idea what kind of birds there were in Minoan days, so I had the research department investigate. Perhaps, I was told, there were peacocks—but that was nothing more than a conjecture. I knew C.B. would like the gaudy effect of peacock feathers, so I sketched them. I designed a long, draping cape covered with the regal plumage, and DeMille liked my idea very much. In fact, it was the first costume that I did for him that evoked anything more than a demeaning grunt of approval. "That *I like*," he said.

The trick was to find all the peacock feathers. Knowing well that he wasn't one to listen to excuses, I had my staff try to locate a bulk load of the precious plumes, but they were scarce. Finally I went to him and explained that we would have to go to Europe to get the finest feathers. He informed me that he had several peacocks on his ranch, so we could just wait until they molted. It occurred to me then that he had approved the cape sketch in the first place so that we would be forced to use his birds' feathers. We waited for peacock molting season and then my wardrobe people trudged up to his ranch to collect almost two thousand feathers. The cape, which attached at the shoulders and formed a train several yards long, was covered with the iridescent feathers, each hand-sewn or glued in place.

As I understand it, that peacock cape still remains in DeMille's "castle on the hill," his home high in the Hollywood

Hills on a street aptly named DeMille Drive. The mansion is now a Hollywood landmark and a museum of sorts where people can view the cape along with other DeMille memorabilia. I have no desire to see that costume again. It was just another means of feeding his already inflated ego.

I have always had the feeling that it was entirely wrong. I doubt very much that there were any peacocks around or nearby in the days of Samson and Delilah. Nor would anyone, even Delilah, have worn the kind of cape that I designed—or any of the other costumes, for that matter. I suppose only scholars would know that the costumes were not historically correct, but it bothered me terribly. I was never able to find anything authentic to indicate what Samson and Delilah looked like, so I improvised. And I won an Oscar.

The five designers worked separately on the film, with occasional meetings to make sure everyone was working on costumes from the same era. With DeMille giving each one separate directions, it was a miracle that the cast members looked as if they came from the same era. While Edith dressed Lamarr and Angela Lansbury, Gile Steele and Elois Jenssen attended to the lead males, and Dorothy Jeakins and Gwen Wakeling dressed the remainder of the huge cast. DeMille was always convinced that his costumes demanded the work of several artists, that one or two designers would burn out on one of his epics.

According to Edith, DeMille's habit of overstaffing costume designers was merely another of his ways of maintaining complete control. If he had several artists attempting to costume the whole film, *he* became the unifying factor.

In *Samson and Delilah* the men's costumes, by Steele and Jenssen, were far superior to anything worn by the women. The artful use of gilded fabrics and metals was striking, even when juxtaposed against an alluringly clad Hedy Lamarr. Lamarr's garb, shimmering and revealing as it was, was all too reminiscent of costumes shown in films of the past, including DeMille's original *Ten Commandments* (1923), *King of Kings* (1927), and *Madame Satan* (1930) with costumes by Adrian. Somehow, even a few of the

Latin American touches Edith had employed in *The Lady Eve* turned up on Delilah. The famed feathered cape was all too obviously inspired by a cape laden with peacock plumes that Theda Bara had worn in the 1917 version of *Cleopatra*. When Edith admitted that she wasn't proud of her costumes in the DeMille epic, she was undoubtedly recalling the lack of original design that went into her portion of the Academy Award-winning wardrobe.

Edith's name became the one most frequently associated with the film, despite the fact that four other designers had dressed all but two members of a cast of hundreds. When DeMille's head of publicity for the film, Richard Condon, planned an expensive and high-powered national promotion for the epic, he asked Edith to speak to women's groups and to hold fashion shows of the film's pseudo-Minoan designs. Seventh Avenue manufacturers produced Delilah-inspired gowns, some even bearing an Edith Head signature on the hangtags, implying that Edith had helped design them. In actuality, Paramount had sold the rights to the use of her name in conjunction with the marketing of the film and the clothes; Edith had done nothing but approve the manufacturer's sketches. Tie-ins had been arranged with more than seven hundred manufacturers to flood the market with everything from Delilah sandals to perfumes and costume jewels. Edith received no financial reimbursement for these design exploitations, but her name was fast becoming a household word.

Condon, the press agent, had turned in ninety-five single-spaced pages filled with promotional ideas before convincing DeMille to hire him for *Samson and Delilah*. Ignoring the sexual overtones of the film, Condon aimed his publicity deluge at schools and churches as well as women's clubs, fashion and retail outlets, the press, and movie exhibitors. In the name of the Bible and history, DeMille's flack sent out hundreds of packets filled with educational materials on Minoan civilization. (Though the research was impressive, little of it was reflected in the film.) Condon and the entire DeMille publicity office were fighting an uphill battle against groups like the Legion of Decency, which chastised DeMille for producing a film portraying Samson and Delilah as a morally corrupt couple yet billing it as a religious film.

Condon's blitz worked. The tale of love and deceit in the land of Zorah became one of the largest moneymakers in film history.* As part of the publicity campaign, Henry Wilcoxon, a star of the film, delivered hundreds of lectures around the country. After traveling to fourteen cities in twenty-eight days, he collapsed with pneumonia. Condon continued the tour without him, giving lectures, making personal appearances, posing with fashion editors to promote the newest lipstick tube shaped like a Minoan fan or discussing the decorative history of the Danite dagger with local museum groups.

After prerelease showings in major cities, *Samson and Delilah* was polled by *Box Office* magazine as the American public's favorite film of 1950.

Following such a huge and successful publicity campaign, the peacock-cape story became a legend. DeMille even told *The New York Times* that he had personally followed molting peacocks around his ten thousand-acre ranch, catching feathers as they dropped and saving only the best for his Delilah's cape. With the circulation of such embellished tales, it was not surprising that film costume critics began to doubt the validity of the whole story. Some even opined that the cape was not designed by Edith Head, that it was merely a "leftover" from some other DeMille epic. Herb Steinberg, now a vice president at Universal, and a PR man at Paramount when the peacock stories started spreading, claims the tales are true. "No, DeMille didn't go out and pick up feathers, and Edith didn't either, but I watched those wardrobe people coming back with bushels of peacock feathers. They collected them, for the cape, at the ranch in Tujunga." Edith bristled when the cape topic came up one too many times.

It's not surprising that people doubted DeMille's veracity. Of course, he didn't go out to his paradise and gather dirty bird feathers. But when people start saying I didn't design the cape,

---

*In its day, of course. Its $11.5 million in rental receipts is small compared with those of *E.T.* (1982), *Star Wars* (1977), and *The Godfather* (1971). As of January 1983, rental receipts for those films were $187 million, $193 million, and $86 million, respectively.

or we didn't hand-glue those damn feathers on, I get furious. My own staff helped collect them and bring them in. We sorted them by size, color, and brilliance. It took days. A "leftover," indeed. DeMille never used anything that was left over from something else; he was too egotistical for that. I wish I never had to talk about that cape again. I've often said Samson and Delilah *is a film I'd like to forget, but nobody will let me because of that damn cape.*

Billy Wilder's *Sunset Boulevard* (1950), which was released shortly after *Samson and Delilah,* became a film classic almost before it was made. Notoriety had surrounded the script, written by Wilder and his partner Charles Brackett, about the decline of an aging Hollywood star. Wilder, as director, had contacted Mae West, Mary Pickford, and Pola Negri to play the part of Norma Desmond, a once-great screen beauty who cannot accept the Hollywood rites of passage and refuses to admit that she is a has-been. All three stars, each of whose lives in some ways paralleled the main character's, flatly rejected the role and implied that Wilder had insulted them by asking.

Gloria Swanson, whose heyday had been in the 1920s, when she was Paramount's highest-paid star, accepted the part. Her portrayal of the declining Norma Desmond was critically acclaimed, and Swanson received an Academy Award nomination for her work.

Costuming played a very important part in the film, and Wilder carefully identified the subtleties he wanted Edith to capture.

Billy explained to me that he wanted Gloria to convey a feeling of the past, but he didn't want her to re-create it. He didn't want anything ridiculous or laughable. She was to be a poignant, sad character, a woman who didn't realize that she had passed her prime by thirty years. Although her greatest moments were in her silent movie days, Norma Desmond tried to be as contemporary as possible by wearing fashionable hairstyles, clothes, and makeup; yet there was something about her that connoted a sense of the past, a bit of déjà vu.

What Billy was telling me was that he wanted me to find some way of combining Jazz Age clothes with the New Look. I knew it could be done, but actually doing it was one of the greatest challenges of my entire career. Everything about her clothes, her hair, her accessories, her negligees, and her furs had to convey a feeling that they weren't exactly from the current era, despite the fact that they were obviously fine, new clothes worn by a woman of wealth and style to whom image meant a great deal.

To accomplish this, I added a touch of the bizarre to each costume to remind audiences that she was living in a dream world of the past. In one scene she wore a hat rimmed in peacock feathers, a trim that was de rigueur in the 1920s but passé in 1950. In another, she wore a piece of costume jewelry that was obviously left over from her flapper days, yet the dress in that scene was completely contemporary. Even in the last scene, when she is descending the stairs following her crime of passion, I defined her wide waist only very slightly, recalling the shapelessness of the 1920s, rather than giving her that whittled hourglass silhouette that characterized the early 1950s.

Because she was an actress who had become lost in her own imagination, I tried to make her look as if she was always impersonating someone. Ironically, although the film was nominated for ten Oscars and although the clothes I designed for Gloria were my toughest assignment and were critically acclaimed by movie and fashion people alike, I was not nominated for an Academy Award for Sunset Boulevard.

Many of the scenes in the film were shot at The Phantom House, a Los Angeles mansion once owned by J. Paul Getty. The remainder was filmed on the same Paramount back lot where Swanson had starred in DeMille films of the early 1920s. Though Edith had caught glimpses of Swanson when she first started at the studio in 1923, she did not formally meet the actress until work began on *Sunset Boulevard.* In 1926, Swanson had taken a brief vacation from her glittering career to marry a French nobleman and become the Marquise de la Falaise de Coudray. Edith recalled that when the star returned to Paramount after her honeymoon, the studio had handed out roses and ordered the staff—sketch artist Edith Head included—to toss them as Swanson emerged from her Rolls-Royce. The designer also remembered the days when it was her task to wash out Swanson's hosiery after a day on the set. Times and roles had changed, but Edith still adored Swanson.

While we were working on Sunset Boulevard, *I was apprehensive about working with Gloria. Yes, I had dressed a great number of stars, but in my mind Gloria represented the greatest from the days when I was just a beginner. She was a legend when I was walking around with stars in my eyes. Dressing her meant dressing an idol; that was frightening. She had been dressed by my teachers, Banton and Greer. They had told me that she was especially meticulous about her costumes—that she fancied herself a designer as well as an actress. I knew, too, that she had owned her own apparel manufacturing company in New York for a while, so she actually was savvy about design and construction. Since she had worked with all the great designers of Hollywood's past, I wondered how she would like me, a relative newcomer. It was not until many months later that I learned she had requested me.*

The first day we met was in Billy Wilder's office at Paramount. I immediately noticed her tiny feet. I had forgotten how small they were. I had seen the size 2 1/2 shoes marked Swanson in wardrobe stock, but to see such a small shoe actually on a foot was extremely impressive. She complimented me by saying that she was aware of my work and glad that we were finally doing a film together. I found her not only easy to work with but particularly helpful because she had so many costumes already planned in her mind. It became a project where I actually designed with the star instead of for her, because she was re-creating a past that she knew and I didn't.

She showed me how she would be moving in each scene and she was careful to point out the differences between how she would have done things in the early days of Hollywood and how they were being done in 1950. She didn't want me to be confused. She was very aware of the nuances that were involved in this role.

I attended the initial screening of Sunset Boulevard *at Paramount, along with a number of top stars, including Barbara Stanwyck. Gloria made a grand entrance wearing a floor-length silver lamé dress. As everyone watched the film, the screening room was silent. The credits rolled, the screen went black, and still there was silence. Then there was thunderous applause. A few people walked out, murmuring that the film would be the ruination of Hollywood, but the rest swarmed around Swanson and Wilder. Stanwyck had tears streaming down her face as she pushed her way up to congratulate Gloria. I heard later that Barbara had knelt down and kissed Gloria's lamé skirt in reverence. I only saw them embrace. I wanted to hug Gloria too, but there were so many people around that I couldn't get near her. I don't recall if I ever had the chance to tell her how much her performance had moved me.*

Hollywood's introspective mood in filmmaking continued with *All About Eve* (1950), written and directed by Joseph L. Mankiewicz. Though the story was set in New York, it might have easily taken place in Hollywood. It told the tale of a fortyish stage actress who realized all too harshly that young actresses mean competition. Where *Sunset Boulevard* had been cynical, biting, and devastating, *Eve* was poignant. Bette Davis, as the declining star Margo Channing, gave what some critics called the performance of her career, and Anne Baxter, as the scheming Eve, projected deceit so well that she shared Academy Award nominations with Davis and Swanson for best actress that year. (Judy Holliday won, for her role in *Born Yesterday.*)

A number of stars, including Stanwyck, had been offered the Margo Channing part but had turned it down, afraid of being typecast as a declining star in her forties. Claudette Colbert accepted the role, but when she was confined to bed with a bad back, Mankiewicz had to find a replacement. Bette Davis claimed she understood Margo Channing very well—too well, perhaps—and won the part just days before shooting was to begin. Fox's costume design master, Charles LeMaire, had already completed the costumes for the other women in the cast, but Edith persuaded her friend Davis to convince Mankiewicz that she should design Margo Channing's wardrobe.

Edith and LeMaire had been social and professional friends for years. As the executive director of wardrobe at Fox, LeMaire was as busy as or even busier than Edith. When he heard that Davis wanted the Paramount designer to design her wardrobe, he personally called Frank Richardson to arrange for Edith's services. "Sure I would have liked to have dressed Davis too, but there was no time. I was already on another film. I had confidence that Edith could do it, so I asked for her on loan," recalls LeMaire.

In the old days it wasn't very common for a designer to be loaned out because each studio had a stable of stars whom we dressed over and over. Occasionally one of those stars would be loaned to another studio, and that studio would also borrow a designer since he or she was familiar with the star's taste and form. When I was loaned out I made a point of meeting all the important people—of getting to know them—so that whenever they thought in terms of an outside designer, mine would be the first name that came to mind. If the stars liked you, they requested you. Some, such as Stanwyck and Davis, had the pull to get whomever they wanted as their designer. Since Bette and I had done a few films already, we had a good working relationship and she trusted me.

Charles LeMaire and I were friends and we worked things out. He dressed Anne Baxter, Celeste Holm, Thelma Ritter, Barbara Bates, and a very sexy unknown blonde named Marilyn Monroe. I did Bette.

However unfortunately, the characteristic look of the 1950s was the cocktail dress—the tight-bodiced, wasp-waisted, full-skirted, shoulder-baring, calf-skimming cocktail dress. Margo Channing, a cliché of the 1950s actress, was the perfect candidate for "the look." Davis wore it well.

Bette Davis is a perfectionist when it comes to costumes. So am I. That's why we work together so well. She tests her clothes, she takes time with the fittings to make sure everything works well for the requirements of the script, and she discusses any problems long before she goes on camera. But there was a major exception in All About Eve. *The off-the-shoulder dress for the big party scene was an accident. My original sketch had a square neckline and a tight bodice. I had extremely high hopes for this dress because the fabric, a brown* gros de Londres *(a heavy silk), photographs magnificently in black and white, and it was trimmed in rich brown sable.*

Because we were working on such a tight deadline, the dress was made up the night before Bette was scheduled to wear it. I went in early the day of the filming to make sure the dress was pressed and camera-ready. There was Bette, already in the dress, looking quizzically at her own reflection in the mirror. I was horrified. The dress didn't fit at all. The top of the three-quarter-length sleeves had a fullness created by pleats, but someone had miscalculated and the entire bodice and neckline were too big. There was no time to save anything, and a change would delay the shooting. I told Bette not to worry, that I would personally tell Joe Mankiewicz what had happened.

I had just about reached the door, my knees feeling as if they were going to give out, when Bette told me to turn around and look. She pulled the neckline off her shoulders, shook one shoulder sexily, and said, "Don't you like it better like this, anyway?" It looked wonderful and I could have hugged her. In fact, I think I did. With a few simple stitches I secured the neckline in place so she could move comfortably, and she left for the set. Above all, I did not want to delay the shooting.

Although many people thought that Davis's character was patterned after the aging actress Tallulah Bankhead, writer-director Mankiewicz insisted that he had modeled her after the Austrian actress Elisabeth Bergner. But Edith still saw Bankhead as the role model, so she had her researchers pull every still of the star they could find.

Some of the costumes were very extravagant, sexy evening gowns. Some of them were rather simple sport or daytime clothes. I had steeped myself in Tallulah, and everything looked as if it was made for her, yet the clothes complemented Bette. What you must understand is that Bette was becoming Tallulah Bankhead or Margo Channing, or whoever the hell she was supposed to be. That is her marvelous talent. She becomes her character. She is such a good actress that she makes clothes belong to her. When she puts on something you don't think it's a costume designed for her—you say, "It belongs to Bette Davis." To me that's a rare achievement—a very rare achievement.

Despite the tight shooting schedule, director Mankiewicz demanded costume tests, to make sure his stars looked perfect. Each principal in the cast was photographed wearing each costume. Then director and designer indicated any necessary changes right on the photo. In one scene Edith had planned that Davis wear a gray suit with a handkerchief in the pocket, a tailored white blouse with a black bow tie, and strapped black patent leather pumps. After the costume test showed her looking too tailored, Davis appeared in the film wearing a different blouse with a frilly white tie at the neck, no handkerchief, and black kid pumps. By the 1960s, costume tests had become so costly that most directors chose not to use them.

The last of the major films Edith had designed in the 1940s was *A Place in the Sun,* starring Elizabeth Taylor, who was seventeen when Edith met her for the first costume fittings. Taylor's roles in *National Velvet* (1944), *A Date with Judy* (1948), and *Little Women* (1948) had made her one of the most exciting new starlets in Hollywood. Her violet eyes, slightly clipped speech, and exquisite face were extremely endearing to her newfound public. Since the face was a perfect draw for fan magazine covers and other important forms of publicity, her beauty—coupled with some talent—made her a major box-office success before she was twenty.

In *A Place in the Sun,* director George Stevens had cast Taylor as Angela Vickers, a beautiful, but spoiled heiress who loved everything about life. Without even trying, she would steal Montgomery Clift away from a plain, plump, and pregnant Shelley Winters.

When Taylor came in for her fittings, she brought an entourage—usually a pet, a teacher (she was still underage and had to spend a certain number of hours per day studying), and, quite often, her mother or another companion to sit with her between takes. During fittings Taylor was extremely quiet, listening to whatever Edith had to say as if it were the last word in design, even though she had already been dressed by such great MGM designers as Irene, Walter Plunkett, and Helen Rose, who was to become MGM's status designer in the 1950s.

I fell in love with Elizabeth immediately. The reason is totally unrelated to films: I love animals and so does she. Elizabeth would always bring pets with her, even to a fitting, which was sometimes a little upsetting to the fitter. She would bring dogs, cats, parakeets, squirrels—whatever her latest fancy was. What a picture! Here's this beautiful, exotic, and very sexy girl listening to a schoolteacher tell her about the Seven Wonders of the World or whatever, with all the animals around and the fitter being very cautious because one of the dogs was cavorting about. It was like a three-ring circus; it was lovely.

Given the opportunity, Taylor joined Edith and her staff for lunch in the commissary and asked Edith about all the stars she used to dress—Lombard, Dietrich, Colbert, Mae West, and Clara Bow. Edith recalled her sitting at the lunch table wide-eyed, speaking adoringly of the stars of the past, quite unaware that she was destined to be as legendary as any of them. Just before Edith's secretary, Jean Tanner Full, was replaced, she, Edith, and Elizabeth had spent an entire lunch hour discussing the young star's impending marriage to hotel-fortune heir Nicky Hilton. "When I think about it now I laugh," recalls Jean. "There I was, giving Elizabeth Taylor advice about marriage. She'd say, 'What should I know about being married?' and Edith and I would just say that it involves a lot of compromise. But Edith was married to the same man for forty years and I've been married to the same man for thirty-seven years. I guess Elizabeth just didn't listen."

Costumes for *A Place in the Sun* were completed in the early part of 1949, but the film was not released until 1951. Because it was a fashion picture, with contemporary costumes that were essential to the story line, it was critical that Edith's designs not look dated when the film hit the theaters.

Elizabeth's clothes were quite sensational and quite re-markably in fashion. But I was not forecasting fashion when I made them. In fact, it was a case of taking the styles that were current in early 1949 and translating them into something timeless. She was a bewitching debutante who was to attend her coming-out party. The dress had to be white and important. Dior's New Look employed very slender waists and full skirts; I knew that when I was working on the costumes. I also knew that the only time something is out of fashion immediately is if the public doesn't buy it.

By the time I was planning the Angela Vickers wardrobe, the public had already shown its acceptance of the New Look, so I was convinced Dior's style would be around long enough for me safely to dress Elizabeth in full skirts. What I couldn't predict was how collars, sleeves, jewelry, and other details would change, for these are the subtle things that make costumes look dated. The clothes in the film had very few details. I made the silhouette the most important aspect of each outfit.

For the debut gown, I relied on flowers, little violets, to accent the bodice, and I sprinkled them on the skirt. It's very difficult to look dated with flowers. The dress became especially dramatic because I made the skirt exceedingly full, with yards and yards of tulle over a pastel underskirt, and the flowers made the bust look fuller. The combination of the full bust and wide skirt accented the waist, making it appear even smaller than it was. Elizabeth prided herself on her tiny waist and was always willing to wear her gowns very tight to achieve a waspish look. I can still hear her telling me, "Tighter, Miss Head, tighter."

96

That dress was such a success; it was beautiful on camera. And Elizabeth was radiant. Some clothing manufacturers copied it—"knocked it off," as they say in their trade—and the dress was mass-produced to hang in every department store in the country. And even though I had designed it two years before, it looked very current.

Fortunately I had not been swayed by any faddish details of late-1940s fashion. It's very difficult for a designer in a motion picture studio to keep from following fashion slavishly. Fad is a great temptation, especially if it's a particularly beautiful fad. Take Yves Saint Laurent's styles, for example. He has designed some beautiful clothes for his couture collection. I loved his Russian look in the 1970s, but to incorporate the styles into a film that was being designed in 1976 would have been a disaster. By 1977 the Russian look was terribly passé, and any film that premiered in late 1977 or early 1978 with stars dressed in those Cossack styles would have been criticized.

Once I did a picture where I designed a dress in a butterfly-print fabric. Butterflies were "in" that year. I liked the design, and used the fabric. Two years later I saw the film in a theater and a woman sitting near me told her husband that she knew it was an old picture because she had had a blouse in that same print two years before. From then on I stuck to plaids or checks or polka dots if I wanted a patterned fabric. I never get myself tied into a certain period.

People have said that my clothes for A Place in the Sun *were prophetic and that I was a great fashion trendsetter in 1951. That's very funny. My clothes were middle of the road in terms of the current fashion trends.*

Elizabeth Taylor, looking ravishing in the film, quickly became the industry's new screen goddess. Since she played a teenager, a whole new age group took on an importance it had never had. It was just the kind of change Hollywood was looking for. Teens had an idol they could copy. Thanks to those quick-thinking garment manufacturers, they could dress like her. In various newspaper interviews Edith noted that anywhere from seven to thirty-seven girls had turned up at the same party looking exactly like Angela Vickers. Despite Edith's exaggerations, the fact remained that the Liz Taylor dress, as it came to be known, was 1951's most popular style at high school proms. As usually happens when garment manufacturers knock off styles from other designers, the original designer is rarely credited and never financially compensated.

Edith received other compensations, however. Despite heavy competition from Walter Plunkett and Gile Steele for their costumes in *Kind Lady* (1951), Charles LeMaire and Renie for *The Model and the Marriage Broker* (1951), Edward Stevenson and Margaret Furse for *The Mudlark* (1951), and Lucinda Ballard for her designs in the very popular Marlon Brando film *A Streetcar Named Desire* (1951), Edith was awarded the Oscar for black-and-white costuming for her work in the Taylor/Clift classic. The same year, Orry-Kelly, Plunkett, and Irene Sharaff, three of Hollywood's most respected costume designers, were honored for their costumes in the Technicolor film *An American in Paris* (1951), which was also named best picture.

The coming of television put a temporary crimp in moviemaking style, but Edith made good personal use of the popular new medium. In September 1952 Art Linkletter's *House Party* started simultaneous TV/radio broadcasts. The radio spots had finally become a comfortable routine for her. Linkletter had taught her to project and to slow down her speech. But now Edith would have to face the camera, and she was frightened at the prospect of putting herself on display before 8.5 million viewers. As she noted in an earlier book, *The Dress Doctor:*

That I was neither young nor beautiful I was well aware; but now a camera was my adversary and I was as paralyzed as a prize fighter by the first punch. When the bell clanged and we took to the air, I wouldn't fight; I tried to hide behind Art Linkletter. Letters poured in criticizing my clothes, my hats, and my dark glasses, especially the dark glasses. And it was true, I wore dark glasses—because, subconsciously, I didn't want people to think I needed to wear glasses at all; I wanted them to think I *was wearing sunglasses. "If you're blind, get a tin cup," one letter said. "If not, take 'em off."**

After viewing herself on kinescope recordings of those early shows, she labeled herself "horrifying and bug-eyed." Ready to abandon her TV career, she turned to Linkletter for advice. "I had tried for years to get Edith to abandon the dark glasses," Linkletter recalls. "She finally agreed, after I explained that the eyes were an important part of body language. She had kept those glasses on as a means of hiding from the world. Edith was a very hidden, timid person. At first she wouldn't look at me or the camera or even at the audience. After each show we'd critique her performance, and I was like a doctor at her bedside, taking her pulse, telling her how to feel better. I told her to be conversational—not that she had to be a great speaker—but just to be friendlier. I told her to be proud of who and what she was, that the audience was interested in what she had to say.

"As she went on camera year after year she gained confidence," Linkletter notes. "Then she went around the country making personal appearances, and she told me that she got more feedback about her spots on my show than she did about her work in motion pictures. Even though she was the outstanding authority on costumes in the motion picture industry, her designs meant very little to the motion picture public. People appreciated the gowns, but they didn't immediately associate them with Edith Head. She wasn't that flamboyant. On TV she became a personality for the first time in her life. And once she realized that she was being appreciated for who she was, she grew as a person."

If Linkletter is right, it was not Edith Head's talent for design that made her into a celebrity. With the possible exception of Adrian, the public has never recognized costume designers as celebrities. And yet a five-foot-tall female costume designer who was over fifty, with a severe chignon, schoolteacher bangs, Coke-bottle specs, and a decidedly rigid demeanor was suddenly making

**The Dress Doctor, Edith Head and Jane Kesner Ardmore (Boston: Little, Brown, and Company, 1959), p. 167.

more than just inroads to stardom. She was attracting huge crowds wherever she went. Her fan mail was piled as high as Elizabeth Taylor's, but relatively few letters asked about the costumes she designed or the stars she dressed. Her fans wanted to know how to look prettier, how to unleash the glamour girl in themselves. Hollywood had taught Edith how to do it for the stars, so now the public wanted her to share the secrets. Art Linkletter had given her the forum, and it was her turn to dish out the information—spiced, of course, with a little juicy Hollywood gossip.

She appeared on *House Party* as frequently as three times a month, strolling through the audience with Linkletter, offering instant solutions to the busty lady from San Diego who wanted to know how to minimize her endowments and the bowlegged teenager from the San Fernando Valley who loved toreador pants but looked like a keyhole in them. The *coup de grâce* would come when she'd take a dumpy grandmother from Pacoima and give her a new, more sophisticated look. She'd simply untuck the woman's blouse and add a belt. Then she'd take off her own simulated pearls and trade them for the grandma's gaudy gold chain. A quick switch of handbags, and *voilà!* Mrs. Pacoima looked ten pounds thinner, smiled ear to ear, and received an ovation from the audience.

I wasn't always nice to those ladies. I tried to be, but sometimes I'd have to be blunt. They didn't know how they looked best and I did. So I'd tell them to "go on a diet, but in the meantime wear solid navy or charcoal gray. They're far more slimming than the hydrangea print you're wearing." They asked for it. If people want to be made over, they must accept criticism. Sometimes the advertisers would request that I be nicer to the ladies, so I'd ease up for a while. Art would always soften things a bit by making a joke if he thought I was getting too abrupt.

My segment was one of the most popular spots on the show. Do you know why? Because every woman in the world— and every man, for that matter—wants to look better. Nobody feels 100 percent confident about herself or himself. So there I was with easy answers, and it helped that I wasn't beautiful. They probably thought, "Here's a very average-looking woman who's a big success, so she must know what she's talking about. If I listen, I can look at least as good as she does."

Edith had more time for television and fashion shows in the 1950s, since she was designing an average of sixteen films a year instead of forty or more, as she had in the 1930s and 1940s. Besides, after more than two decades in one department of a major studio, she knew her job very well. She was an excellent administrator, adept at surrounding herself with capable people and able to delegate responsibility. According to those who worked closely with her in that period—the fitters, sketch artists, and seamstresses—she had no compunction about claiming others' work or ideas as her own if she thought it necessary. A fitter who worked with her for twenty years recalls, "We all decided she should run for President. She had an answer for everyone and everything. She was uncanny. Some days she would start selling a director or star on a particular design and then she'd realize the person didn't like it. In the same breath she'd start *un*selling the very same design, suggesting it was *her* idea that the sketch was wrong for the part. It was almost like a game for her. She liked to sweet-talk her way in and out of things. She would tell little fibs and then threaten you so you wouldn't reveal the truth. But she was so diplomatic that she made you feel good when you helped her. I always felt sorry for her, because it seemed she was always alone. She thought the stars were her friends, then all of a sudden they'd wind up requesting another designer. That hurt her, I know it did."

Such was the case with another new face of the 1950s, Audrey Hepburn. If Marilyn Monroe and Elizabeth Taylor were to be the sex goddesses of the decade, Hepburn was the antigoddess. She was the antithesis of anything that fit the sexy 1950s stereotype. She was skinny in an era of voluptuousness, flat when everyone else was round. Her neck was too long, her face was too innocent. By 1950s standards she was all wrong, yet she was about to enchant the world. William Wyler found the ballerina-thin, Belgian-born actress in London and immediately cast her as the disgruntled princess in *Roman Holiday* (1953). Edith Head was the first Hollywood costume designer to dress Hepburn.

When I first met Audrey she was doing Gigi *on Broadway in New York. I had to go east to have our initial costume discussions for* Roman Holiday. *I was completely enchanted by her. She was intelligent and had a strong sense about fashion, but what impressed me most was her body. I knew she would be the perfect mannequin for anything I would make. When clothes are designed to be sexy, you need a shapely form to flaunt them. But when clothes are designed for art's sake you need a shapeless body to display them. I knew it would be a great temptation to design clothes that would overpower her, the actress. I could have used her to show off my talents and detract from hers, but I didn't. I considered doing it, believe me. Another designer might have taken advantage of her, but I made her look even more beautiful.*

Audrey played Her Royal Highness Princess Anne, and the first time she appears on screen she is regally dressed in a brocade gown, with the correct jewels, the correct orders, even the correct gloves. She is the epitome of royal protocol; everything about her is flawless. In true Hollywood form she hates her state of affairs and wants to be free of her crown and everything that goes along with it. She runs away from the palace and becomes something of a street urchin.

To create the contrast, I put her in funny little flat shoes, a gathered cotton skirt, and a plain blouse with the sleeves rolled up. She even goes to the barber and has her regal crown of hair chopped off. Suddenly she is the kind of girl you wouldn't look at twice. It sounds easy to do, but it wasn't. Trying to make someone like Audrey, who has so much hauteur, *look anything but chic is very difficult. I had to adjust the length of the skirt, for instance, making it too long so that she looked somewhat dowdy. I used fabric that was limp to create the impression that she just didn't care what she wore. The costuming was very important in this film—it told the story. First she was a fairy-tale princess, then she became a sporty, wild, happy, very* real *person who had no regard for her appearance.*

The simpler the clothes, the better for Audrey. I tried to design things that would accentuate the novel qualities of her body. I called attention to her long neck so that people began to describe her as "swanlike" and "graceful" instead of "gangly." I emphasized her broad shoulders to draw the eye up toward her face, but nobody ever said she looked like a football player. And instead of trying to pad her hips, I put her in skin-tight pants. I didn't try to use camouflage on Audrey or to make her look like something she was not. Isn't it interesting that the Audrey Hepburn look, the reed-slim silhouette, is still the most sought-after look?

Edith won a fifth Oscar for her *Roman Holiday* designs. Hepburn was named best actress, and Ian McLellan Hunter received an Oscar for the script of this delightfully light, romantic comedy.*

After Hepburn's overwhelming success in *Roman Holiday*, Billy Wilder was delighted that he had tabbed her to play the lead in *Sabrina,* his upcoming adaptation of Samuel Taylor's stage play *Sabrina Fair.* Obviously aware of Hepburn's sex appeal, he told *Life* magazine, "This girl singlehandedly may make bosoms a thing of the past." He instructed Edith to do exactly what she had done in *Roman Holiday,* only better.

Every designer wishes for the perfect picture in which he or she can really show off design magic. My one chance was in Sabrina, *directed by Billy Wilder and starring Audrey, Humphrey Bogart, and William Holden—it was the perfect setup. Three wonderful stars, and my leading lady looking like a Paris mannequin.*

Audrey played the daughter of a chauffeur on a rich family's estate. She falls madly in love with one of the sons (Bill Holden), who never notices her. To him she is just the tacky

*Several years later film historians determined that the blacklisted writer Dalton Trumbo, in need of money, had actually written the script using Hunter's name. Hunter was also blacklisted in the wave of McCarthyism that struck Hollywood, but not until after he was awarded the Oscar for *Roman Holiday*. Even after the truth was learned, Trumbo was never recognized by the Academy of Motion Picture Arts and Sciences for that script.

daughter of a servant. With her hair hanging down straight and her clothes extremely simple and ill-fitted, she isn't particularly noteworthy. Then the Cinderella story begins. She goes to Paris to learn to be a lady. She comes back as the most chic creature that ever stepped off a plane, dressed perfectly in the most beautiful French clothes the world has ever seen.

In *The Dress Doctor,* Edith described the design process for *Sabrina* this way:

Planning the clothes this time, I went up to San Francisco, where Audrey was playing on stage. I took with me pages and pages of "little Audreys"—the Hepburn face and figure in miniature, on which Audrey could doodle dresses. She loves to design, and we worked as a team on the Sabrina *clothes. . . . The director broke my heart by suggesting that while the "chauffeur's daughter" was in Paris she actually* buy *a Paris suit designed by a French designer.* *

As a novice in Hollywood, Hepburn had given Edith little input about her costumes for *Roman Holiday,* but by the time the two were ready to begin work on *Sabrina,* Hepburn realized she was a star and wanted more say about what she wore. Just back from Paris, she walked in to Edith's initial costume meeting armed with a wardrobe designed by Hubert de Givenchy, the noted couturier, who had also provided her with a notebook of suggested sketches. When Edith presented her sketches to the actress, instead of the quiet, accepting young thing who had greeted her the year before, an assertive Audrey Hepburn pulled out the sketch pad and samples to show Edith exactly what she wanted.

One of the most famous dresses of Edith's career appeared in *Sabrina.* The black cocktail dress featured a high, geometric neckline which was secured at both shoulders by tiny bows. The design was immediately copied by clothing manufacturers and dubbed the "Sabrina neckline." Edith took singular credit for it.

*The Dress Doctor, p. 119.

However, Hepburn's friend and, by then, personal designer, Givenchy, quietly claimed that the black dress was his design. He was surprised that the Paramount designer had not given him credit for his work. Other Hollywood costume designers were dubious about the origins of the Sabrina dress, claiming that it was too innovative to be one of Edith's designs. Her critics charged that since Edith Head relied on feminine, face-framing necklines, the *bateau* neckline on the disputed black dress and the tiny jeweled hat were too high-fashion to have come from Edith's conservative sketch pad. Edith scoffed at the notion that she would copy someone else's designs and accepted her Oscar proudly. (After her death in 1981, people who worked with Edith at Paramount confided that she actually had not designed the black dress, that it was made at Paramount, under Edith's supervision, from Givenchy's sketch.) In 1983, Hubert de Givenchy reconfirmed that the black dress and a white ballgown Hepburn wore in *Sabrina* were both his designs.

Eventually, Edith bought the black dress and the white gown Taylor had worn in *A Place in the Sun* to add to a small costume collection she had begun in the 1940s. That collection grew and Edith began presenting retrospective fashion shows all over the world.

The designer did not work on an Audrey Hepburn film again until *Funny Face* (1957), but in that film Givenchy designed the star's fashionable wardrobe, and Edith dressed her in her first, dowdy costumes in the film. In *Breakfast at Tiffany's* (1961), Givenchy dressed her again, while New York designer Pauline Trigère dressed Patricia Neal, and Edith costumed the rest of the women.

While brunettes such as Hepburn and Taylor were bringing their own kinds of sex appeal to 1950s films, blondes were making their marks too. After Marilyn Monroe's small but notable appearance as "Miss Caswell of the Copacabana School of Dramatic Arts" in *All About Eve* (1950), she embarked on a short, tragic film career that would establish her as one of the immortal screen goddesses. Her clothes, most often designed by William Travilla, were as guileless and lascivious as her image. Though Travilla would occasionally opt for décolletage, he usually carefully covered her, letting her voluptuous body do what it would to her audiences. Having worked with most of the screen's greatest stars since 1923, Edith Head always regretted that she had never dressed Monroe.

I was sorry that I had begun work so late on All About Eve. *Maybe if I had been loaned out for it earlier, I could have designed all the costumes, including Marilyn's.*

I met her socially several times and we always talked about clothes. She was extremely knowledgeable about fit and fabric, which surprised me. She frequently asked me about ways to make her legs look longer and prettier. I suggested that she wear shaded hosiery when she was dressed in anything that revealed her calves. Shaded hose, very popular in the 1950s, were darker along the sides of the legs, creating the illusion of a slimmer calf. Not that she had chubby legs, but they weren't perfect, and Marilyn was always striving to look perfect.

When a star comes along who is so famous, so beautiful, and so lovable, every designer wants to make clothes for her. Travilla was the man of the hour. He knew every inch of that woman's body and how to make it look its best, so she stuck with him. I tried to get a chance to dress her. I used every contact I had, from Alfred Hitchcock on down, but Marilyn was specific. She wanted Travilla, or Helen Rose or even Dorothy Jeakins, but she never asked for Edith Head.

I never thought she looked especially comfortable in what she wore, and she once told a reporter that she didn't feel comfortable in clothes. Naturally the press made a big production of the sexual angle of her remark, but I think she really meant it seriously. Every designer who worked with her cinched her and harnessed her. Marilyn was a free spirit who should have been dressed in such a way that she would be able to forget about her clothes. When a woman is sexy, she knows it and she doesn't need clothes that constantly remind her. Marilyn should have been a star in the late 1960s—she could have been devastating as a sensual flower child. I hated the hippie look, but Marilyn would have loved it.

SEVEN

If Edith couldn't have Monroe in the 1950s, she got the next best blonde: Grace Kelly. As Hepburn was the brunette antithesis of Elizabeth Taylor's seething sexuality, innocent Grace Kelly was in pristine contrast to Marilyn Monroe.

If I had to pick a favorite actress (which I really don't like to do, but people always want to know), it would be Grace Kelly. We don't have many great women stars anymore, but in the 1950s Grace was tops. She was an ex-model and she knew how to wear clothes. Every actress's contract should specify that she be trained in modeling or dancing, or at least go to school to learn how to wear clothes.

When I first saw Grace in High Noon *(1952), I was struck by her beautiful face and perfect carriage. We worked together on* The Bridges at Toko-ri *(1954), but that wasn't really a costume picture. I was very excited when I was assigned to dress her in* The Country Girl *(1954) opposite Bing Crosby—that is, I was happy until I read the script. She was to play a woman who had been married for years and had lost interest in clothes, herself —everything. The character had absolutely no resemblance to Grace Kelly. I put her in housedresses and skirts and blouses, and made her look dumpy.*

I realized immediately when I showed the costumes to her that Grace was not at all comfortable. I used my best psychiatrist's voice and said, "Grace, I didn't think we could do it, but you look truly depressed. I congratulate you." She understood, from my words and manner, that she looked right for the part, so she stopped worrying about her appearance and concentrated on her acting. At the end of the film, Grace's character saves herself from a humdrum existence and takes a renewed interest in life. She spruces herself up. So for a few scenes, at least, I could dress Grace stylishly.

Grace was delightful to work with because she was very well educated and we could talk about anything together—art, music, literature. She enjoyed museums. She would get excited about classical music and she loved to converse with me about those kinds of things. Sometimes she would come into my salon with her lunch and the two of us would talk and laugh for hours at a time. It was always a pleasure to see her kick off her shoes and relax.

Off screen she was not the best-dressed actress in Hollywood, but she was always very fastidious about the way she looked. She wore white gloves and very sheer hose, and always carried a hankie. She was quite a contrast to the new stars. People today would call her manner "uptight," but she wasn't. Grace had a very cool, reserved demeanor which tended to put off people who didn't know her. Actually she was quite shy. Since she was so beautiful, men were always flirting with her and she wasn't especially comfortable with such superficiality. She felt safe in my salon, as if it was a quiet refuge from the studio commissary.

I had a more complete opportunity to dress her in Rear Window *(1954), which was my second experience working with Alfred Hitchcock. (The first had been* Notorious, *in 1946.) In* Rear Window, *Grace was cast as a high-society type, so her part called for an extremely stylish wardrobe. Hitchcock told me it was important that Grace's clothes help to establish some of the conflict in the story. She was to be the typical sophisticated society-girl magazine editor who falls in love with a scruffy photographer, Jimmy Stewart. He's insecure and thinks that she thinks he isn't good enough for her.*

Hitch wanted her to look like a piece of Dresden china, something slightly untouchable. So I did that. Her suits were impeccably tailored. Her accessories looked as though they couldn't be worn by anyone else but her. She was perfect. Few actresses could have carried off the look the way Grace did.

Since all the action took place in one room, everything that happened within that room had to have impact. Grace's clothes often provided that impact. The clothes also helped advance the narrative.

The black-and-white dress I used in the first love scene had a simple neckline, which framed her face in closeups. Then, as the camera pulled back, the beaded chiffon skirt immediately told the audience she was a rich girl.

Grace appeared in a nightgown and peignoir in Jimmy Stewart's bedroom, yet it was still a very innocent scene. Why? Jimmy's leg was in a cast, and he was virtually helpless when it came to romance. Grace was just showing him what he was missing by not marrying her. That was a perfect example of Hitchcock's offbeat sense of humor.

When people ask me who my favorite actress is, who my favorite actor is, who my favorite director is, and what my favorite film is, I tell them to watch To Catch a Thief *(1955) and they'll get all the answers. The film was a costume designer's dream. It had all the ingredients for being fun, a challenge, and a great product. The director was Hitchcock. The stars, Cary Grant and*

Grace Kelly. The location, the Côte d'Azur in the south of France. Grace played the part of possibly the richest woman in America, with the most fabulous clothes and the most fabulous jewels. Her mother, played by Jessie Royce Landis, was equally elegant.

The story evolved around a world of people with great taste and plenty of money. Even the extras were meticulously dressed. At the end of the picture we had a fancy masquerade ball, presumably at the court of one of the great kings of France, so every woman was running around dressed like Marie Antoinette. That was the most expensive setup I've ever done. Grace wore a dress of delicate gold mesh, a golden wig, and a golden mask. Hitchcock told me that he wanted her to look like a princess. She did.

To Catch a Thief *was not a difficult assignment, however. I had a big budget, perfect people to dress, and a perfect director, as well as a great story. I couldn't have planned it all better if I'd tried.*

There were certain scenes where the clothes had to help tell the story. Since Cary Grant was supposed to be a jewel thief, some of the gowns had to be designed around a piece of jewelry. When the camera did a closeup on a certain necklace, the dress formed a background for it. Sometimes the dress was strapless, but there had to be enough fabric showing in the tight shot so that the audience knew the woman had clothes on. Now this may sound simple, but it wasn't. The strapless gown had to have simple lines, so that it did not detract from the necklace, yet it had to emanate an haute couture *quality that matched the luxury of the jewels. Hitch was very explicit about such things.*

Hitchcock was constantly aware that we were filming the story in one of the fashion capitals of the world. He told me, "Edith, we are now in France. People dress *here. It's the place where style is created—so do it."*

When Grace went to the beach, she wore a huge sun hat and the most beautiful black-and-white sun costume that I've ever done. It was striking—almost too striking. But the script said that she was the kind of American who liked attention, so

I gave her attention-getting clothes. (She probably would have caught more eyes in one of the French bikinis that were so popular in the south of France in the 1950s, but Hitchcock wouldn't let Grace bare that much.)

I was nominated for an Academy Award for To Catch a Thief *and, unfortunately, I forgot the lesson I had learned in 1948, when I was convinced I would win for* The Emperor Waltz. *Once again, I got my hopes up. I had done an outstanding job and, in my estimation, the competition was very slim. Somehow I lost, and that was the single greatest disappointment of my costume design career.*

After that loss, I never cared very much about winning or losing an Oscar. I realized that so much depended upon the popularity of the film, not the quality of the designs. Charles LeMaire is a good friend of mine and I would tell him to his face that his designs for Love Is a Many Splendored Thing *(1955) were blah compared to my gowns for* To Catch a Thief. *All the costumes Jennifer Jones wore were Chinese cheong sams, the traditional Chinese dress, which could have been purchased in Chinatown if Charles had wanted to. He is such a professional that I'm sure he designed the clothes. He was nominated for another film that year,* The Virgin Queen *(1956), which he co-designed with Mary Wills, and to my mind those costumes were more impressive than those that won.*

The point is Love Is a Many Splendored Thing *was an extremely popular movie. It did very well at the box office, and it had a very popular theme song, so it carried a number of awards that year, including what should have been my costume design award. That may sound egotistical, but a creative person must have a healthy ego.*

Grace Kelly was under contract to MGM when Paramount began production on *To Catch a Thief.* It took a major persuasive effort by Kelly, Alfred Hitchcock, and his *Thief* star Cary Grant to convince MGM to loan out its hottest property. Kelly wanted the part badly, threatening to give up her entire career if MGM didn't loan her out. Even before her studio bosses conceded, Kelly called

Edith and told her to get started on the costumes in her size. It was on location for *To Catch a Thief* that Kelly met Prince Rainier.

While in France, Edith and Kelly spent long days shopping for the finishing touches to her wardrobe. A stopover in Paris led them to the expensive French boutique Hermès, where Grace had heard she would find the world's finest gloves. Edith recounted their Hermès experience to one of Kelly's biographers:

Like two girls in an ice cream shop, we fell in love with everything we saw. We chose gloves with little roses embroidered on them, gloves with openwork trim, all kinds of gloves. Grace got more and more excited—she got the same kind of joy collecting gloves as other women did diamonds. Finally they presented her with a package and an astronomical bill. Gloves and shoes are the only things where Grace loses count of money.

For a moment she looked confused and said, "I haven't got that much on me." We pooled our resources and it still wasn't enough. In the end they let us go back to the hotel, and the gloves were delivered later. . . .

The story illustrates that in spite of all her intelligence and business ability about contracts, in those days she still had this rather charming childish exuberance about her when it came to shopping.

*Two years ago I was again shopping in Paris for a Hitchcock film and picking out shoes for the star. Guess who I met? Grace was there, at it again, buying shoes. Our eyes met and we laughed. The lovely thing about Grace is that she never changes with her old friends.**

Although Edith claimed to have dressed Cary Grant in *To Catch a Thief,* Grant recalls the costuming of the motion picture differently. "Edith dressed the women but she didn't design my costumes. I planned and provided everything myself. In fact, I

*From *Princess Grace,* by Gwen Robyns (New York: David McKay, 1976), p. 101.

Barbara Stanwyck wore a white crepe bolero
and tie-on skirt over a gold lamé sheath in
The Lady Eve. The Latin American influence
behind the ensemble rocked
the U.S. fashion world in the 1940s.
Called a *guayavera*, the short jacket
is tied high and tight under the bust, giving
the illusion of a round, full bosom.
Stanwyck incorporated the gold-braid-trimmed
ensemble into her personal wardrobe,
wearing a black gown underneath.

A pregnant and petite Veronica Lake had to be dressed like a young boy in *Sullivan's Travels* (1941), so Edith hid her bulges in an oversize jacket and stashed her famous tresses underneath a paper boy's cap.

Edith often complained that wedding dresses were the most boring gowns to design, since they all looked alike. For Stanwyck in *The Lady Eve*, however, the designer fashioned the ultimate in sexy satin, with as proper a neckline as any church would demand. The veil incorporated four layers of imported bridal net and the gown featured a seven-foot, cathedral-length train.

Edith's designs frequently turned up in the newspapers and fan magazines of the 1940s. This trio of photographs displaying one of her classic suits was sent out to the press with the following caption: "A secretary's dream is this triple-duty dressmaker suit of bright renaissance blue wool, designed by Edith Head for Margaret Hayes to wear in Paramount's *Sullivan's Travels.* The basic suit has a straight skirt with front fullness. The jacket has a high-crossed neckline and fastens at one side. With a few simple changes, the suit meets the needs of the office, the shopping tour, and the cocktail hour. Made with concealed snaps, it is perfect for the office when worn with white piqué collar and cuffs. For shopping, a snap-on leopard collar, matched by a leopard muff, creates a second ensemble. Worn plain, with three golden arrows pinned at the collar, the suit makes a smart appearance at the cocktail hour."

(LEFT)
Road to Morocco (1942), a particularly funny entry in the Lamour-Hope-Crosby series, was lightly criticized for its extravagant wardrobe in a time of war. Publicity releases focused on the money-saving procedures used in making Lamour's gowns, such as hand-painting leather to simulate gold trim. But budgets were obviously not skimped on this hand-beaded *souffle* gown and turban.

(RIGHT)
Chiffon and braid define this *Road to Morocco* gown for Dorothy Lamour.

(LEFT)

For her dream sequence in *Lady in the Dark* (1944), Ginger Rogers wore a sequinned leotard with built-in gloves. To please the censors, Rogers's deep V-neckline was inset with a piece of nude-colored *souffle.* The mink overskirt, originally lined with several pounds of imitation emeralds, was relined with a paisley pattern of featherweight sequins so that Rogers could easily dance in the costume.

Costuming Barbara Stanwyck as a 1940s-style burlesque queen in *Ball of Fire* (1941), Edith combined prints, sequins, and baubles in an extremely uncharacteristic gaudy design. Stanwyck played a modern-day Snow White in this Billy Wilder story, and Gary Cooper, cast as a college professor, was one of her eight pseudodwarves.

(LEFT)
This black crepe dinner suit with its sprays of glimmering wheat on the back shoulder and front hip was designed by Edith Head for Barbara Stanwyck's personal wardrobe. Stanwyck had asked Edith to design something special to wear with her new topaz and gold jewelry.

After her fashionable appearance in *The Lady Eve*, Stanwyck became something of a clotheshorse, both on the screen and off. Edith designed this white crepe suit with flamboyant mink-tail accents for the star's personal wardrobe. In the early days of the film industry, stars were frequently allowed to keep their costumes as a perquisite of the job. The practice stopped when the studios started realizing the value of the clothes. By the early 1930s, stars paid wardrobe departments for their offscreen services. At one point, according to Hedda Hopper, Stanwyck's son Dion secretly offered Edith six dollars to make "a nice dress" for his mommy's Christmas present. When Edith agreed, Stanwyck supplied the remaining several hundred dollars.

Red strawberries on a field of
navy blue crepe highlight this
outfit designed for Stanwyck's
luncheon-circuit wardrobe. Edith
rarely used prints in her film
costumes, but employed them
frequently for personal
wardrobes.

(ABOVE, LEFT)
In *Tender Comrade* (1943), Edith, on loan to RKO, dressed Ginger Rogers in brief shorts to show off those famous legs. Renie dressed the rest of the cast.

(ABOVE, CENTER)
In *The Stork Club* (1945) hat-check girl Betty Hutton becomes a rich woman and gets a fabulous Head wardrobe in the process, including this slinky black crepe evening dress. The broad-shoulders, a look that MGM designer Adrian gave Joan Crawford in the 1930s, became a signature of the 1940s. Edith disliked the silhouette, calling it "the lady football-player look," but used it at the request of many stars.

(ABOVE)
Since Paramount stayed away from big-budget extravaganzas in the 1940s, Edith rarely had the opportunity to indulge her design fantasies. Occasionally a film like *The Stork Club* came along and she was able to have some fun. With the war nearing its end, studio executives became less conservative with costume budgets, so ermine, leopard skin, and gold lamé once again found their way to the screen.

(LEFT)
The uniforms worn by hat-check girls Betty Hutton and Iris Adrian in *The Stork Club* were later adopted as the official dress for hat-check girls at the posh New York club. Barry Fitzgerald looks on.

(BELOW, LEFT)
Edith and director/costume designer Mitchell Leisen collaborated on Dorothy Lamour's extravagant costumes in *Masquerade in Mexico* (1945), but she was on her own dressing the rest of the cast. Silent-screen star Mae Busch made a cameo appearance as a party guest wearing Edith's ethnic skirt and halter-top design.

(BELOW, CENTER)
A simple ribbon at the neck offsets the black satin and chiffon gown that Edith designed for Stanwyck in *The Bride Wore Boots* (1946).

(BELOW, RIGHT)
Black velvet reflected just enough light to offset Ingrid Bergman's blond hair and ivory skin in *Notorious* (1946). Edith rarely gave Bergman jewelry or clothes with intricate details, noting that the star was not comfortable with lavish designs.

In the opening scenes of *Notorious*, Edith dressed Ingrid Bergman in a shocking mix of bare midriff and zebra stripes that drew all eyes to her. Cary Grant has his back to the camera. *Dead Men Don't Wear Plaid* (1982) incorporated the same scene, with Steve Martin sitting in for Grant.

(OPPOSITE)
Hitchcock's eerie imagination was evident even in this publicity still from *Notorious*. Here, a shadowed Ingrid Bergman wears Edith's simple white crepe dinner suit, with only a touch of jewelry at the neck.

Edith, at left, discusses a costume with Alfred Hitchcock, while Bergman and an unidentified woman listen in. The gown in the sketch was rejected for *Notorious*, since the script called for a demure and extremely simple wardrobe for the star.

The negligees worn by Loretta Young in *The Perfect Marriage* (1946), with David Niven, inspired a layout in *Life* magazine, showing its women readers what to wear to bed to keep their marriages perfect. Macy's bought the rights to a number of the designs and made Young's bedtime wardrobe a mass-market affair.

Dorothy Lamour was one of Edith's most elegant clotheshorses, a perfect mannequin for the designer's simple silhouettes and sometimes garish details. In *My Favorite Brunette* (1947), Lamour carried off this strapless moiré gown and its waterfall of fake flora.

Lamour and Edith both seemed most comfortable when a slight ethnic touch was added to the star's gowns. The Latin American influence turns up more than once in Lamour's wardrobe for *My Favorite Brunette* (1947).

In *Sorry, Wrong Number* (1948), Barbara Stanwyck spent many scenes in bed, giving Edith the opportunity to create some of the world's most elegant negligees. Throughout the film Stanwyck wore fabulous jewels, many from her personal collection.

In *The Emperor Waltz* (1948), Joan Fontaine wore an Edith Head gown as lavish as the period it represented: 1901 Austria under Emperor Franz Josef.

(LEFT)
In this still from *The Emperor Waltz*, Joan Fontaine wears a Head-designed
riding outfit while Bing Crosby, dressed in lederhosen created by
menswear designer Gile Steele, looks on.

(RIGHT)
Edith was crushed when the gowns she created for Joan Fontaine in *The
Emperor Waltz* failed to earn her the first Academy Award offered for costume design.
The print in this gown was inspired by a carpet in Edith's mother's home.

(LEFT)
Edith received her first Academy Award for *The Heiress* (1949), a film that
brought Olivia de Havilland her second Oscar as best actress. Here,
her moiré gown fits tightly across the bust and wrinkles at the sleeve—fitting
techniques designed to convey a woman uncomfortable with herself.

(RIGHT)
Olivia de Havilland's role in *The Heiress* as a spinster who never really
knew how to dress called for costumes that expressed her fashion
insecurities. Here Edith added one too many gewgaws to separate the rich
from the elegant.

(LEFT)
In a later scene in *The Heiress*, a confident and radiant de Havilland,
dressed to take revenge on a fortune-hunting Montgomery Clift, appeared in
one of Edith's most beautiful period gowns.

(RIGHT)
Director William Wyler insisted that Edith research even the undergarments
for de Havilland's costumes in *The Heiress*. "He wanted accuracy down to
the number of ruffles on her petticoat," Edith recalled.

(LEFT)

Even Edith's lavish costumes for *Samson and Delilah* (1949) could not overshadow Hedy Lamarr's exquisite beauty. Lamarr played opposite the brawny and often barechested Victor Mature. Groucho Marx once commented, "It's the only movie I ever saw in which the male lead's tits were bigger than the female's." Lamarr's cleavage and navel were never exposed in the film. "The censors had a thing about women's bellybuttons," Edith explained.

(RIGHT)

Edith won an Academy Award in color costuming for her designs for Lamarr and Angela Lansbury in *Samson and Delilah*, which was released in 1949 but considered a 1950 film for award purposes. The same year, the designer also took black-and-white costuming honors for *All About Eve* (1950), with Bette Davis.

Edith's famed peacock cape for Lamarr in *Samson and Delilah* is still on view at the Cecil B. DeMille estate in Los Angeles. The cape is made from two thousand peacock plumes, reportedly gathered from peacocks that roamed freely on the movie mogul's ranch.

(LEFT)
Gloria Swanson helped Edith conceptualize the costumes for her comeback role in *Sunset Boulevard* (1950). All the designs were overdone to reflect the film's dramatization of an aging silent-screen star's faded career.

(RIGHT)
Together, Edith and Gloria Swanson created a 1920s look, updated only slightly to the 1950s, for Swanson's role as Norma Desmond in *Sunset Boulevard*. The trailing fox stole topped a dress with a lowered waistline and the exaggerated drape of the late 1920s.

Edith Head captured Oscar honors for her work in the Joseph Mankiewicz film *All About Eve* (1950). The brown cocktail dress worn by Bette Davis in this scene became one of her most famous costumes. Originally designed with a square neckline, the dress fit improperly but pleased Davis as it fell seductively off her shoulders. At left is Anne Baxter, who played the deceitful Eve. The blonde is Marilyn Monroe. George Sanders looks on.

This sketch, from Edith's personal collection, is not the drawing submitted to director Joseph Mankiewicz for Bette Davis's role as Margo Channing in *All About Eve*. Edith's original rendering showed the dress to have a square neckline, not the off-the-shoulder style Davis wore in the film. Edith often asked her artists to render sketches after a film was completed and used these finished pieces of art for promotional purposes. (Academy of Motion Picture Arts and Sciences)

A beaming Elizabeth Taylor shows off her trim waist and ample bosom in another New Look adaptation by Edith Head for *A Place in the Sun*. (Stacy Endres Collection)

Edith met Elizabeth Taylor when the seventeen-year-old star began work on *A Place in the Sun* (1951). Taylor prided herself on her tiny waist, which Edith enhanced in strapless gowns with bouffant skirts—a hallmark of the New Look created by Christian Dior in the late 1940s. The white gown, shown in both sketch and photo, was copied by manufacturers all over the country and became a favorite prom dress among American teenagers.

When Edith wasn't taking full advantage
of Elizabeth Taylor's shoulders, she
was accenting her bosom, another of Taylor's
fine endowments. Edith designed this
overskirted ensemble for *Elephant Walk*
and used the silhouette frequently
throughout the 1950s. (Stacy Endres Collection)

Edith often said that Elizabeth Taylor
had the most beautiful shoulders in
Hollywood, so she liked to show them off.
Edith draped chiffon over one gorgeous
shoulder, leaving the other for the
audience to savor. This was one of many
white dresses the star wore in
Elephant Walk (1954).
(Stacy Endres Collection)

Audrey Hepburn's figure became one of the most influential forces in American fashion in the 1950s. Her lean, almost gangly appearance set a fashion trend that still has women the world over dieting to achieve the Hepburn look. In this still from Paramount's publicity campaign for *Roman Holiday* (1953), Hepburn wears a prim white shirt and circle skirt, as a gray-suited Gregory Peck approaches at right. The film brought Edith her fifth Academy Award.

Audrey Hepburn made her U.S.
film debut in *Roman Holiday*,
directed by William Wyler.
Cast as a princess, in one of
the film's earliest scenes
she is shown in a regal ball
gown and jewels before running
off to hobnob with more common
folk. (Academy of Motion
Picture Arts and Sciences)

Controversy surrounded the black dress Audrey Hepburn wore in *Sabrina* (1954).
One of Edith's most famous costumes, the gown was copied by manufacturers all
over the country, but many critics charged that it was actually designed by
Hepburn's personal couturier, Hubert de Givenchy. Humphrey Bogart didn't own
a chic tuxedo, so Edith designed his sleek afterhours garb for *Sabrina*.

Grace Kelly won her only Academy
Award for her performance in
The Country Girl (1954), playing
opposite Bing Crosby. As the
depressed wife of an alcoholic
singer, she wore dowdy, boring
clothes early in the film.
Then, as she and her husband put
their lives back together,
her wardrobe, complete with hats
and gloves, changed to reflect
her new spirit.

For one of the more dramatic
scenes in *Rear Window*, Hitchcock
wanted Grace Kelly dressed in
black and white, so Edith
designed this sophisticated
cocktail dress, one of the most
revealing gowns ever worn
by the star.

Rear Window (1954) was Edith's
first opportunity to put Grace
Kelly in a fabulous wardrobe. Since
the star was cast as a fashion
editor, director Alfred Hitchcock allowed
the designer to inject a great deal
of high fashion into the costumes.
Kelly liked to wear gloves, so
Edith indulged her, even
with this simple floral-print
afternoon dress.

bought everything in Cannes, just before we began shooting. She didn't go with me when I purchased the clothes, nor did she approve anything. I was the only one who approved my clothes. Hitch trusted me implicitly to select my own wardrobe. If he wanted me to wear something very specific he would tell me, but generally I wore simple, tasteful clothes—the same kinds of clothes I wear off screen."

In the film industry, according to Grant, men traditionally supply their own wardrobe. "It's often written into the contract. You work with the costume designer if the film is a period picture or if many copies of the same suit are required. In *North by Northwest* (1959), I needed six identical suits because of the shooting sequence." Most directors require that costumes be provided in duplicate, since an actor or actress may have to fall into a swimming pool in one scene and then be called upon to shoot the preceding scene in the same costume, thus necessitating a dry duplicate. Duplicates also ensure a fresh, clean change for messy stars who spot their costumes during lunch breaks or nervous ones who perspire on the set. In the case of an extravagant costume such as Grace Kelly's golden ballgown in *To Catch a Thief*, the cost of a spare would be prohibitive. Any accidents to the gown would require holding up shooting while the costume was rushed to the wardrobe department for immediate dry cleaning or repairs.

Less than a year after the film was released, Grace traded her Hollywood career for a jeweled crown and a palace in Monaco. During the months before the wedding every designer in Hollywood who knew the soon-to-be princess had begun sketching wedding gown designs, hopeful that he or she would be chosen to dress the royal bride. It should have been obvious, however, that Helen Rose, the Oscar-winning designer at Kelly's home studio, MGM, who had dressed her in *Green Fire* (1954), *The Swan* (1956), and *High Society* (1956), would design and supervise the production of the historic wedding gown. Still, Edith Head hoped that she would be asked to design her friend's wedding dress. Crushed by the news that Rose was given the coveted job, Edith immediately informed Kelly that she would design her going-away suit and that the ensemble would be a gift from Paramount Studios. The light gray silk suit was topped with a white overcoat and worn with a tiny white hat and long white gloves.

After the wedding little mention was made of the full-skirted gray suit Princess Grace wore as she waved adieu to her new and adoring subjects and headed for a blissful honeymoon. But it was months before women stopped talking about the *peau de soie* wedding gown with its eleven-foot train strewn with Brussels lace that was said to be 125 years old. The exclusive Dallas specialty store Neiman-Marcus dressed the eight bridesmaids in sunlight-yellow silk gowns and the flower-girls in white Swiss organdy with embroidered daisies and yellow petticoats. Even the attendants' attire received more press than the princess's going-away suit. For several years after the wedding, Edith was erroneously acknowledged as the designer of the wedding gown, a credit that she would intermittently accept, deny, or ignore.

Edith and the Royal Family of Monaco would continue to keep close ties, despite the royal slap in the face she had felt when she was passed over as the designer of the gown. Edith was received at the palace on several occasions, and whenever Her Serene Highness and Prince Rainier were entertained at Alfred Hitchcock's home in California, Edith and her husband Bill were always invited. When Princesses Caroline and Stephanie became of curtsying age, Edith gifted them with their first pairs of tiny white gloves, a tribute to their mother's charming tradition.

The 1950s were Edith's glory years. By the middle of the decade she had won six Academy Awards, four of them for contemporary fashion pictures. She was the most popular guest on Linkletter's *House Party*, she and her close friend June Van Dyke had made a business out of staging Hollywood costume fashion shows for the public, and she was continually asked to dress the most prestigious stars of the day. She and Bill were working on the second decade of a happy, placid marriage, comfortably established in a splendid Early-California manse just north of Beverly Hills on swank Coldwater Canyon Drive. She was living the life of the Hollywood star, the kind of life she had envied in her early days in the business. She had shown the beauties how to look like stars

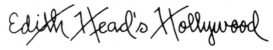

and she had become as sought after as any one of them. Edith had proved that fame could come to a plain little woman with spectacles if she was smart enough and politic enough to persevere. So it was perfectly fitting that in 1955 Edith should actually appear in a movie, playing, no less, herself.

The film, *Lucy Gallant* (1955), starred Charlton Heston and Jane Wyman. Though critics panned the film for being a prolonged soap opera and too much of a "woman's movie," Edith, even with her split-second part, proved to be a star. Her fabulous costumes, meant to be *haute couture* designs from Paris sold in Wyman's chic clothing store, were featured in a long fashion-show segment of the film, complete with an Edith Head narrative.

This was the first time Edith's designs were showcased strictly for fashion's sake, so she incorporated every creative idea she and her staff could evoke to present a remarkably elegant display. Since both *Lucy Gallant* and *To Catch a Thief* were color films released in 1955, and since the latter starred the popular Grace Kelly, Edith was nominated for *To Catch a Thief* instead of her fashion extravaganza. Many of her peers told her that her designs for *Lucy Gallant* were superior to the costumes for *Thief*, but Edith's opinion never changed: No work she had done, before or after, compared with her gowns for the Hitchcock film.

Edith and Hitchcock had developed a mutual respect that continued throughout the rest of their careers. After her successes costuming *Rear Window* and *To Catch a Thief*, he requested her for *The Trouble with Harry* (1955), with a young starlet named Shirley MacLaine; *The Man Who Knew Too Much* (1956), with Doris Day; and *Vertigo* (1958), with Kim Novak, his major films of the 1950s.

In *The Man Who Knew Too Much*, Edith dressed Doris Day to suit her part as the doctor's wife. "The clothes weren't right for me," Day later told a reporter. "But they were just what a doctor's wife would wear. And that's what I was playing. Edith dresses actors for the part, not for themselves alone."

In Hitchcock's *Vertigo*, one scene called for Kim Novak to wear a gray suit, a costume that figured prominently in the hero's obsessive reconstruction of what he presumes to be his dead lover.

Edith designed a tailored, rather boxy but fashionable gray ensemble for Hitchcock's newest blonde.

Kim was a bit intimidated by me at our first costume meeting, I suppose, so she immediately told me that she would be delighted with anything I designed for her. I remember her saying she would wear any color except gray, and she must have thought that would give me full rein. Either she hadn't read the script or she had and wanted me to think she hadn't. I explained to her that Hitch paints a picture in his films, that color is as important to him as it is to any artist. I then proceeded to stick the sketch of the gray suit off to the side so she wouldn't see it and to show her some of the other designs. We had a very amicable meeting and I told her we would need one more meeting to make final fabric and color selections.

As soon as she left I was on the phone to Hitch, asking if that damn suit had to be gray and he explained to me that the simple gray suit and plain hairstyle were very important and represented the character's view of herself in the first half of the film. The character would go through a psychological change in the second half of the film and would then wear more colorful clothes to reflect the change.

Even in a brief conversation, Hitch could communicate complex ideas. He was telling me that women have more than one tendency, a multiplicity of tastes, which can be clouded by the way they view themselves at any particular moment. He wasn't about to lose that subtle but important concept just because Kim Novak didn't like to wear gray. "Handle it, Edith," I remember him saying. "I don't care what she wears as long as it's a gray suit."

When Kim came in for our next session, I was completely prepared. I had several swatches of gray fabric in various shades, textures, and weights. Before she had an opportunity to complain, I showed her the sketch and the fabrics and suggested that she choose the fabric she thought would be best on her. She immediately had a positive feeling and felt that we were designing together. Of course, I knew that any of the fabrics would work well for the suit silhouette I had designed, so I didn't care which one she chose.

In 1956, when *That Certain Feeling* with George Sanders, Bob Hope, and Eva Marie Saint was released, Edith found a lucrative opportunity to promote her work. Saint, cast as a secretary, wore a wardrobe that changed the fashion flavor of offices from coast to coast. Although she was attired in a simple charcoal-gray flannel suit in many of her scenes, her beauty gave a new, professional credence to the women who anchored the front offices of America. Hooking up with a major specialty store on New York's Fifth Avenue, Edith designed a suit and a wardrobe of blouses that were advertised in a full-page spread in *Life* magazine, featuring Saint as the model. Edith made personal appearances to promote the collection, and secretaries turned out in droves, not just to see the queen of Hollywood costumes but to buy the clothes.

During the latter part of the 1950s Edith would turn her sights to publishing, a longtime dream she had never realized. Though she had tried to write a how-to-dress book in the mid-1940s, her frantic schedule (she designed forty or fifty film wardrobes a year) didn't leave much time for writing. Now that she was designing an average of sixteen films each year, she had the spare hours to devote to an autobiography. Working with an accomplished young journalist, Jane Kesner Ardmore, Edith compiled a 250-page volume filled with dressing-room talk about her favorite stars as well as hundreds of *House Party*–style tips on dressing—hints on what to wear to everything from amusement parks and christenings to garden weddings and wrestling matches.

Due in large part to Edith's countrywide tour to promote the book, *The Dress Doctor* became a best-seller in less than two months. She often incorporated costume fashion shows into the promotional tour, drawing huge crowds wherever she went. Six months after it was published, the book had sold twenty-five thousand copies, had been reviewed in hundreds of journals, and was serialized in dozens of major newspapers. The number of fan letters and beseeching requests for wardrobe guidance skyrocketed, forcing her to employ a full-time secretary to answer her mail.

When I look back on the 1950s I think of them as the highlight of my career. I received so much response from my public that I finally realized I was a celebrity in my own right. That was difficult for me to accept. Until the 1950s, I saw myself as just another costume designer, a title I didn't particularly like, but I was stuck with it. After working with Howard Greer and Travis Banton, I knew I was not a creative design genius. I was never going to be the world's greatest costume designer, but there was no reason I could not be the smartest. When you can make an actress beautiful or an actor handsome, you can succeed in Hollywood, as long as you know the right people to please. That's why I have always said that I am a better politician than I am a designer. I know who to please.

There are probably dozens of better designers on New York's Seventh Avenue, but they wouldn't last a day in Hollywood. You have to know when to say yes and when to say "I'm not sure it will work, sir, but I'm certainly going to try!" And you'd better know when to smile and when to be serious. I spent my first thirty years in Hollywood learning all these things.

My favorite era in Hollywood costume design was the 1930s, with Dietrich and Lombard and their glamour, but the films of the 1950s came about as close to that kind of glamour as Hollywood will ever see again. The films of the decade did not have the look of the 1930s, where everybody was rich and totally unrealistic, but they offered an opportunity to show different levels of society as well as different values.

In the 1950s pictures, you could almost tell the story by the way clothes were handled. This was no costume design magic —it was pure, straight designing to help tell a story without any satire or tricks. Costume designing was pure fashion. And we had female stars who were truly glamorous.

When people think of the 1950s they think of Grace Kelly, Audrey Hepburn, Elizabeth Taylor, Sophia Loren, and, of course, Marilyn Monroe. I remember Grace's posture, how perfectly erect she would stand while my fitter adjusted a hem. I recall Audrey's waist being so small that we could put a dog collar around it. And I remember the days when Elizabeth's figure was so trim and beautiful.

In Elephant Walk *(1954), she replaced Vivien Leigh and wore the costumes I had made for Vivien. We refit most of them and remade only two to accommodate Elizabeth's larger bust. The film was shot in the tropics, so I dressed her predominantly in white and showed off her beautiful back and shoulders. She was so gorgeous.*

I often dressed Sophia Loren; I can still see her looking somewhat chubby after a holiday feast, and then slipping into her fabulous handmade Italian corset to become the tiny-waisted, voluptuous siren in Houseboat *(1958). I like to think I played a major part in creating the images of all these stars.*

These glamour girls were not the only stars of the 1950s. Male stars returned to the screen after a wartime absence and began to establish themselves as important artists. Bing Crosby and Bob Hope continued to be the big names at Paramount, but Charlton Heston, Kirk Douglas, Burt Lancaster, and William Holden were becoming sought-after stars, often teamed with Edith's most popular leading ladies. For years men had been prohibited in the women's costume salon, and except for her dear friend Bob Hope and his colorblind cohort Crosby, Edith was called upon to dress only the superstar women. But as male actors became increasingly popular, she designed costumes for more of them, from Danny Kaye's black velvet doublets and suits of armor in *The Court Jester* (1956), to Clark Gable's conservative suits in *Teacher's Pet* (1958), to Cornel Wilde's spangled leotard in *The Greatest Show on Earth* (1952) and Yul Brynner's embroidered pirate getup in *The Buccaneer* (1958). Also, the new comedy team of Dean Martin and Jerry Lewis was appearing in producer Hal Wallis' films that required as much creative and humorous costuming as Crosby and Hope's *Road* pictures had. Edith developed such a strong professional rapport with Jerry Lewis that he later selected her as costume designer on several films he directed in the 1960s.

When Elvis Presley made his second film, *Loving You*, in

1957 (his first film was *Love Me Tender,* in 1956, at Twentieth Century-Fox) Hal Wallis asked Edith not only to dress the female leads, Lizabeth Scott and Dolores Hart, but to improve on the wardrobe Presley's personal valet had chosen for him.

Elvis was playing a hillbilly singer in the film, so he was at least at home in the role. He was famous for his tight trousers, so I couldn't change those. (Of course, when I look back at the film now, they look like baggy pants. They were tight across the pelvis, but the legs were full.) Since the film was in Technicolor, I made a few color adjustments, but basically nobody dressed Elvis Presley better than Elvis.

Elvis' wardrobes were extremely simple in all nine of the Hal Wallis productions. For his stage and album cover costumes, Elvis, his manager, Colonel Tom Parker, and his personal valet chose his wardrobe. On the jacket of his second album of gold-record hits, Elvis wore his most famous costume, a 24-karat gold lamé suit that in 1959 cost $10,000 to tailor at Nudie's, Hollywood's most famous cowboy clothier. He was never dressed in anything as flamboyant on the screen.

Before I met Elvis, I was totally prepared not to like him. I had seen more than I wanted to see of him on a series of Saturday night specials on television and then I watched him vibrate on The Ed Sullivan Show. *I realized why Hal Wallis wanted him—he excited young women. What I could not understand was why those girls were so attracted to him. Before our first meeting I told myself to be open-minded and to try to treat this fellow with the respect due a star, but I had my doubts about pulling it off. Hal Wallis brought him and his entourage to the studio. He was very charming and shook hands with everyone in the room, but when he was introduced to me he very daringly kissed me on the cheek. I guess one of my claims to fame is that I have been kissed by Elvis Presley.*
He played opposite so many different leading ladies that it got to be a joke. Elvis Presley making love to so and so in

Loving You *(1957),   Elvis Presley singing to somebody else in* King Creole *(1958), and Elvis Presley caressing yet another star-let in* G.I. Blues *(1960). But he was a wonderful movie lover—he looked comfortable with all those women. Of course, he wasn't as comfortable being a Romeo as he was singing, but I think his audiences preferred seeing him as a lover.*

Basically Elvis wore a uniform in all his films. For casual scenes he'd open his shirt at the neck and wear tight pants— black jeans were a favorite of his. Then when he'd go out with one of his ladies, he'd put on dark pants, dark shirt, and a lighter jacket. There was always a striking contrast between his shirt and his jacket. Since every film had a theme, I'd have to design something that fit in. In King Creole *(1958) he played a boxer, so I worked up sketches for satin robes and trunks. In* Blue Hawaii *(1961), it was swim trunks with a racing stripe to match his surfboard. The script called for him to get married in tradi-tional Hawaiian groom's garb, so I had a hand in that too. I thought of Elvis' costumes as gimmick clothes, so it was easy for me to dress him. Also, his image was very well established, and I wasn't about to tamper with it. In that sense he was like a male version of Mae West: He knew the Elvis look.*

The girls were always sweet, innocent blondes who wore full skirts and petticoats, or they were sultry, not-so-innocent brunettes who wore tight dresses with slits on the sides. These films did not present great design challenges.

We were all very sad when he was drafted. Working on his films had become more fun than we had expected. I cringed when every detail about his induction became a news item. When the Army cut his hair, Colonel Parker collected the shorn tresses and sent them to fan clubs. It was a relief when he finally re-turned from duty. He had fallen in love with a very young and beautiful girl named Priscilla, and he seemed mellower than the man who had been drafted.

When we went on location to the Hawaiian Islands to shoot Blue Hawaii *(1961), there were so many girls crowding around our hotel that we had to have policemen guarding the place, and most of us were afraid to go out. I would not have*

*believed the size of the crowds if I had not seen them myself. Elvis
had a suite next to mine and there were guards posted outside
his door, as well as policemen posted outside under his windows
in case girls tried to climb up the vines.*

*He had learned to take all this hysteria in stride. Yet
whenever I dealt with him, he was still as sweet and seemingly
innocent as you could hope for—always the Southern gentle-
man. Since I was so much older, I suppose he was treating me
the way he would treat a friend's mother or a grandmother.*

By the end of 1959 Edith Head had turned sixty-two. She
could look back on a decade that included Academy Award nominations every year. (She received a total of fifteen nominations, including two each for the years 1950, 1952, 1955, 1956, and 1959; in
those years she was honored for both her color and black-and-white
film work.) She was a best-selling author. She had a permanent
guest spot on one of America's best-loved TV shows. She had
dressed almost every major star in Hollywood, including a future
President of the United States. (Ronald Reagan starred with
Rhonda Fleming in *Hong Kong* and *The Last Outpost* in 1951 and
Tropic Zone in 1953.) She had built a collection of screen costumes
that would grow to be the most important in the world, and she was
a sought-after guest lecturer. She had achieved a kind of fame she
had only dreamed about in her earliest years at Paramount.

EIGHT

Shortly after the end of World War II, Edith Head had commented that the only people who seemed to be making a personal fashion statement in America were the beatniks who huddled in smoky coffeehouses in San Francisco and Greenwich Village. As the mid-1950s approached, Edith still equated "offbeat" with black turtleneck sweaters and berets, a look that became a clichéd symbol of passive rebellion against the establishment. A corporate artist who had spent her working life pleasing her bosses, Edith expressed her respect for the intellectuals who would rather write poetry than make money.

I always thought I would make a good beatnik. I even had the long hair, if I was willing to let it down. But I could never give up success—success is a trap. Inside I was a prima donna who insisted that a costume be made my way or not at all; outside I was the model employee, easy to get along with and always on time. Sure I got frustrated at times, but I was making lots of money. And who could complain about getting paid to dress the most beautiful women in the world? A career like mine keeps you going to the office, day in and day out. I learned to suppress my artistic needs.

Edith had understood the 1950s very well—its movie stars, its beatniks, its tiny waists and full skirts. With the onset of the 1960s, she had to accept the fact that even beatniks were passé and that Jacqueline Bouvier Kennedy was introducing a world of women to a new and rather shapeless fashion design, offset by sophisticated bouffant hairdos. Fashion magazines such as *Vogue* and *Harper's Bazaar* experienced a boost in circulation as American women began to take a renewed interest in what to wear and how to look. These women weren't going to movies to discover trend-setting fashion. If anything, now Mrs. America wanted to see the same clothes on the screen as she saw in the pages of the fashion monthlies.

Times had definitely changed. High-fashion names such as Saint Laurent, Pucci, and Givenchy were becoming far better known than film-design names such as Plunkett, Sharaff, and Rose. Had Edith not continued to appear on *House Party*, her name might have lost instant recognition too. MGM's designer Helen Rose had opened her own high-priced ready-to-wear company, and she was becoming more celebrated for her retail designs than for the costumes she made for some of Elizabeth Taylor's most famous roles. Rose reasoned that she could express herself more creatively and make a better living as a ready-to-wear designer. Manufacturers were constantly approaching Edith, asking her to do the same.

I could never be a retail designer. They are pressured by the whims of the public, and their livelihood depends upon whether or not a collection sells. They do four or five collections a year, and if one doesn't sell they have a good chance of going broke. When I design for my films it's like doing a new collection for each one, but I am always sure the clothes will be right, or I redo them before it's too late.

Costume designers and retail designers are in totally different businesses. My costumes are made with one individual character in mind. They are created to tell a story and to reflect a time period. A retail designer strives to make clothes that will fit the trim career girl, the housewife who has had three children, and the grandmother who has grown stooped with age but who still wants to look young. The dress that sells well in California might flop in New York, and a hit in Atlanta is a loser in Minneapolis. I don't want that kind of pressure. I much prefer to dress Natalie Wood and Joanne Woodward and Shirley Mac-Laine. With them, I know what I'm doing.

Shirley MacLaine first walked into Edith's salon to be fitted for her role in Alfred Hitchcock's *The Trouble with Harry* (1955). Edith met the young actress again after producer Hal Wallis put her under contract. MacLaine had the difficult duty of playing the female lead opposite Dean Martin and Jerry Lewis in *Artists and Models* (1955), a zany story about a fellow who starts receiving top-secret government information during his too frequent nightmares. For one of her first big scenes, MacLaine was supposed to be dressed as a bat.

She was not the least bit pleased about being cast as a bat, but she already had a professional attitude about acting. Instead of bitching, she told me she didn't know the first thing about bats. "Are they mammals or reptiles? And how do they have babies?" she asked. I wasn't sure, so I called the research people and asked them to send me all they could about bats. Once she knew that a bat was a tiny flying mammal that catches its prey by reflected sound waves—research called it "echolocation"—she had a new respect for the creature she was supposed to play. She started flying around the room flapping her wings until I told her she was going to have to light so I could continue the fitting process.

Next Hal asked me to dress her in Hot Spell *(1958), where she played another kind of bat—the twenty-year-old kind who steals husbands away from unsuspecting wives like Shirley Booth. The same year, 1958, I dressed her and Shirley Booth again in* The Matchmaker, *which was a period piece. It wasn't until 1959 that Shirley and I finally got a fashion vehicle,* Career *(1959), a contemporary story set in New York. The* Career *wardrobe earned an Academy Award nomination for best black-and-white costumes that year, but I lost out to Orry-Kelly for Tony Curtis' and Jack Lemmon's drag getups in* Some Like It Hot. *(I was also nominated that year for* The Five Pennies *in the color-costume category, but* Ben-Hur *swept that award and just about everything else.)*

Shirley and I got to be very good friends. I loved dressing her, and I sincerely believe she had respect for my work. We rarely had any disagreements about costumes—in fact, I can't think of a single instance. She knew that she had gorgeous legs and liked to show them off. Any designer would be a fool not to take those legs into consideration with every Shirley MacLaine costume.

Shirley came into her own in the 1960s. She was no glamour girl; in fact, Hal Wallis usually ended up putting her in character roles. That was very perceptive of him. I think he realized that Shirley was the first of a very new breed of actress.

In the early days of the motion picture industry, and even as late as the 1950s, stars had trademarks: Jean Harlow with her white satin dresses; Dietrich with her tailored slacks; Garbo with her slouch hats and trenchcoats; and Marilyn Monroe with her slightly tousled hair and tight clothes. But as we moved into the 1960s, the female stars didn't really care what they wore on the set or off. If two stars showed up at a party wearing the same dress, neither of them cared. Nobody cared. It was as if individualism had been thrown out the window in the name of realism. Shirley MacLaine was one of the first stars who truly exercised that kind of freedom of expression. I wasn't used to that in the

1960s; I'm not even sure I am now. I just wasn't "brought up" that way.

Edith worked with MacLaine consistently through 1965, dressing her in *All in a Night's Work* (1961), with Dean Martin; *My Geisha* (1962), for which Edith received yet another Oscar nomination; *John Goldfarb, Please Come Home* (1965) at Twentieth Century-Fox; and *The Yellow Rolls-Royce* (1965), with Ingrid Bergman and Jeanne Moreau at MGM. But it was a Twentieth Century-Fox film in 1964, *What a Way to Go*, that gave Edith an opportunity to dress MacLaine as she had never been dressed before.

By 1964 Shirley was a very big star. Some people said she was making $800,000 per year, plus percentages. One poll rated her the number-six box-office draw in the country. Doris Day was number one, but then came four men—Jack Lemmon, Rock Hudson, John Wayne, and Cary Grant. So Shirley was one of the two most important women in Hollywood. Obviously, she could have had any designer she wanted, so I was very pleased that she decided to have me written into her contracts.

In the early stages of her career, when she was doing all those Martin and Lewis films, she was working for Hal Wallis. And Hal believed that an audience should never notice clothing unless it made a plot point. He hated anything that was the least bit ostentatious. Even though I consider myself to be a fairly conservative designer, he was always telling me, "Tone it down, Edith," or "The shoulder is too wide" or "Her skirt is too full." Shirley had the potential to be a clotheshorse, but not in a Wallis film. He didn't believe in fashion-show motion pictures.

What a Way to Go *was produced by Arthur P. Jacobs, who gave me one of the largest budgets I'd ever had for costumes. We spent more than $500,000 on Shirley's clothes, and she wore $3.5 million worth of jewels, which we borrowed from Harry Winston, the famous Fifth Avenue jeweler. In case anyone has forgotten, that was a damn fortune in the early 1960s.*

This picture was a designer's dream. There I was with

Shirley MacLaine, who wears clothes beautifully, and a budget that seemed limitless. The script was a funny story about a rich young woman who gets married six times—to husbands played by Paul Newman, Gene Kelly, Dean Martin, Robert Mitchum, Dick Van Dyke, and Robert Cummings. She tries to mold her personality to each one, so she is like six different women. As each one dies she becomes even richer.

We had great fun with the costumes. In one scene Shirley was dressed head to toe in pink. In another, she looked like she was clad totally in diamonds. (The dress may have been rhinestones, but those sparklers from Harry Winston were real!) I did more than seventy-two costumes for her in that film. Sidney Guilaroff, who will probably go down in history as Hollywood's most famous hairstylist, did seventy-two different hairdos to match my costumes. Moss Mabry did the rest of the cast, since I was busy enough trying to dress Shirley.

One reviewer called my costumes tasteless and gaudy, but when I phoned him to talk about it, he never returned my calls. He wasn't absolutely wrong, because at times Shirley's character was supposed to be tasteless and gaudy. Shirley was very pleased with the costumes and so was I. Moss and I were nominated for an Academy Award for the film, but this time we lost to My Fair Lady *(1964), with its extravagant costumes by Cecil Beaton.*

I won only one Oscar in the 1960s and that was for The Facts of Life *(1960), with Bob Hope and Lucille Ball. It was a black-and-white film. Without exception the color films that were awarded Oscars for costume design in the 1960s were all big-budget musicals and/or period films. That pattern continued well into the 1970s.*

For her award-winning work on the bedroom farce *The Facts of Life* (1960), Edith was teamed with Edward Stevenson, the man who had dressed Lucille Ball as Lucy Ricardo for so many years on *I Love Lucy*. Though Ball had requested Stevenson, producers Norman Panama and Melvin Frank had insisted on using Edith, the biggest name in Hollywood costume design. Not wanting to interfere with the relationship between the star and her chosen designer, Edith suggested that Stevenson supervise the production of each costume, and that the clothes be made at Ball's studio, Desilu, where Stevenson worked.

Lucille Ball's costumes in the film reflected both designers' touches. The lace-trimmed chiffon negligees and prim, white-collared daytime dresses were typically Head, while the point d'esprit cocktail dresses and sheer organdy evening coats were Stevenson at his best. (Pleased that Edith had given Stevenson creative control on the costumes, Lucille Ball always spoke highly of Edith. "Edie knew the truth about all of us," Ball told a reporter after Edith's death. "She knew who had flat fannies and who didn't—but she never told.")

Film reviewers who were not aware of the close ties between Stevenson and Ball often gave singular credit to Head for the star's wardrobe. Several years later, an Oscar statuette turned up behind a bar in a midtown Los Angeles saloon. The inscription read "To Edith Head and Edward Stevenson for best black-and-white costume design for *The Facts of Life*—1960." The bartender said a man had left it in payment for some drinks and had never returned. Stevenson died shortly thereafter.

Around the same time that she and Stevenson collaborated on *The Facts of Life*, Edith plunged into one of her favorite assignments, another film with Bette Davis. The costumes for *Pocketful of Miracles* (1961) were a definite contrast to what Edith had done with Davis in *All About Eve* (1950), a decade earlier. This time Davis was cast as a bag lady, Apple Annie. She was clad in what Edith lovingly called a bundle of rags, while the extras wore priceless gowns from Western Costume—gowns that had once been worn by Dietrich, Lombard, and Lamarr. Since Apple Annie was temporarily transformed into a woman of means by a few caring gangsters, the script allowed Edith to have fun with a rags-to-riches story.

I love stories with happy endings and this was one of them. Bette played a tattered, old apple seller, and Ann-Margret —it was her first big film break—was supposed to be her long-lost *daughter. Bette, of course, was marvelous and cared as much about the ragged clothes as she did about the fashionable ones. We spent $25,000 on her magnificent clothes for her day as a rich woman, and I doubt that we spent $5 to dress her as Apple Annie.*

The biggest surprise for everyone was Ann-Margret. She was wonderful as a very sweet teenage girl. She wore clothes so well that it was a pleasure to dress her. I had to keep her wardrobe extremely simple, but at the same time I had to let the audience know that she was wealthy. Because of Ann-Margret's red hair and blue eyes, I kept her in bright and medium greens, blues, violets, and purples. She had great fun at the fittings. Try to imagine working on your first major film and being in fittings with Bette Davis and Hope Lange. She tried to be very serious and adult about the whole experience, but you could tell that she was bubbling over with delight about being there.

Anxious to expand her work beyond the movie screen, Edith accepted an offer to dress a stage production in the late 1950s. She designed the costumes for Broadway's *The Pleasure of His Company*, with Cornelia Otis Skinner. Although many successful stage costume designers have become well known for their film work, the reverse has rarely been true. Costumes for the stage are dependent on shape rather than on the small design details that a closeup camera can capture. To endure night after night of quick changes, stage wardrobes must be made very carefully, with much attention given to inner construction as well as to what's visible. The seam of a simple daytime dress for a film need not be carefully reinforced with double rows of stitches, but such a precaution must be taken with a stage costume. And although a delicate silk crepe de Chine might be used to make a screen costume, stage designers would opt for heavier, more serviceable cloths such as velvet and brocade. The price of these luxurious fabrics and the labor involved force up the prices of stage costumes, thus limiting the size of wardrobes. In her role as a stage designer, limited budgets and superior construction were new concerns for Edith.

Both Samuel Taylor's play and Edith's costumes received

good reviews from New York critics, so when George Seaton decided to direct the film version in 1961, it was only natural that Edith should be assigned to dress its stars, Lilli Palmer and Debbie Reynolds.

Although my stage costumes for The Pleasure of His Company *were very sophisticated, I was still more pleased with my work for George Seaton's film. My biggest problem doing costumes for Lilli Palmer was that she was in Europe and I was in Hollywood while the costumes were being made and fitted. She wasn't due in town until just before the filming was to begin. We had to send my sketches for the designs back and forth across the Atlantic so that Lilli's personal dressmaker could make measurement notations. Then when the clothes were made, we sent them over so that they would be perfectly fitted. Despite the awkward logistics, the costumes looked beautiful on her.*

Debbie Reynolds played Fred Astaire's about-to-be-married daughter. She was a perfect size 7 and had kept her 23-inch waist, even though she had had a beautiful daughter, Carrie, four years earlier. Debbie and I worked together very well and I must admit that as I dressed her for the wedding scenes, I began to feel like a mother-of-the-bride.

For her own wedding to Eddie Fisher in 1955, Debbie had worn a suit, so even though this was just a costume it was her first full-length wedding gown. I went all out. I searched through my huge collection of one-of-a-kind fabrics until I found what I wanted: the heirloom-quality, handmade lace I had purchased at a Parisian flea market for a pittance. When I bought it I knew that I would someday have the perfect use for it. I decided that with Debbie's youthful good looks and the character's sweet innocence, she should have a very classic gown. I used the lace for a beautiful bolero top, which drew attention to her tiny waist. I used layers and layers of white net in the skirt, making her waist look even tinier.

I even had a small part in the film, as the bridal consultant at I. Magnin, where the bride-to-be was having her dress fitted. My only line was, "Doesn't she look lovely?" George Sea-

ton let me wear my glasses, so at least I could see what I was doing. About five hundred newspapers carried the story when I announced that I was going to be in the film. (I know that because I employed a private clipping service that went through most of the country's newspapers and clipped articles pertaining to a specific subject.)

Unfortunately the film received terrible reviews. The New Yorker, *a magazine that rarely condescends to notice film costumes, called the film "a shoddy piece of work" but said my costumes were "lovely." The wedding dress was the most famous of the fifty-five costumes I did for that film. After the picture was released, many stores held promotional contests offering copies of the gown as prizes. The original gown was given to Debbie, who wanted to save it for Carrie's wedding. Debbie also received many pieces of the film trousseau to spruce up her wardrobe after she was named to one of those infernal worst-dressed lists.*

In another 1961 picture, *The Ladies' Man*, Jerry Lewis played opposite thirty-one leading ladies, all of whom were young starlets.

These girls were budding stars, not bit players. I immediately began getting phone calls, notes, bunches of flowers, and boxes of candy from the girls and their mamas. The messages were worded differently, but the essence was always the same: "We've always loved your work. . . . So thrilled she has the part. . . . P.S. With her hair she never wears . . ."

When Edith was nominated for an Oscar for her work in *The Man Who Shot Liberty Valance* (1962), some of the people who worked closest to her were surprised. "There wasn't a new costume in the entire movie—everything was taken out of stock. There just weren't enough costume films to choose from that year," commented a wardrobe woman who had worked with Edith at Paramount. One of the few criteria for the best costume design award is that the clothes be designed expressly for a film.

While 1962 was a lean year for costumes, 1963 was bulging.

Edith was so busy that she was forced to hire yet another sketch artist, bringing the total to three. She had seen the work of a young man who was sketching for another film designer and she sought him out. She hired Bob Mackie to work with Grace Sprague and Leah Rhodes. "Edith gave me a great deal of freedom in the design area," Mackie reminisces. "She was extremely open to new ideas. We all did what we wanted and then turned the work in to Edith. Even though she had a number of artists working for her, by the time she edited the sketches everything looked like Edith Head designed it. That's what was important. *That* was a big part of her talent."

Edith used Mackie for *Donovan's Reef* (1963), with Elizabeth Allen, Dorothy Lamour, Lee Marvin, and John Wayne. Mackie recalls that Edith was displeased with the casting of Allen and took it upon herself to get the woman off the movie. "She wanted Vera Miles to have that part, so she spent days on the phone trying to convince the producers and director John Ford to get Allen out. She failed. But if she didn't like Allen, that didn't affect the costumes she designed for her. Edith was too much of a professional to let her personal feelings get in the way of what she designed."

I have known designers who have been vindictive. If they didn't like a girl, they created dresses that weren't right, just to make the girl look foolish. That always backfires. A designer's job is to make an actor or actress look like the character. If the look is wrong, the designer is at fault. When I go into that fitting room, no matter what has happened between me and the star, I put the past aside and go by the script.

Edith's recollections of *Donovan's Reef* have little to do with the costume process or with Elizabeth Allen. Instead, she recalls the time she spent with director John Ford.

I fell in love with John. Every day that I wasn't busy and he was not directing, I would have tea with him. He was exactly like the male leads in his movies: strong, virile, passionate. You'd expect him to drink slugs of straight whiskey. Instead, he drank tea. Tea was one of his passions. I thought that I knew how to drink it, but he showed me the fine points. I felt like an idiot, but he told me not to feel bad, that most people didn't know how. The trick, he said, was in lifting both the saucer and the cup simultaneously, one with the left hand and one with the right— never just the cup. I have a wonderful memory of husky, burly John Ford showing me how to lift a teacup and saucer properly.

Grace Sprague, who had been Edith's sketch artist for years, was extremely proficient at turning out the "Edith Head look." With just minor adjustments at the hem and shoulder, these bread-and-butter classics looked as good in the 1950s as they had in the 1940s. But when director Mel Shavelson asked Edith to do *A New Kind of Love* (1963) with Joanne Woodward, Paul Newman, and Maurice Chevalier, she assigned young Mackie to sketch the high-fashion dresses called for in the script. Mackie's designs were incorporated into the film along with *haute couture* apparel from some of the most prestigious French designer houses, including Lanvin, Saint Laurent, Dior, and Cardin. Woodward's twenty costume changes in this color film earned Edith an Academy Award nomination. (She was also nominated that year for her designs for *Love with the Proper Stranger* and *Wives and Lovers*, both black-and-white films.)

Love with the Proper Stranger (1963) was Edith's first assignment with the young and beautiful Natalie Wood. Though Wood had become a hot property through her successes in *Rebel Without a Cause* (1955) and *Splendor in the Grass* (1961), she did not yet have a designer she called her own. No one had created a "Natalie Wood" image for the star, and Edith was anxious to do it. She hoped to woo the actress at the first fitting for *Love with the Proper Stranger*, but schedules were working against her. Mackie recalls the instance.

"Edith needed a new actress to keep her career going strong, and Natalie was very hot, so Edith wanted her. She was prepared to give her the full star treatment when they first met. The trouble was that Martha Hyer, who is married to Hal Wallis and who was an important star in her own right, was scheduled for a fitting in the main salon in Edith's suite at the only time that Natalie was available for an appointment. Edith was frenzied. But all of a sudden she had a wonderful plan and we all helped her. We took over Leah Rhodes's office and fixed it up to look like Edith Head's salon. We moved everything—the Oscars, the sewing machine collection, the fabric swatches, the furniture. We had food brought in. It was an instant set change. It worked—Natalie went for it. Edith got Natalie and they proceeded to do movies together for years."*

In *Wives and Lovers*, the second black-and-white film for which she received an Academy Award nomination in 1963, Edith dressed Janet Leigh, Shelley Winters, and Martha Hyer.

This was one of the few Hal Wallis movies in which I had an opportunity to truly create some beautiful clothes. Hal was particularly careful to approve each sketch. He even asked to see fabric swatches, and when the clothes were finished he personally checked each costume as it was worn.

In this film, he requested that Martha wear the gold gown Grace Kelly had worn in To Catch a Thief. *I was more than delighted to use it again. We took the birds off and added roses, narrowed the skirt, and enlarged the whole dress very slightly to fit Martha. Since Shelley Winters didn't want to look the least bit plump appearing on the same screen with Janet Leigh and Martha, she went on a diet and fit into a perfect size 10 for the film. She said it almost killed her, but I'm sure she was exaggerating. She looked fabulous in the twelve costumes I designed for her new figure.*

*Bob Mackie left Edith's Paramount design rooms after only a few months to work with a freelance film designer, Ray Aghayan. The two formed a partnership that eventually became one of the most important costume-producing companies in Hollywood. When Mackie gained fame designing for Cher and Carol Burnett in the 1970s, Edith called him "one of the biggest talents in Hollywood." Though she often spoke of him as still "learning" his craft, he was nominated for an Academy Award in 1972 for *Lady Sings the Blues*. They were competitors for the Oscar in 1975 for his work with Aghayan on *Funny Lady* and hers for *The Man Who Would Be King*, but both lost to Ulla-Britt Søderlund and Milena Canonero for their costumes in *Barry Lyndon*.

Lana Turner rarely made films at Paramount, but tempted by a humorous script and the promise of a glamorous wardrobe, the star came to the studio to make *Who's Got the Action?* (1962) with Dean Martin. Edith fitted her for eighteen costumes.

When we heard Lana was coming, everyone in the department got pretty excited. I had met her socially, but we had never worked together on a film. She canceled several appointments with me, and the day she finally came in she was in a hurry to finish. I explained that we had many things to go over, letting her know that I wanted these to be the most beautiful costumes she had ever worn. Realizing that I was sincere, she calmed down a bit and took more of an interest in what I had to say.

Although all her costumes in the film were important, the two nightgowns she needed were the most difficult to engineer. In doing what I call a superglamour nightgown, we start by making a clinging foundation exactly the color of the star's skin. This takes intricate dressmaking and many fittings, because it cannot have a wrinkle and must follow the exact contour of the star's body. With a nude-colored foundation, we can get around any censorship problems. To further insure ourselves against any possible censorship, we use two layers of sheer silk soufflé as lining for a lace gown. Lana's negligees were made of reembroidered Alençon lace, the same type used in bridal gowns. The lining was dyed to her exact skin tone, so the gown seemed sheer and alluring but was not vulgar. By the time we made the foundation, the two underlinings, and the lace gown, it was as if we had constructed four garments. With that much labor involved, the cost of the gowns was $750 each.

So many films bearing the Edith Head costume credit were released in 1963 that Edith told people she felt Hollywood was getting back on its feet. She complained that she was tired after working on fifteen films, but elated that so many of her assignments that year had been with major stars. In addition to Wood, Turner, and Woodward, she had dressed Lucille Ball in *Critic's*

Choice (1963), Debbie Reynolds in *My Six Loves* (1963), and Judy Garland in *I Could Go on Singing* (1963).

Judy went from a size 6 to a size 16 during the filming, and not *because the script called for such a change. And since the film wasn't shot in sequence, she'd be fat in one scene and look terrific in another. This didn't escape the critics' eyes, believe me. When the film was released,* Time *(which is one of the few magazines whose reviews I take seriously) said that Judy's voice was marvelous, but that in one of her "Edith Head gowns" she looked like an "overripe tomato." I was horrified to find out that although I had put her in a black gown for one scene that was filmed on stage at the London Palladium, one of her designer friends over there convinced her to wear red. She was at her heaviest in that scene and she* did *look like a tomato—so did my face when that review ran. So I immediately wrote a letter to the editor, disclaiming any credit for that dress, and the magazine printed it. Of course nobody reads those letters, but at least I felt that I had done something.*

One of the most acclaimed films of 1963 was *Hud,* starring Paul Newman and Patricia Neal. Neal was named best actress that year for her role. Edith dressed both stars, under the strict guidance of director Martin Ritt.

I was not sure that Mr. Ritt liked me. He was very charming, but he continually went over and over what he wanted for costumes, as if he didn't think I understood the concept of an antihero or the extreme realism of the script. Patricia Neal and Paul Newman played two people without much money, people who lived a totally unfashionable life—a real life. Mr. Ritt was very careful and emphasized the fact that he did not want the audience to notice the clothes.
Paul's clothes were supposed to suggest a very egotistical man who was vain about his appearance. Yet I had specific direction that there were to be no fancy cowboy boots or belt

buckles in Paul's wardrobe. Mr. Ritt said that above all he wanted honest clothes, nothing theatrical.

Sufficiently primed about what he wanted, I set about doing plenty of sketches and I went over them time and again with the director. When I took the drawings to him, I would also bring in several shirts, pairs of jeans, and different hats to see which ones would make Paul look just cocky enough. We even did costume test photos, something that most film budgets no longer allow. But Mr. Ritt felt that the costumes were extremely important.

When it came to Pat's wardrobe, he was equally explicit. She took more of an interest in her wardrobe than Paul did (he really doesn't care too much what he wears, as long as he's comfortable). I didn't do any sketches at all for her. Instead, she and I went through wardrobe stock together, analyzing each piece of clothing that we pulled out. "Would you really wear this?" and "Is it too nice?" and "Is the fabric too sophisticated?" were the most common questions we raised. I remember that one old housedress she wore actually needed to be mended before she could put it on. We didn't want her to look tacky, but at the same time it was important that she look slightly haggard, tired of her existence and hopelessly stuck where she was. It took six weeks to complete Pat's wardrobe, and I doubt that we spent more than $2 creating anything new for her. Pat modeled all the costumes for Mr. Ritt, and after all our long, hard work, he made very few changes.

While she was working with numerous other directors, Edith continued her important collaboration with Alfred Hitchcock. In one of his most memorable 1960s films, *The Birds* (1963), the designer was asked to dress another of Hitch's blondes, Tippi Hedren, whom the director had spotted on television in a dietary drink commercial. Hitchcock contacted Hedren immediately and put her under personal contract soon afterward. When he decided to cast her as Melanie in *The Birds,* Hitchcock and his wife took her to dinner at Chasen's and presented her with a small gold-and-pearl brooch in the shape of three birds. Then he announced his plan. The next day

Edith was called in for wardrobe consultation, and the difficult process of making the film began. In her first motion picture, Hedren's loyalty to her craft was often put to the test. At one point, she was asked to lie down and let live birds (which were tied to her with nearly invisible threads) peck at her and her Edith Head suit.

In The Birds, *the fashion was not too important because we started out establishing the girl as a well-dressed person with taste and money. Later, as she became more terrified, Hitchcock preferred that the audience not notice her clothes. He didn't want any distractions from the terror. I can barely remember what she had on myself.*

He virtually restricted me to two colors, blue and green. We had worked together for so many years that I was well aware of his feeling about garish colors. He didn't like anything bright unless it made a story point. He preferred "nature colors," as he called them: beige, soft greens, and delicate turquoises. He had strong feelings that color should never be so strong that it overpowered the scene or the actress. If the script called for a girl in a red dress, that was one thing, but to put her in a red dress for no reason was out of the question in a Hitchcock film.

The Birds was extremely successful, so Hitch went on to use Tippi in Marnie *(1964), a role he had originally planned for Princess Grace, who was considering a return to the screen. When Her Serene Highness decided that the part was not suitable for her, Tippi got it. Though the movie turned out very well, it was the last time she and Hitch made a film together.*

Loyalty was extremely important to Alfred Hitchcock. He was as loyal to his craftsmen as he expected them to be to him. When he died in 1980, Hitch and I had made a total of eleven pictures together: Notorious *(1946),* Rear Window *(1954),* To Catch a Thief *(1955),* The Trouble with Harry *(1955),* The Man Who Knew Too Much *(1956),* Vertigo *(1958),* The Birds *(1963),* Marnie *(1964),* Torn Curtain *(1966),* Topaz *(1969), and* Family Plot *(1976).*

Edith's work on Elvis Presley films continued into the mid-1960s, and his leading ladies continued to be young starlets whose names were rarely heard of again. But in *Roustabout* (1964), he was teamed with one of the grande dames of the screen, Barbara Stanwyck. Edith liked to think of Stanwyck as the young beauty in *The Lady Eve* (1941), and she noted to newspapers all over the country that the star was as well shaped in 1964 as she had been in 1940. She had a figure suitable for jeans.

For many years I felt that dungarees should be relegated to the rodeo and the garden. Very few women over the age of sixteen had the figure to wear them. But now, with the youth fetish that has swept our country, many women are in as good shape at forty-five as they were at sixteen. Barbara is one of those women. I'm not. I have a roll above my waist and my rear sags a bit, so I wear dungarees only at home when I'm taking care of my orchids. But Barbara looks terrific in a pair of blue denims, so I had no qualms about putting them on her. She has so much presence that no matter what she wears, she owns the screen. Teaming her with Elvis was a stroke of genius. It gave him credence as an actor and it brought in some of the older audiences who would never have watched a Presley film otherwise.

In 1965 Joan Crawford was asked to present the Academy Award for best director. Though Edith had never dressed the star in a film, they had become close social friends, and the designer often fashioned gowns for Crawford's personal wardrobe. When the actress asked Edith to design the gown she would wear to the ceremony, both of them agreed that the dress had to be the most dramatic gown of the evening. It was Crawford's first appearance on the Academy Award stage in years, and she hoped to be able to present the Oscar to her 1940s mentor, George Cukor, for his work in *My Fair Lady* (1964). Since most of Cecil Beaton's costumes in that film were either black or white, Edith and Crawford decided that her gown should be either black or white, in subtle homage to Cukor.

Joan's appearance on the stage, at the end of the evening, had to be a stunning climax to the long stream of actors and actresses who were chosen to present the preceding awards. As the biggest star making a personal appearance at the Academy Awards, Crawford couldn't be anything less than sensational. I designed her gown accordingly, a lovely slim sheath of shimmering beads from Spain, with a matching coat. There was still a question as to whether it would be black or white, however. We had found out that the actress who was to present the Oscar just ahead of Joan had sampled both black and white fabrics, but she refused to tell us what color she was going to wear. Joan's solution was simple—do the dress in both colors. "If she comes out in white, I'll wear black, and vice versa."

As the other awards were presented, we stood backstage with two wardrobe girls, one holding the black dress and one holding the white dress, all of us waiting for the secretive actress presenter to come on stage. She entered from the other wing— in white. We zipped Joan into the black gown and she radiantly made her entrance. "And the winner is . . . George Cukor." Joan gave an emotional tribute to him and the audience rose to its feet. It was one of the most memorable moments in all my years at the Academy Awards.

Natalie Wood continued to be Edith's most important star in the 1960s. After *Love with the Proper Stranger,* she followed up with *Sex and the Single Girl* (1964). Natalie took Edith with her to Warner Brothers to design her period costumes for *The Great Race* (1965), with Jack Lemmon and Tony Curtis.

Another consistent source of assignments was Jerry Lewis, the comedian/actor/director who asked for Edith on most of his Paramount films. Although she was required to dress him as a blundering goof, his co-stars were always pretty young women in stylish (but never *too* stylish) contemporary clothes. Lewis often commented that Edith had a knack for designing clothes that were perfectly suited to actresses' roles. He told one reporter that his leading ladies' costumes had an important effect on his own work and that he always felt confident that Edith would please his eye.

Harlow (1965), directed by Gordon Douglas and starring Carroll Baker as actress Jean Harlow, forced Edith to employ many of the same designs that were in vogue when she first started on the Paramount lot—those slinky satin gowns that exposed everything they ostensibly covered. The new aspect of this loosely biographical film was that Baker would appear on screen apparently in the nude.

Those beautiful clinging clothes that Jean Harlow wore in her day—that was sex. People don't understand that it is far more exciting to see a woman dressed in clothes that suggest gorgeous breasts and alluring hips than to see her bare bosom or buttocks. Naked bodies have very little personality. Clothes are symbols that provide identification—especially in a film. If everyone walked around without clothes, it would be very difficult for people to remember each other, or even to notice each other.

The trouble with films that rely on nudity for impact is that a nude scene provides impact the first time only. Then what? With costumes I could provide impact scene after scene, if the director wanted that much effect. It takes more imagination to create costumes with shock value than it does to show a woman in the raw. But isn't imagination what filmmaking is all about?

The British youth revolution of the early 1960s rocked the world. Enter the Beatles. Enter Mary Quant and her knee-baring minis. But it was 1964 before Hollywood took notice. By then, the French designer André Courrèges had recognized the importance of the British thigh exposure and raised his skirts four inches above the knee. The French fashion nod gave the short skirt international acceptance, but Edith waited until 1965 to use a mini in a film. Her first thigh-high skirt appeared on Natalie Wood in MGM's *Penelope* (1966). It was designed by sketch artist Richard Hopper, who had joined Edith shortly after Bob Mackie departed.

By 1966 both Helen Rose and Walter Plunkett had resigned from MGM and retired to Palm Springs. The great designers with whom Edith had grown up—Adrian, Travis Banton, Howard Greer, Orry-Kelly, and Irene—were all dead. Charles LeMaire had been freelancing since leaving his job at Fox in 1959. Dorothy Jeakins was about to be named curator of the textile and costume department of the Los Angeles County Museum of Art. Jean Louis, the Frenchman who had been Columbia's head designer, was now working for Universal Studios, but he had also begun concentrating on a private costume design business. And there was Edith at Paramount.

The studio designer, as Edith had known the job, was suddenly a thing of the past. More and more contemporary costumes were simply being purchased in Los Angeles and Beverly Hills department stores—and that was a job for an increasingly important person in the wardrobe department, the shopper. Shoppers scour the stores for clothes that meet a designer's request, charge them on a studio credit card, and then return anything the designer rejects. When she had the time, Edith accompanied her shoppers to I. Magnin, Saks Fifth Avenue, and Bullock's-Wilshire to select wardrobe pieces. Occasionally, if time was short, a star would meet Edith at the store, where they would make selections and do fittings on the spot. When she had the luxury of a few extra hours or days between shopping and shooting, Edith would often request that her seamstresses change a collar or slim a skirt, to make the garments more individually suited to an actor or actress.

Freelance designers were getting temporary assignments with independent production companies, and some lucky ones landed steady positions with television shows. As Paramount began producing fewer and fewer films, there were fewer assignments to justify Edith's salary.

Alfred Hitchcock and his good friend Lew Wasserman, president of MCA-Universal, had spoken to Edith about coming to work for Hitchcock, who had moved his production company to Universal. Although she had enjoyed working with Hitchcock on their most recent effort, *Torn Curtain* (1966), with Julie Andrews and Paul Newman, she told them she was extremely sentimental about Paramount and would leave only when she was forced. Health problems had slowed her somewhat, but she was still twice as active as most women in their late sixties. "I'll probably die in the design salon at Paramount," she told one of her closest friends. "But you may as well die where you've lived."

In 1966 Adolph Zukor, one of the few people who had been at Paramount longer than Edith, was named chairman emeritus of the studio. Barney Balaban, longtime president of the firm, was put into Zukor's figurehead position as chairman of the board. Within a very short time, two major stockholders, Ernest Martin and Herbert Siegel, sold their shares to Charles Bluhdorn, chairman of the board at the conglomerate Gulf + Western. Shortly thereafter, Paramount stockholders voted to merge with Gulf + Western.

When Edith's contract expired in 1967, she was told it would not be renewed. At least six months earlier she had confided to her sketch artist and friend Richard Hopper that she thought they would be moving to Universal Studios. He didn't ask questions, but after her contract expired, he was not at all startled by the move. There was no major announcement at Paramount and, after forty-four years, not one official tribute to Hollywood's most famous costume designer.

Though Edith never dressed Joan Crawford in a film, the two were friends and Crawford often turned to the designer for her off screen clothes. In the 1950s, Edith fashioned an entire wardrobe for Crawford, including this form-fitting white lace formal with red satin trim and a green wool dinner ensemble with mink cuffs.

Edith dressed Shirley MacLaine as a sexy
black bat and Dorothy Malone as a
lavishly feathered bird in Hal Wallis's
Artists and Models (1955), with
Dean Martin and Jerry Lewis.

Grace Kelly's black-and-white beach
ensemble for *To Catch a Thief* (1955) was
"as fashionable as anything we saw
on the sand in the south of France,"
Edith recalled.

Alfred Hitchcock told Edith to make Grace Kelly look "like a fairy princess" in the lavish masquerade ball sequence in *To Catch a Thief*. Edith wrapped her in imported gold lamé, covered her blond tresses with a golden wig, and crowned her with golden doves (which also lighted at her hip). Cary Grant bought most of his own clothes for the film, but Edith designed the masquerade ball costume shown here. (Academy of Motion Picture Arts and Sciences)

(LEFT)
Grace Kelly was so impressed with this ombre-blue silk chiffon gown from *To Catch a Thief* that she bought it for her personal wardrobe and wore it out to dinner with her then-suitor, Prince Rainier.

(CENTER)
When Danny Kaye was told he was to wear a suit of armor in *The Court Jester* (1955), he threatened to quit the film. Edith soothed him by making it of flexible, lightweight aluminum.

As Jane Wyman and former Governor of Texas Allan Shivers (playing himself) look on, a model displays one of Edith's interpretations of *haute couture*, part of the fashion-show extravaganza in *Lucy Gallant* (1955). The white gown has a matching coat lined in scarlet.

The definitive Edith Head suit was worn by Marlene Dietrich in *Witness for the Prosecution* (1957). The initials *G.S.* at the foot indicate the sketch was rendered by Edith's longtime sketch artist Grace Sprague.

Since Edith was called upon to create numerous high-fashion designs for *Lucy Gallant*, it is no surprise that she borrowed ideas from her past. The all-over pleats and banded hip in this cocktail ensemble are reminiscent of early 1930s styles.

Another high-fashion ensemble from Edith's *Lucy Gallant* collection, this suede and tweed suit was featured in the film's fashion-show sequence.

If there was one Edith Head signature look, it was the clean, classic suit. She wore it and almost every woman she dressed wore it at one time or another. As the fashion editor who "discovers" Audrey Hepburn in *Funny Face*, Kay Thompson wears a simple textured silk suit, distinguished only by its three buttons at the bust.

In *Vertigo* (1958), Kim Novak played a woman with a double identity. Although she told Edith at the outset of the film that she would wear any color but gray, her most important costume turned out to be a tailored gray suit.

Hubert de Givenchy designed Audrey Hepburn's high-fashion clothes in *Funny Face* (1957), but Edith dressed the star in the early scenes when Hepburn played a shy clerk in a bookshop.

Bette Davis was transformed from the ragtag street vendor Apple Annie to a bejeweled lady of means in *Pocketful of Miracles* (1961). Edith was nominated for an Academy Award for the film's extravagant costumes.

(OPPOSITE)
Lilli Palmer's extensive wardrobe in *The Pleasure of His Company* (1961) included this black *point d'esprit* cocktail dress with bateau neckline. Attached to the sketch is a sample of the delicate net fabric.

Lilli Palmer
as Kate

Edith Head

The Pleasure of
his Company

A the Int. Living room
and garden

(RIGHT)
In *What a Way to Go* (1964),
a large portion of the film's
reported $5 million budget went
to Shirley MacLaine's incredible
wardrobe. This hostess gown
of gold Persian tapestry, banded in
rare sable, is accessorized
with antique Persian gold jewelry.

(BELOW)
To make Tippi Hedren utterly
peckable in *The Birds*
(1963), Edith chose a textured
wool fabric that could be
easily snagged and torn during the
terrifying attack sequence.

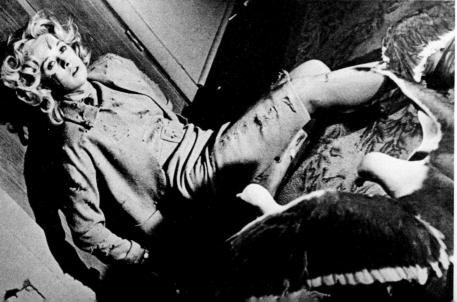

(LEFT)
A nautically clad Shirley MacLaine poses for a wardrobe test for *What a Way to Go*. Although wardrobe tests were commonplace in the film industry until the late 1950s, those photo sessions became an expensive—and expendable—luxury in the 1960s.

(RIGHT)
During a bedroom fantasy sequence in *What a Way to Go*, Shirley MacLaine's negligee was completely covered with handmade, mint-green organza chrysanthemums.

Lana Turner's wardrobe for *Love Has Many Faces* (1965) became the subject of a five-minute color film called "Million-Dollar Wardrobe." The short played in theaters the week before the Turner melodrama opened, an attempt to entice audiences back the next week. Even posters for the film plugged Edith's endeavors, but she was not nominated for an Academy Award for her extravagant costumes.

A rose, a raised waistline, and sheer lace all combine to make Natalie Wood's bosom the focal point of her wedding gown in *The Great Race* (1965).

Edith coordinates Natalie Wood with her shaggy dog in *Penelope*.

European fashion designers introduced the miniskirt in the early 1960s, but Edith did not raise her stars' hemlines until 1966, when she dressed Natalie Wood in *Penelope*.

Edith created this miniskirted outfit for
Jane Fonda's role in *Barefoot in the
Park* (1967). The designer described Fonda
as "a joy to dress because she has
fabulous legs that look great even in
miniskirts and boots." Edith didn't design
Robert Redford's wardrobe in the film, "but
I did tell him what clothes he should
wear—and when to go barefoot," she recalled.

For the 1969 Academy Award ceremonies,
presenter Liz Taylor asked Edith Head to design
a gown that would showcase the huge diamond
pendant her then-husband Richard Burton
had given her. The gown showed off more than
just the diamond, however, and started a trend
toward exposed cleavage at the award ceremonies.

(© AMPAS®)

Shirley MacLaine was one
of only a few women Edith liked
to put in miniskirts. "She
has fabulous legs," she told
reporters. Edith's designs for
Sweet Charity (1969) earned
an Academy Award nomination.

Once Edith dressed them, the "boys" looked pretty dapper in *Butch Cassidy and the Sundance Kid* (1969). The entire male wardrobe was rented from Western Costume Company, Hollywood's largest stock costume house.

Flannelette
wrapper

Bare foot —

It was imperative that Katharine Ross's flannel robe allow enough freedom of movement for her to ride tandem on Paul Newman's bike. A button-front skirt provided that freedom. Ross ended up wearing shoes instead of going barefoot, as indicated on the sketch. The theme song "Raindrops Keep Falling on My Head" serenaded the pair as they rode across fields in *Butch Cassidy and the Sundance Kid*.

Only the length of the skirt distinguishes this classic Edith Head suit as a 1960s style. The sketch was for Joanne Woodward in *Winning* (1969), costarring Paul Newman.

Mae West often said that Edith was the only woman in the world who understood her, so she had Edith written into her film contracts as her personal wardrobe designer. In *Myra Breckinridge* (1970), Edith showed her design genius, adapting the Mae West look to a contemporary setting.

(LEFT, BELOW)
In *Myra Breckinridge*, Mae West's contract specified that she would be the only star to wear black and white. As Letitia Van Allen, she visits a hospital ward in black French velvet and white mink designed by Edith Head. For the director's reference, a swatch of the black velvet is attached to the sketch. (OPPOSITE)

Complete with high platform shoes and fur-trimmed pantsuit, Elizabeth Taylor played Henry Fonda's facelifted wife in *Ash Wednesday* (1973). Edith was loaned to Paramount to dress Taylor, the designer's first return to the studio since leaving it for Universal in 1967.

al Newman "The Sting" Robert Redford
1974

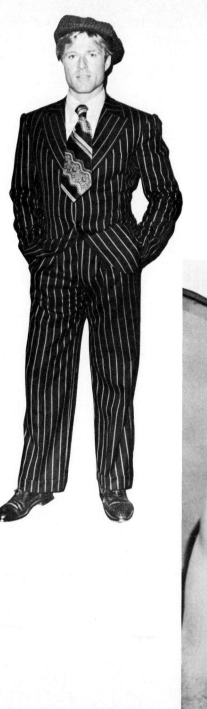

(LEFT)

By the time she dressed Paul Newman and Robert Redford in *The Sting* (1973), Edith had already costumed each of them separately in several films and she had dressed them as a team in *Butch Cassidy and the Sundance Kid* (1969), so she knew their likes and dislikes. Director George Roy Hill instructed her to give Newman (left) a macho look and to keep Redford looking dapper.

(CENTER)

Director George Roy Hill demanded absolute accuracy in the 1930s period costumes for *The Sting*. Redford's chalk-striped suit, wide-patterned tie, and wing-tip shoes were true to the era.

(BELOW)

In her designs for Paul Newman and Robert Redford in *The Sting*, Edith paid close attention to the effect of hats. To achieve Redford's impish naïveté, she gave him a newspaper boy's cap. A sophisticated fedora helped maintain Newman's sly arrogance, even when he was dressed in well-worn coveralls.

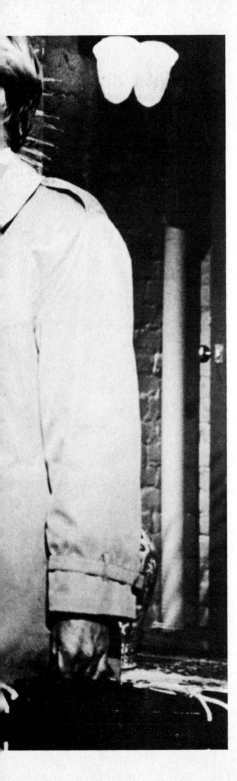

Edith's eighth Academy Award, for *The Sting*, was the first Oscar presented for costumes in a film with no female leads. The film set many fashion trends for men, including the return of the wing-collared tuxedo shirt.

When Natalie Wood needed a gown to wear to the Academy Award ceremonies in 1978, Edith sketched this fluid red jersey sheath with matching ruffled cape. (Betty Goodman Collection)

For years Edith relied on fur
trim to dramatize many of
her timeless designs. Here,
in two sketches for Jill
Clayburgh in *Gable and
Lombard* (1976), fur enhances
very simple, classic lines.

Edith studied the
W. C. Fields look and
copied it line for
line to dress Rod Steiger
in *W. C. Fields and
Me* (1976).

As the villain, Night, in *The Bluebird*, Jane Fonda was dressed in black while her beneficent counterpart, Light, played by Elizabeth Taylor, was in pure white.

The Soviet Union and the United States joined creative forces to produce *The Bluebird* (1976). Edith traveled to Moscow to dress Liz Taylor as Light, Mother, Maternal Love, and Witch. (Stacy Endres Collection)

Steve Martin, as Rigby Reardon in *Dead Men Don't Wear Plaid* (1982), played
a 1940s detective dressed in everything from traditional linen suits to
a duplicate of a dress worn by Barbara Stanwyck in *Double Indemnity* (1944).
This was the last screen wardrobe designed by Edith Head.

NINE

The bungalow at the end of Main Street in Universal City became Edith's. The two parking spaces outside were occupied by her shiny late-model car and a canopied golf cart in which she could zip around the lot. Her shingle, a bronze plaque shaped like a woman and etched with her signature, identified the designer's new salon. Inside the bungalow, her seven golden Oscar statuettes lined the entry hall. At the reception desk, Edith's new secretary greeted clients and accepted the flowers and calls, a job that kept her busy for months after Edith's arrival at the studio. Well-wishers wanted Edith to know just how happy they were that she hadn't decided to retire after the unhappy ending to her Paramount career.

The people closest to her mused on the idea of a retired Edith Head. "I don't know what Edith would have done if she had stayed home," explains June Van Dyke, the fashion-show promoter who had worked with Edith since 1951 and had become almost a surrogate daughter to her. "She was a career woman, a corporate woman. She was so ahead of her time. Going into that office and designing was her life. She didn't like to socialize. She didn't want to be one of the retired ladies' lunch bunch. How could she slow down after half a century of Hollywood?"

Edith's pace did slow down, however, because of a factor over which she had no control—the number of films to which she was assigned. Her first Universal releases were not seen until 1968, and there were just five: *Madigan*, with Richard Widmark; *The Secret War of Harry Frigg*, with Paul Newman; *What's So Bad About Feeling Good?*, with Mary Tyler Moore and George Peppard; *In Enemy Country*, with Anthony Franciosa; and *The Pink Jungle*, with James Garner. None was a memorable film.

In *What's So Bad About Feeling Good?*, she was asked to transform Mary Tyler Moore, with her TV goody-two-shoes image, into a hippie.

I turned Mary Tyler Moore into the lowest possible hippie. She looked like a badly tied-up Christmas bundle that had been given to the poor. Her hair was peculiar. She wore funny sandals and jeans, of course. I purposely draped fabrics on her poorly, and I chose patterns that looked somewhat dated. She looked terrible, but she was right for the part.

The invasion of the hippies was the worst thing that ever happened to fashion. The look was all right for the young, for college kids who had no responsibilities. But all of a sudden, as if afflicted with a strange disease, people of all ages began trying to look like hippies. It was "fashionable" to be uncombed and disheveled. It was chic to go to secondhand stores and find something old. This trend was disastrous to the film industry, because we had to adapt quickly and get out of it in time to avoid looking dated.

The costumes in Edith's last Paramount films (all released in 1967) had been as unexciting as her first Universal offerings in

1968. The result was that, for the first time since the costume category was introduced in 1948, Edith was not among the Academy Award nominees—either in 1967 or 1968. Determined to get her name back on the list for a 1969 release, she phoned directors and producers who were scheduled on Universal's newest and biggest projects.

Before long, she was entrenched in many promising projects. *Sweet Charity* (1969), a film starring Shirley MacLaine—whom she hadn't dressed since 1964 in *The Yellow Rolls-Royce* (1965)—was on Bob Fosse's agenda. Hitchcock's *Topaz* (1969) was in production. Katharine Ross, a newcomer, was scheduled to star with Robert Redford and Paul Newman in a George Roy Hill Western, *Butch Cassidy and the Sundance Kid* (1969).

Edith's aggressive approach was rewarded. Fosse's *Sweet Charity*, though not a financial success, put the designer's name back on the nomination list. Ironically, it was Hal Wallis' first film for Universal, *Anne of the Thousand Days* (1969), with costumes by Margaret Furse—not Edith Head—that won the costume Oscar. Until 1964, Edith had done costumes for almost every picture Hal Wallis produced.

I was crushed when I didn't get to do Becket *(1964), but I assumed that I would have another opportunity to do a big-budget period film for Hal Wallis. I was wrong. At the time, Hal was making a number of historical dramas on location in Britain, and because of the labor laws I couldn't work there. A wonderfully talented Englishwoman named Margaret Furse designed* Becket *and then did* Anne of the Thousand Days *(1969), for which she won an Academy Award. The same designer did* Mary, Queen of Scots *(1971) for Hal and was again nominated for an Oscar. I grew very frustrated. I always felt there was some way I could have gotten around the labor laws if Hal had given me the chance. Margaret Furse died in 1974. She did a magnificent job for Hal.*

Dressing Katharine Ross in *Butch Cassidy and the Sundance Kid* (1969) proved to be more fun than work for Edith.

Katharine has the same kind of beguiling innocence that Ingrid Bergman had when I first met her. Her beauty is so pure. I became acquainted with her when she starred with John Wayne in The Hellfighters *(1969). We were on location in Wyoming. At first she was a bit intimidated by Duke and me. We were such legends to her. But by the time she came to my salon to discuss her period clothes for* Butch Cassidy, *she had confidence, ideas of her own, and a sincere interest in what she was going to wear.*

There was an important scene early in the film where she was to strip down to her camisole and then slowly take that off, too. We discussed the garment thoroughly and she tried on several different types to see which would be the easiest and the sexiest to remove. William Goldman had been very explicit in the script about what Etta, Katharine's character, wore. That made it easier for me.

Butch and Sundance were both dressed out of stock wardrobe at Universal and Western Costume. The only discussions I had with Robert Redford and Paul Newman were about their hats—which of course are very important to a couple of cowpokes. Since I had dressed so many horse operas in my early days in the industry, I was able to tell them about the various styles cowboys wore. Paul's hat was a lot more macho, the cocky cowboy hat, while Bob's hat was more functional and worked very well with his square jaw and mustache.

In terms of sheer entertainment, not in terms of my designing, Butch Cassidy and the Sundance Kid *was my favorite movie. It had everything—humor, action, romance, and the two handsomest men in Hollywood.*

Shortly before the first Redford/Newman film was released, in September 1969, the last Art Linkletter's *House Party* show was aired. Soap operas were becoming increasingly more important to daytime TV audiences than anything Edith had to offer about how to dress. Her second book, *How to Dress for Success,* written with Joe Hymans and published by Random House in late 1967, had not been as successful as *The Dress Doctor,* a fact that was indicative of the public's changing taste. With the demise of *House Party,*

Edith was no longer a regular fixture in American homes. If she was going to stay in touch with her fans, she had to find other ways to reach them.

Edith told her friend June Van Dyke that those appearances on the show had kept her young and in touch with the public. She didn't want to lose that contact. Together they decided to increase the number of costume fashion shows, both to supplement their incomes and to keep Edith's name in circulation. With Universal's blessing and financial support, Van Dyke and Edith traveled all over the United States and occasionally to Europe to produce the shows. By 1970 the relentless team was doing eighteen shows a year.

I felt as if I had made a career change. Now I'm a part-time designer and a full-time traveling Hollywood museum. I love doing those shows, despite how much work they require. We have to find models who look like the stars who wore the gowns. Then I have to show the models how to wear the costumes. A girl can't just put on Mae West's dress from She Done Him Wrong *(1933) and jiggle down the runway as so many models do today. She has to carry that gown the way Mae carried it—with class. She has to take the walking stick and thrust it out in front of her with every step. When her head moves, her bosom had better move in the same direction. That's the way Mae did it. I show the girls how to walk like Crawford and Dietrich and Lombard and Lamour and Harlow and Stanwyck and Taylor and Lamarr and Davis and Loren and Taylor and Wood—all of them. My stars.*

When I first started doing the shows I got very caught up in the nostalgia of it. Now it's a business. I have to worry about the cost of all the models, about refurbishing those gowns (some of them have been totally remade), and about the appropriate music. It's like any other job—you have budgets and schedules and headaches. And many rewards. I love to talk to the people who come to the shows; I love to hear the applause; I love to visit the towns. It's remarkable how many people enjoy seeing old costumes.

With three popular films to her credit in 1969—*Butch Cassidy;* Robert Redford and Katharine Ross again in *Tell Them Willie Boy Is Here;* and Hitchcock's *Topaz*—Edith entered the 1970s with a renewed interest in her "part-time" endeavor, designing. She began her sixth decade of filmmaking with a so-called disaster film, *Airport,* the first of three *Airport* films she would do in the next seven years. The 1970 adaptation of the best-selling Arthur Hailey novel featured Burt Lancaster, Dean Martin, Jean Seberg, Helen Hayes, Jacqueline Bisset, and Maureen Stapleton. Edith dressed the women in the all-star cast, while producer Ross Hunter designed the men's wardrobes.

There's no set uniform for what people wear when they fly. It would have been easier if we had been doing Airport '*55 instead of an* Airport *set in 1970 (followed by* Airport '75 *and* Airport '77*). In the 1950s, people dressed up to fly. Women wore elegant clothes and men were very debonair. There was no such thing as a pair of jeans on an airplane. Flying was for the fortunate folks and it was respected. Now with coach fare and economy fare, anyone can fly—which is wonderful, don't misunderstand me. However, when I see young people getting on a plane in a ratty pair of cut-off jeans and a tank top, it disturbs me. Comfort has become so important to people that they forget what they look like. When I was doing the first* Airport, *I had to study how people regarded travel from a fashion point of view. Every time I went to an airport I watched the people around me. It was probably the first time I realized just how much the world had changed. There was very little regard for dress. To incorporate that feeling into the film, I asked all my actors to bring in an outfit they would wear if they were flying. From there, taking their characters into consideration, I did my sketches.*

My basic concerns became comfort and action. My designs were not travel clothes—that is an outdated concept—but rather clothes that travel well, presumably selected from average wardrobes.

Jacqueline Bisset played a stewardess, and dressing the stewardesses was extremely fun. I had actually designed uni-

*forms for United Airlines in the 1960s, so I knew the basic re-
quirements. Stewardesses are dressed to please the men on the
plane. Men travel more than women, so a smart airline offers
pretty girls in pretty clothes. I'm sure women would prefer to see
stewardesses wear something more practical. It doesn't give a
woman passenger a feeling of security to see some cutie pie in
a dress cut up to her rear. Skirts were so short in the early 1970s
that stewardesses ran the risk of some rather embarrassing ex-
posures. We call them "crotch shots" in the industry.*

*I tried to make my stewardesses sexy but respectably cov-
ered. I put them all in polyester-knit fabric—a symbol of the
1970s. I did jumpsuits and pants and trenchcoats. All were extremely practical. What happened? Again, a major airline
adopted my uniforms.*

After the film was released, both Hunter and Edith endorsed
collections of men's and women's wear that were marketed for a
short time in American department stores. Edith had often told the
press that she would not be a successful retail designer, and the
Airport collection confirmed her predictions. A few months after
it first appeared in stores, the collection was withdrawn. Edith did
not attempt to design clothes for her public again until 1974, when
she entered the home-sewing business, selling her designs to the
Vogue Pattern Company.

When Mae West sent Edith the script for *Myra Breckinridge* (1970), Edith admitted to the aging star that she didn't like
the story. Out of loyalty to Mae, Edith allowed herself to be
loaned to Twentieth Century-Fox to dress her old friend. West
was cast opposite Raquel Welch, whose wardrobe was designed
by the newest status designer in Hollywood, Theodora Van Runkle. Van Runkle had begun the late-1960s wave of nostalgic fashion by creating the wardrobe for Faye Dunaway in *Bonnie and
Clyde* (1967).

*Gore Vidal's story was worse than pornographic; it was
unpleasant, unreal, and contrived. I did Mae's clothes and saw
her costume tests, but I did not view one foot of the film. I hear*

it was pretty horrendous—but it could not have been as bad as all the goings-on on the set.

Mae had written into her contract that she was the only one who would appear on screen dressed in black, white, or black and white. She always did that, because whoever wears black and white in a Technicolor film immediately gets the audience's eye. When Raquel found out, she was furious. Raquel was the star, but Mae was getting special attention because everyone at the studio loved her. Tempers exploded when Raquel showed up in a black dress with the palest blue ruffle on it—anyone who has ever photographed a Technicolor film knows that pale blue shows up as white. The shooting was held up until Raquel won, on a technicality—the ruffle was *blue.*

Myra Breckinridge, which was based on Gore Vidal's novel of the same name, received terrible reviews, though many praised West's acting ability. Most critics guessed that this would be her final picture, but West surprised everyone, including Edith, by taking yet another project. In 1978, with educated guesses setting her age at eighty-six, she filmed *Sextette*, a picture based on the play she had written in the 1920s. Another miserable failure, it was her last film.

Whoever thought Mae West would die? She was supposed to go on forever. There was never anyone like her and there never will be. One of a kind—that's what she was. I still remember the first day I met her, and believe it or not, she looked just as beautiful a month before she died. Her hands were as soft and pink as ever. Her skin was flawless. She always knew exactly what it meant to be a woman and how to get what she wanted. I think she died without a regret in the world.

Edith watched another legend's career hit highs and lows in the 1970s. Elizabeth Taylor had become a very close friend of Edith and Bill Ihnen. She stayed with them often when she was in Los Angeles and eventually earned a sign over the guest room door that read "Elizabeth Taylor Slept Here." She requested that Edith do her costumes whenever there was an opportunity. When Taylor and Burton did a TV guest spot on *The Lucy Show* in 1970, Edith was called in for the costumes.

Later, when the couple made *Hammersmith Is Out* (1972), director Peter Ustinov approved Edith as Taylor's designer. She also dressed her in the made-for-TV film *Divorce His, Divorce Hers* (1973), a title that seemed all too descriptive of Taylor and Burton's much publicized personal life.

In June 1973, Taylor and her daughter, Maria, moved into the guest house on Ihnen's ranch. Always protective of Taylor, as rumors surfaced about the couple's separation, Edith made a rare comment about a star's personal life. She told the *Chicago Tribune*'s Norma Lee Browning: "I've been with Elizabeth and Richard all over Europe, and I can tell you I have never seen two people who are so compatible. It's much more than just being in love. They complement each other, they need each other, but they're taking a little vacation from each other.

"I know that Elizabeth is so much in love with Richard, and I know from the way she talks that she is looking at this as only a temporary separation. When a picture of her and Peter Lawford came out, she said, 'I know Richard won't believe it. I've never thought or dreamed of looking at another man since Richard.' Does that sound like a woman who is walking out on her husband?"

On location in Italy with Taylor, Edith selected an expensive wardrobe for her role as the facelifted wife-turned-sexpot in *Ash Wednesday* (1973), with Henry Fonda. Edith's last film with Taylor was *The Bluebird* (1976), which presented the designer with her most exciting adventure of the 1970s—a trip to Russia. The film, directed by George Cukor, was a joint production between the United States and the Soviet Union. Though the film was not the success either country had hoped, Edith took great pleasure in dressing Taylor.

Elizabeth Taylor is the most beautiful woman I've ever fit. She is not as easy to dress as Grace Kelly or Audrey Hepburn, because she is a short woman—only 5'2". She's also extremely curvaceous and has short legs. But, you see, those are the kinds *of minor imperfections that make for classic beauty. A woman's individual beauty is created by little mars in the state of perfect beauty.* * *Elizabeth's fascination lies in those little discrepancies. She has aged gracefully, despite what her detractors have said. She is beautiful when she is plump and she is lovely when she trims down. A faulty figure can be changed by foundations and the proper use of dark and light colors. But no makeup can create a face like Elizabeth's. She is exquisite.*

To Edith, Elizabeth represented the last vestige of "stardom," the last of the screen's sex goddesses. She obviously missed this dying breed.

The majority of female stars today deliberately do not project an image. Their point of view is that the star idea is old-fashioned. I'm talking about Jane Fonda, Katharine Ross, Jacqueline Bisset, and Sally Field. Faye Dunaway may be one of the only exceptions—she realizes that glamour and having a consistent look mean something to the public. But these other girls, these new stars, couldn't care less. There isn't one of them who doesn't have the potential to be extremely glamorous. Now they're more interested in projecting themselves as artists, as serious actresses. I give them credit for that, but it doesn't make my job as exciting. When a woman tells you she thinks the character would buy her clothes from Sears, not Saint Laurent, you approach your work differently.

When the girls come in for fittings now, they come in jeans, and many of them don't even bother with underwear. No more Grace Kelly with white gloves. They talk about the movie

*At one point in the 1950s, Edith listed Grace Kelly's flaw as "a waist that was much too small." She called Audrey Hepburn's neck "too long and thin" and her feet "too big." And Monroe was "entirely too voluptuous." On the other hand, she told a reporter, "these flaws are always coupled with marks of perfection. Elizabeth Taylor has a perfect face and perfect hair. Loren's eyes are perfect." Edith went on to list the "perfect" qualities of her favorite stars: Marilyn Monroe, nose; Ingrid Bergman, mouth; Deborah Kerr, neck; Leslie Caron, arms; Debbie Reynolds, hands; Jane Wyman, shoulders; Brigitte Bardot, bosom; Audrey Hepburn, waist; Janet Leigh, hips; Shirley MacLaine, legs; Grace Kelly, posture.

they want to direct, *not the movie they want to* star *in. It's a different world.*

Men are so much easier to dress. Maybe it's because there are so many good parts available to them that men don't have to struggle anymore, so they aren't as temperamental. Women are all fighting to get the best roles. They're all being "assertive" —that's the buzzword now, "assertive." Once they get the part, they argue with me, to keep in practice. They argue over minute details. They don't like sashes . . . Would I make the neckline lower? . . . Am I sure the hem is the right length? This is after they've spent thirty-five minutes telling me how much costumes don't matter. Give me a man to dress any time.

Perhaps director George Roy Hill considered Edith to be a good-luck charm. Or maybe he realized that her talent was best used in period films. Whatever his reasons, Hill liked to have Edith dress the men in his movies. "She's extremely dependable, detail-oriented, and efficient," he once told an interviewer. After the success of *Butch Cassidy and the Sundance Kid* (1969), he asked her to dress Redford and Newman again in *The Sting* (1973).

A movie like The Sting *is often dressed right out of stock. It could have been done that way. Here's where the director makes such a difference. George Roy Hill is a stickler for authenticity. He wants everything to be accurate right down to the last collar button. So we made everything new. I dressed the six principals and had their sixty costumes made at Western Costume Company. The whole process took only six weeks. But it wasn't easy. Mr. Hill wanted to see every fabric swatch I was planning to use. He okayed everything personally.*

Fittings can take hours with women, but on this film it took only an hour to dress the world's two handsomest men. At Universal we do our fittings in little bungalows, so Bob was in one, Paul in another. Though they both have superb figures, they are extremely modest, so they didn't want me to see them until they were completely dressed. They both have a fine sense of humor and play off each other very well.

I waited in the wings for them to come out in each outfit. They constantly teased each other. One would say, "I don't think I look right in this" and the other would say, "Oh, you mustn't wear that, it looks terrible." They both have blue eyes, so they'd argue over which one was going to wear the blue necktie or the blue shirt. It was all in fun. I would have shown favoritism if I gave one of them a blue tie, so I ended up giving them both blue ties.

Both of them look extremely sophisticated in suits. To keep Bob from looking too worldly, I gave him a newsboy's cap and a garish wide-patterned tie. Coupled with his impish grin, they made him look rather naïve. When I wanted Paul to come across as a tough guy, I made sure his undershirt was showing. He'd pull his hat down low on his forehead to look rather menacing and sly.

Both actors had brought in their own tailors to speed up the fitting process—they are very busy men and can't afford to waste time. Bob is more meticulous than Paul about what he wears. He likes to look a certain way, but Paul just wants to be comfortable. The Sting was the first time in the history of the Academy Awards that a predominantly male film won a costume award. I was very proud of that fact. But the truth is that no matter how good the costumes are, if the actors aren't good or the film isn't a success, nobody will notice them. In the case of Redford and Newman, who have such big names and such large followings, the costumes started a whole new trend in male fashion. Suddenly men were wearing shirts with band collars, two-tone shoes, and newspaper-boy caps. They brought back chalk-stripe suits. It was fascinating. I don't ever remember a male cast having such an impact on fashion.

When Edith accepted her Academy Award for the George Roy Hill film, it was not without some question from her costume design colleagues. Rumors were flying that Peter Saldutti and Vincent Dee, both working in Universal's men's wardrobe department at the time costumes for *The Sting* were designed, were irked that she did not publicly credit them for their contributions to the wardrobe of the film. Even after Edith's death, Saldutti "graciously declined" to confirm or deny those rumors, and Dee, who had retired, could not be reached for comment. Until she died, Edith claimed that *The Sting* was one of her "greatest achievements" and that her fondest memories came from "working with George Roy Hill to create a wardrobe which was perfectly accurate."

In 1974, the same year she was awarded her Oscar for *The Sting*, the Hollywood Chamber of Commerce honored her by engraving her name on one of the stars imbedded on the touristy Walk of Fame. It had taken Edith a long time to claim her star, which was placed between the bronze name plates honoring two of her closest friends, Alfred Hitchcock and James Cagney. Rather than complain about the Chamber of Commerce's tardiness, Edith approached the event with her usual flair for publicity. In an exclusive interview, she told her close friend Marylou Luther, the *Los Angeles Times*'s fashion editor, "My motto is never to be caught inactive, so figuring that it would be difficult for photographers to get all of my 5′ 1¼″ in the same picture with the sidewalk, I stooped to polish the star—with my Gucci scarf." The picture ran on the country's major wire services and turned up in more than 350 newspapers all over the world. At seventy-six, Edith still knew how to attract media attention.

Her next assignments were all major productions. In 1975 Hal Wallis asked her to design Katharine Hepburn's wardrobe in *Rooster Cogburn* with John Wayne. The same year, she dressed Robert Redford in *The Great Waldo Pepper,* and Michael Caine and Sean Connery in *The Man Who Would Be King.*

I felt renewed in 1975. I was back doing big stars and great movies. I loved the excitement of it all.

Katharine Hepburn, one of the great actresses of all time, can look any way she wants. In Rooster Cogburn, *she and I had worked out a wonderful wardrobe that was perfect for the part, but Hal didn't like the hat and bag we had selected. She ended up wearing a battered old hat and added her own personal touch by tying an old length of scarf around it.*

She's a great one for collecting old pieces of material. Kate will often say, "Let's wear this . . ." and then pull a scrap of cloth out of her bag, telling me she bought it at a thrift store. She always brings along a bag of fabrics to costume meetings. She did the same thing on Olly Olly Oxen Free (1978), *a children's story we did together.*

In Rooster Cogburn *we had to solve the problem of how a very proper Bible-toting lady in a period skirt was going to ride a horse bareback. We solved it by bringing a fake "horse"—a rounded saddle attached to a sawhorse—into the fitting room. We experimented with a number of skirts from wardrobe until we found the one that worked best. We still had to split a side seam of the skirt so that it would function properly. Some of the newcomers in the wardrobe department asked why she didn't just ride side-saddle, but that simply showed that they didn't understand the script. She played the daughter of a poor missionary who had died, leaving her alone in the world. She didn't have the money to own a side-saddle or riding clothes, so she had to ride bareback. Kate did all her own riding scenes; she's an excellent horsewoman.*

My next big picture was The Great Waldo Pepper *(1975), another George Roy Hill film. This was a labor of love for Mr. Hill. He's an aviator and knows everything about the history of flying. The film took place about the time of World War I, so the research was very interesting to me—I'm one of those people who remember both wars. It wasn't a big hit, which was a surprise for a Redford picture, but we all had fun making it.*

The biggest challenge of the 1970s and one of the most difficult of my whole career was John Huston's The Man Who Would Be King *(1975). We filmed it in the Atlas Mountains of Morocco, and John made Marrakesh our main headquarters. The script called for thousands of extras, so John hired the Berbers who lived in the area. Sometimes they would go home at the end of the day wearing our costumes, which would upset John Apperson, supervisor of the film's wardrobe. Bright and early the next morning, however, they'd be back, wearing the same costumes.*

*I couldn't blame Apperson for being worried. He had su-
pervised production of all the costumes I designed. He bought all
the materials, had the fabrics dyed to my specifications, and
then watched each seamstress make them stitch by stitch. That's
how precise he was. On location there was no place to sew the
clothes, so the studio rented an old warehouse, sent in sewing
machines, and hired the locals to do the labor. But we quickly
realized that the people sewed by hand, sitting cross-legged on
the floor. Most of them spoke only Arabic, but a few also knew
French. Fortunately, I speak French, so I could help him communicate with them. They ended up sewing everything by hand
—beautifully.*

*The glamorous part of this job was dressing Sean Con-
nery and Michael Caine. I dressed Sean as a whirling dervish,
and while I was fitting him, Michael was there laughing his head
off at Sean's legs. Then they'd reverse positions, and Sean would
laugh while I dressed Michael in rags. Even though we were set
up in a filthy old warehouse, John Huston sat there throughout
the fittings looking very official.*

*I was nominated for an Academy Award for the film, but
lost to another period picture,* Barry Lyndon *(1975). I was also
nominated by the British filmmakers, which is very unusual for
an American designer.*

Comedienne Carol Burnett had become friends with Edith
and Bill after working with the designer on *Who's Been Sleeping
in My Bed?* (1963) and *Pete 'n' Tillie* (1972). Edith had difficulty
dressing the statuesque actress in the latter film.

Carol wasn't supposed to look sophisticated in Pete 'n'
Tillie; *in fact, my director, Marty Ritt, wanted her to be a bit
dowdy. But anything you put on Carol looks fabulous because
she's got a model's body, with terrific legs. So I had to use the
cheapest fabrics and alter the fit so she wouldn't look so good.
Because she's always playing character parts in Bob Mackie's
hilarious costumes, people don't realize what a clotheshorse she
is. It's difficult to make her look bad.*

When Burnett reflects on the time she spent with Edith, she says it's the social situations that come to mind first. "I went to her home one afternoon with Roddy McDowall. We weren't there very long before she blurted out that she had a crush on the football player Larry Czonka. 'People think I love football,' she said, 'but it's him I'm nuts about. What a hunk! Now there's a man I'd like to dress—or better yet, *un* dress.' Bill just laughed and put his arm around her. It was very funny—and sweet at the same time."

In the latter half of the 1970s, Edith was assigned to a few movies, none of them major hits, but all of them with memorable stars. Among them were her last picture for Hitchcock, *Family Plot* (1976), with Karen Black and Bruce Dern; *W. C. Fields and Me* (1976), with Rod Steiger, Valerie Perrine, and Bernadette Peters; *Airport '77* (1977), with Jack Lemmon, James Stewart, Brenda Vaccaro, and Olivia de Havilland, a film for which she received her thirty-fifth Academy Award nomination; *The Big Fix* (1978), with Richard Dreyfuss and Susan Anspach; and *The Last Married Couple in America* (1979), her first film in several years with her once-loyal star Natalie Wood. But it was *Gable and Lombard* (1976), with Jill Clayburgh and James Brolin, that caused Edith to lose some respect for Hollywood.

I hated that picture. The exploitive, derisive, vulgar approach it took to two of the industry's greatest stars was completely repulsive to me. I knew Gable and Lombard; I knew them separately and I knew them together. I laughed with Carole and I cried with Clark when she died. They were both charming, and the script turned them into tacky, oversexed, vulgar people. They were none of those things. Lombard was famous for her off-color quips, but she rarely made them in public. She reserved her witty remarks for friends at parties. That script had her saying the foulest things. In one scene she was stark naked. I was furious, and I will never work for Sidney J. Furie again.

If those were her private thoughts about the film, she hid them well in public statements before the picture was released. She went on tour with costumes and costume sketches. She appeared

on numerous TV and radio interview shows, promoting the movie
as a glamorous tribute to two of her favorite glamour stars. But
once the film came out, Edith devoted herself to her own pursuits,
designing only for those films to which she was assigned and spending as many hours as possible with her husband.

Bill was dying. He spent most of his time lying down, away
from his easel, no longer even able to paint. In 1979 he quietly
passed away at the age of ninety-one. Edith was at his side. Although she attended a charity fashion show the day after he died,
friends said she was privately grief-stricken and withdrawn for
months. They had been very affectionate to each other, more so
than most acquaintances had ever guessed. "She was never the
same after Bill died," recalls Universal's Herb Steinberg. "Her
spirit died with him."

She continued a hectic pace of fashion shows, promotional
events, meetings to discuss her Vogue patterns, and work on the
very occasional film. Her own health failing, she made frequent
stopovers in the hospital, receiving regular blood transfusions and
resting in preparation for her next exhausting spurt.

Her friends couldn't understand why she kept up such a
hectic pace. She took no vacations, even though she had told her
close friend, photographer John Engstead, that she dreamed of
visiting Norway, one of the few places she had missed in her many
career travels. When he and a group of friends planned a Norwegian holiday and made arrangements for her to accompany them,
she blurted out in frustration, "I don't have the money."

After Bill's death, she had been forced to subdivide and sell
portions of the land that housed "Casa Ladera," the Ihnens' home
of thirty years, just to pay taxes. Her income for 1979 had been less
than $50,000, far from enough to support her huge Coldwater
Canyon hacienda and its land. Her contract with Universal included
her car (which her poor eyesight prevented her from driving), her
secretary, her sketch artist, her bungalow (which had become a
regular stop on the Universal Studios tour), and her monogrammed
golf cart, but relatively little money. One of her major sources of
income was her Vogue patterns, but selling them meant promoting
them, a pursuit she would not give up. Since 1974 her alliance with

Vogue had proved to be very successful, with her patterns representing some of the company's best-selling styles.

Edith had hopes for another big motion picture, something that would at least earn another Academy Award nomination: thirty-five still weren't enough. She wanted a picture that spoke well for Hollywood—something to be proud of.

I don't think anybody is quite able to figure out where Hollywood is going. We don't make glamorous movies today, we don't build images. Everything now is very realistic, artistic— and depressing. When is the last time you saw a wonderful musical or a fabulous fantasy? Nobody is going to convince me that Hollywood is going to continue like this. The 1970s were dull, but I have hope for the coming decade. What's ahead should be exciting. I want to make great movies in the 1980s.

FILMOGRAPHY

Listed below are more than 750 films in which Edith Head contributed in some way to the costume process—as designer, co-designer, or assistant designer. Edith claimed to have worked on 1,131 films in her career. To document all of them would be impossible, since so many records of her work are gone. As chief designer at Paramount, she took an interest in every film that carried the studio's logo, and often, even if the film wasn't assigned to her, she made her feelings known about its costumes. For this reason, even if her name did not appear as a screen credit, Edith regarded the film as one of hers.

This filmography was compiled by Scott McAuley and is based on Edith Head's personal list of her credits, supplemented by previously published filmographies, by a listing researched by Malcolm Vance and Tom Tierney, and by personal research. Every effort has been made to give credit to other designers who worked with Edith Head on films. Any omissions are not intentional.

The films are listed chronologically by year, and then alphabetically under each date. The first line of each entry is the title, followed parenthetically by the studio that released the film. The next line indicates co-designer(s), if applicable, followed by director. The last line of each entry lists up to four stars of the film in alphabetical order. Single asterisks indicate films for which Edith Head received Academy Award nominations. Double asterisks indicate films for which she won Academy Awards.

1924　*Peter Pan* (Paramount)
w/Howard Greer
DIR: Herbert Brenon
Betty Bronson

1925　*The Golden Bed* (Paramount)
w/Howard Greer, Claire West
DIR: Cecil B. DeMille
Vera Reynolds, Irene Rich

　　　The Wanderer (Paramount)
w/Howard Greer
DIR: Raoul Walsh
Greta Nissen, Vera Reynolds, Irene Rich

1926　*Mantrap* (Paramount)
DIR: Victor Fleming
Clara Bow, Ernest Torrence

1927　*Wings* (Paramount)
DIR: William A. Wellman
Clara Bow, Gary Cooper

1929　*The Saturday Night Kid* (Paramount)
w/Travis Banton
DIR: A. Edward Sutherland
Jean Arthur, Clara Bow, Jean Harlow

　　　The Virginian (Paramount)
DIR: Victor Fleming
Mary Brian, Gary Cooper

Edith Head's Hollywood

The Wolf Song (Paramount)
DIR: Victor Fleming
Gary Cooper, Lupe Velez

1930 *Along Came Youth* (Paramount)
DIR: Lloyd Corrigan, Norman Z. McLeod
Gary Cooper, Frances Dee

Follow the Leader (Paramount)
DIR: Norman Taurog
Ginger Rogers, Ed Wynn

Only the Brave (Paramount)
DIR: Frank Tuttle
Mary Brian, Gary Cooper

The Santa Fe Trail (Paramount)
DIR: Otto Brower, E. H. Knopf
Richard Arlen, Mitzi Green

1932 *The Big Broadcast of 1932* (Paramount)
DIR: Frank Tuttle
Gracie Allen, Bing Crosby, Leila Hyams

A Farewell to Arms (Paramount)
w/Travis Banton
DIR: Frank Borzage
Gary Cooper, Helen Hayes

He Learned About Women (Paramount)
DIR: Lloyd Corrigan
Susan Fleming, Alison Skipworth

Hot Saturday (Paramount)
DIR: William Seiter
Nancy Carroll, Cary Grant

Love Me Tonight (Paramount)
DIR: Rouben Mamoulian
Maurice Chevalier, Myrna Loy, Jeanette MacDonald

The Sign of the Cross (Paramount)
w/Travis Banton
DIR: Cecil B. DeMille
Claudette Colbert, Elissa Landi, Fredric March

Two Kinds of Women (Paramount)
DIR: William C. DeMille
Wynne Gibson, Miriam Hopkins

Undercover Man (Paramount)
DIR: James Flood
Nancy Carroll, George Raft

Wayward (Paramount)
DIR: Edward Sloman
Nancy Carroll, Pauline Frederick, Gertrude Michael

1933 *A Cradle Song* (Paramount)
w/Travis Banton
DIR: Mitchell Leisen
Gertrude Michael, Kent Taylor

Crime of the Century (Paramount)
w/Travis Banton
DIR: William Beaudine
Michael Browne, Ray Walker

Duck Soup (Paramount)
DIR: Leo McCarey
Marx Brothers, Raquel Torres

Gambling Ship (Paramount)
DIR: L. Gasnier, Max Marcin
Cary Grant, Benita Hume

Hello, Everybody (Paramount)
DIR: William Seiter
Sally Blane, Randolph Scott, Kate Smith

I'm No Angel (Paramount)
w/Travis Banton
DIR: Wesley Ruggles
Cary Grant, Mae West

She Done Him Wrong (Paramount)
DIR: Lowell Sherman
Cary Grant, Mae West

Sitting Pretty (Paramount)
DIR: Harry Joe Brown
Jack Oakie, Ginger Rogers

Strictly Personal (Paramount)
DIR: Ralph Murphy
Marjorie Rambeau

White Woman (Paramount)
w/Travis Banton
DIR: Stuart Walker
Charles Laughton, Carole Lombard

1934 *Ladies Should Listen* (Paramount)
DIR: Frank Tuttle
Frances Drake, Cary Grant

Little Miss Marker (Paramount)
DIR: Alexander Hall
Dorothy Dell, Shirley Temple

Many Happy Returns (Paramount)
DIR: Norman Z. McLeod
Gracie Allen, George Burns

The Notorious Sophie Lang (Paramount)
w/Travis Banton
DIR: Ralph Murphy
Gertrude Michael, Ray Milland

The Pursuit of Happiness (Paramount)
DIR: Alexander Hall
Joan Bennett, Francis Lederer

The Witching Hour (Paramount)
DIR: Henry Hathaway
Judith Allen, Sir Guy Standing

You Belong to Me (Paramount)
DIR: Alfred Werker
Helen Mack, Lee Tracy

1935 *The Big Broadcast of 1936* (Paramount)
DIR: Norman Taurog
Gracie Allen, Wendy Barrie, Ethel Merman

Car 99 (Paramount)
DIR: Charles Barton
Fred MacMurray, Ann Sheridan

The Crusades (Paramount)
w/Travis Banton, Natalie Visart
DIR: Cecil B. DeMille
Henry Wilcoxon, Loretta Young

Father Brown, Detective (Paramount)
DIR: Edward Sedgwick
Paul Lukas, Gertrude Michael

Four Hours to Kill (Paramount)
DIR: Mitchell Leisen
Helen Mack, Gertrude Michael

The Glass Key (Paramount)
DIR: Frank Tuttle
Claire Dodd, George Raft

Here Comes Cookie (Paramount)
DIR: Norman Z. McLeod
Gracie Allen, George Burns

Hold 'Em, Yale (Paramount)
DIR: Sidney Lanfield
Buster Crabbe, Patricia Ellis

The Last Outpost (Paramount)
DIR: Charles Barton, Louis Gasnier
Cary Grant, Gertrude Michael

The Lives of a Bengal Lancer (Paramount)
w/Travis Banton
DIR: Henry Hathaway
Kathleen Burke, Gary Cooper, Franchot Tone

Man on the Flying Trapeze (Paramount)
DIR: Clyde Bruckman
Mary Brian, W. C. Fields

Men Without Names (Paramount)
DIR: Ralph Murphy
Madge Evans, Fred MacMurray

Mississippi (Paramount)
DIR: A. Edward Sutherland
Joan Bennett, Bing Crosby

People Will Talk (Paramount)
DIR: Alfred Santell
Mary Boland, Leila Hyams

Peter Ibbetson (Paramount)
DIR: Henry Hathaway
Gary Cooper, Ida Lupino

Ruggles of Red Gap (Paramount)
w/Travis Banton
DIR: Leo McCarey
Mary Boland, Charles Laughton, Zasu Pitts

Stolen Harmony (Paramount)
DIR: Alfred Werker
Iris Adrian, Grace Bradley, George Raft

Two for Tonight (Paramount)
DIR: Frank Tuttle
Joan Bennett, Bing Crosby

Wings in the Dark (Paramount)
DIR: James Flood
Cary Grant, Myrna Loy

1936   *The Accusing Finger* (Paramount)
DIR: James Hogan
Marsha Hunt, Paul Kelly

The Big Broadcast of 1937 (Paramount)
DIR: Mitchell Leisen
Gracie Allen, Martha Raye, Shirley Ross

Border Flight (Paramount)
DIR: Otho Lovering
Robert Cummings, Frances Farmer

College Holiday (Paramount)
DIR: Frank Tuttle
Gracie Allen, Martha Raye

Collegiate (Paramount)
DIR: Ralph Murphy
Betty Grable, Frances Langford

Hollywood Boulevard (Paramount)
DIR: Robert Florey
Robert Cummings, Marsha Hunt

The Jungle Princess (Paramount)
DIR: William Thiele
Dorothy Lamour, Ray Milland

Lady Be Careful (Paramount)
DIR: J. Theodore Reed
Lew Ayres, Mary Carlisle

The Milky Way (Paramount)
DIR: Leo McCarey
Helen Mack, Verree Teasdale

Murder with Pictures (Paramount)
DIR: Charles Barton
Joyce Compton, Gail Patrick

Poppy (Paramount)
DIR: A. Edward Sutherland
Catherine Doucet, W. C. Fields, Rochelle Hudson

The Return of Sophie Lang (Paramount)
DIR: George Archainbaud
Gertrude Michael, Ray Milland

Rhythm on the Range (Paramount)
DIR: Norman Taurog
Bing Crosby, Frances Farmer, Martha Raye

Rose Bowl (Paramount)
DIR: Charles Barton
Tom Brown, Eleanor Whitney

The Texas Rangers (Paramount)
DIR: King Vidor
Fred MacMurray, Jean Parker

Thirteen Hours by Air (Paramount)
DIR: Mitchell Leisen
Joan Bennett, Fred MacMurray

Three Cheers for Love (Paramount)
DIR: Raymond McCarey
Robert Cummings, Eleanor Whitney

Till We Meet Again (Paramount)
DIR: Robert Florey
Herbert Marshall, Gertrude Michael

Too Many Parents (Paramount)
DIR: Robert F. McGowan
Frances Farmer, Colin Tapley

Wedding Present (Paramount)
DIR: Richard Wallace
Joan Bennett, Cary Grant

Wives Never Know (Paramount)
w/Travis Banton
DIR: Elliott Nugent
Mary Boland, Vivienne Osborne

Woman Trap (Paramount)
DIR: Harold Young
Gertrude Michael, George Murphy

1937 *Arizona Mahoney* (Paramount)
DIR: James Hogan
Joe Cook, June Martell

Artists and Models (Paramount)
w/Travis Banton
DIR: Raoul Walsh
Ida Lupino, Gail Patrick, Martha Raye

The Barrier (Paramount)
DIR: Lesley Selander
Leo Carrillo, Jean Parker

Blonde Trouble (Paramount)
DIR: George Archainbaud
Eleanor Whitney

Blossoms on Broadway (Paramount)
DIR: Richard Wallace
Edward Arnold, Shirley Ross

Borderland (Paramount)
DIR: Nate Watt
William Boyd, Nora Lane, Charlene Wyatt

Born to the West (Paramount)
DIR: Charles Barton
Marsha Hunt, John Wayne

Bulldog Drummond Comes Back (Paramount)
DIR: Louis King
John Barrymore, Louise Campbell, John Howard

Bulldog Drummond Escapes (Paramount)
DIR: James Hogan
Heather Angel, Ray Milland

Bulldog Drummond's Revenge (Paramount)
DIR: Louis King
John Barrymore, Louise Campbell, John Howard

Clarence (Paramount)
DIR: George Archainbaud
Spring Byington, Eleanor Whitney, Charlotte Wynters

The Crime Nobody Saw (Paramount)
DIR: Charles Barton
Lew Ayres, Ruth Coleman

Daughter of Shanghai (Paramount)
DIR: Robert Florey
Charles Bickford, Anna May Wong

A Doctor's Diary (Paramount)
w/William Bridgehouse
DIR: Charles Vidor
Helen Burgess, Ruth Coleman

Double or Nothing (Paramount)
DIR: J. Theodore Reed
Mary Carlisle, Bing Crosby, Martha Raye

Easy Living (Paramount)
w/Travis Banton
DIR: Mitchell Leisen
Jean Arthur, Ray Milland

Ebb Tide (Paramount)
DIR: James Hogan
Frances Farmer, Ray Milland

Exclusive (Paramount)
DIR: Alexander Hall
Frances Farmer, Fred MacMurray

Forlorn River (Paramount)
DIR: Charles Barton
Buster Crabbe, June Martell

Girl from Scotland Yard (Paramount)
DIR: Robert Vignola
Robert Baldwin, Karen Morley

The Great Gambini (Paramount)
DIR: Charles Vidor
Marian Marsh, Genevieve Tobin

Her Husband Lies (Paramount)
w/Travis Banton
DIR: Edward Ludwig
Ricardo Cortez, Gail Patrick

Hideaway Girl (Paramount)
DIR: George Archainbaud
Robert Cummings, Martha Raye, Shirley Ross

Hills of Old Wyoming (Paramount)
DIR: Nate Watt
William Boyd, Gail Sheridan

Hold 'Em, Navy (Paramount)
DIR: Kurt Neumann
Lew Ayres, Mary Carlisle

Hopalong Rides Again (Paramount)
DIR: Lesley Selander
William Boyd, Lois Wilde

Hotel Haywire (Paramount)
DIR: George Archainbaud
Mary Carlisle, Leo Carrillo

Internes Can't Take Money (Paramount)
DIR: Alfred Santell
Joel McCrea, Barbara Stanwyck

John Meade's Woman (Paramount)
w/William Bridgehouse
DIR: Richard Wallace
Francine Larrimore, Gail Patrick

King of Gamblers (Paramount)
DIR: Robert Florey
Lloyd Nolan, Claire Trevor

The Last Train from Madrid (Paramount)
DIR: James Hogan
Dorothy Lamour, Helen Mack, Karen Morley

Let's Make a Million (Paramount)
DIR: Raymond McCarey
Edward Everett Horton, Charlotte Wynters

Love on Toast (Paramount)
DIR: E. A. DuPont
Stella Adler, John Payne

Make Way for Tomorrow (Paramount)
DIR: Leo McCarey
Fay Bainter, Beulah Bondi, Victor Moore

Midnight Madonna (Paramount)
DIR: James Flood
Mady Correll, Warren William

Mind Your Own Business (Paramount)
DIR: Norman Z. McLeod
Mary Boland, Alice Brady

Mountain Music (Paramount)
DIR: Robert Florey
Ellen Drew, Martha Raye

Murder Goes to College (Paramount)
DIR: Charles Riesner
Astrid Allwyn, Marsha Hunt

Night Club Scandal (Paramount)
DIR: Ralph Murphy
John Barrymore, Louise Campbell, Lynne Overman

A Night of Mystery (Paramount)
DIR: E. A. DuPont
Ruth Coleman, Ellen Drew

North of the Rio Grande (Paramount)
DIR: Nate Watt
William Boyd, Bernadene Hayes

On Such a Night (Paramount)
DIR: E. A. DuPont
Karen Morley, Grant Richards

Outcast (Paramount)
DIR: Robert Florey
Karen Morley, Warren William

Partners in Crime (Paramount)
DIR: Ralph Murphy
Inez Courtney, Muriel Hutchinson, Lynne Overman

Partners of the Plains (Paramount)
DIR: Lesley Selander
William Boyd, Gwen Gaze

Rustler's Valley (Paramount)
DIR: Nate Watt
William Boyd, Muriel Evans

She Asked for It (Paramount)
DIR: Erle C. Kenton
Orin Heyward, Vivienne Osborne

She's No Lady (Paramount)
DIR: Charles Vidor
Ann Dvorak, John Trent

Sophie Lang Goes West (Paramount)
w/Travis Banton
DIR: Charles Riesner
Buster Crabbe, Gertrude Michael

Souls at Sea (Paramount)
DIR: Henry Hathaway
Olympe Bradna, Gary Cooper, Frances Dee

Texas Trail (Paramount)
DIR: David Selman
Judith Allen, William Boyd

This Way, Please (Paramount)
DIR: Robert Florey
Betty Grable, Mary Livingstone, Charles ("Buddy") Rogers

Thrill of a Lifetime (Paramount)
DIR: George Archainbaud
Judy Canova, Dorothy Lamour, Eleanor Whitney

Thunder Trail (Paramount)
DIR: Charles Barton
Marsha Hunt

True Confession (Paramount)
w/Travis Banton
DIR: Wesley Ruggles
Carole Lombard

Turn Off the Moon (Paramount)
DIR: Lewis Seiler
Eleanor Whitney

Waikiki Wedding (Paramount)
DIR: Frank Tuttle
Bing Crosby, Martha Raye, Shirley Ross

Wells Fargo (Paramount)
DIR: Frank Lloyd
Frances Dee, Joel McCrea

Wild Money (Paramount)
DIR: Louis King
Louise Campbell, Edward Everett Horton

1938 *The Arkansas Traveler* (Paramount)
DIR: Alfred Santell
Fay Bainter, Mary Boland, Jean Parker

Artists and Models Abroad (Paramount)
w/Travis Banton
DIR: Mitchell Leisen
Joan Bennett, Mary Boland

Bar 20 Justice (Paramount)
DIR: Lesley Selander
William Boyd, Gwen Gaze

The Big Broadcast of 1938 (Paramount)
DIR: Mitchell Leisen
Kirsten Flagstad, Dorothy Lamour, Shirley Ross

Booloo (Paramount)
DIR: Clyde E. Elliott
Suratna Asmaka, Jayne Regan, Colin Tapley

The Buccaneer (Paramount)
DIR: Cecil B. DeMille
Franciska Gaal, Margot Grahame

Bulldog Drummond in Africa (Paramount)
DIR: Louis King
Heather Angel, John Howard

Bulldog Drummond's Peril (Paramount)
DIR: James Hogan
John Barrymore, Louise Campbell, John Howard

Campus Confessions (Paramount)
DIR: George Archainbaud
Betty Grable, Eleanor Whitney

Cassidy of Bar 20 (Paramount)
DIR: Lesley Selander
William Boyd, Nora Lane

Coconut Grove (Paramount)
DIR: Alfred Santell
Harriet Hilliard, Fred MacMurray

College Swing (Paramount)
DIR: Raoul Walsh
Gracie Allen, Betty Grable, Martha Raye

Dangerous to Know (Paramount)
DIR: Robert Florey
Akin Tamiroff, Anna May Wong

Doctor Rhythm (Paramount)
w/Dorothy Jeakins
DIR: Frank Tuttle
Mary Carlisle, Bing Crosby, Beatrice Lillie

The Frontiersman (Paramount)
DIR: Lesley Selander
William Boyd, Evelyn Venable, Clara Kimball Young

Give Me a Sailor (Paramount)
DIR: Elliott Nugent
Betty Grable, Bob Hope, Martha Raye

Heart of Arizona (Paramount)
DIR: Lesley Selander
William Boyd, Natalie Moorhead

Her Jungle Love (Paramount)
DIR: George Archainbaud
Dorothy Lamour, Ray Milland

Hunted Men (Paramount)
DIR: Louis King
Mary Carlisle, Lloyd Nolan

Illegal Traffic (Paramount)
DIR: Louis King
Mary Carlisle, J. Carroll Naish

In Old Mexico (Paramount)
DIR: Edward D. Venturini
William Boyd, Jane Clayton

King of Alcatraz (Paramount)
DIR: Robert Florey
Lloyd Nolan, Anthony Quinn, Gail Patrick

Little Orphan Annie (Paramount)
DIR: Ben Holmes
Ann Gillis, Robert Kent

Men with Wings (Paramount)
DIR: William A. Wellman
Louise Campbell, Fred MacMurray, Ray Milland

The Mysterious Rider (Paramount)
DIR: Lesley Selander
Douglas Dumbrille, Charlotte Fields

Pride of the West (Paramount)
DIR: Lesley Selander
William Boyd, Charlotte Fields

Prison Farm (Paramount)
DIR: Louis King
Lloyd Nolan, Shirley Ross

Professor Beware (Paramount)
DIR: Elliott Nugent
Harold Lloyd, Phyllis Welch

Ride a Crooked Mile (Paramount)
DIR: Alfred E. Green
Frances Farmer, Akim Tamiroff

Say It in French (Paramount)
DIR: Andrew L. Stone
Olympe Bradna, Ray Milland

Scandal Sheet (Paramount)
DIR: James Hogan
Lew Ayres, Louise Campbell

Sing, You Sinners (Paramount)
DIR: Wesley Ruggles
Bing Crosby, Ellen Drew, Donald O'Connor

Sons of the Legion (Paramount)
DIR: James Hogan
Evelyn Keyes, Donald O'Connor, Lynne Overman

Spawn of the North (Paramount)
DIR: Henry Hathaway
Henry Fonda, Dorothy Lamour, Louise Pratt

Stolen Heaven (Paramount)
DIR: Andrew L. Stone
Olympe Bradna, Gene Raymond

The Texans (Paramount)
DIR: James Hogan
Joan Bennett, May Robson, Randolph Scott

Thanks for the Memory (Paramount)
DIR: George Archainbaud
Bob Hope, Shirley Ross

Tip-off Girls (Paramount)
DIR: Louis King
Mary Carlisle, Lloyd Nolan

Tom Sawyer, Detective (Paramount)
DIR: Louis King
Donald O'Connor

Touchdown, Army (Paramount)
DIR: Kurt Neumann
Mary Carlisle, John Howard

Tropic Holiday (Paramount)
DIR: J. Theodore Reed
Dorothy Lamour

You and Me (Paramount)
DIR: Fritz Lang
George Raft, Sylvia Sidney

1939   *All Women Have Secrets* (Paramount)
DIR: Kurt Neumann
Virginia Dale

Arrest Bulldog Drummond (Paramount)
DIR: James Hogan
Heather Angel, John Howard

Back Door to Heaven (Paramount)
DIR: William Howard
Patricia Ellis, Aline MacMahon

The Beachcomber (Paramount)
DIR: Erich Pommer
Elsa Lanchester, Charles Laughton

Beau Geste (Paramount)
DIR: William A. Wellman
Garry Cooper, Susan Hayward, Ray Milland

Boy Trouble (Paramount)
DIR: George Archainbaud
Mary Boland, Charles Ruggles

Bulldog Drummond's Bride (Paramount)
DIR: James Hogan
Heather Angel, John Howard

Bulldog Drummond's Secret Police (Paramount)
DIR: James Hogan
Heather Angel, John Howard

Café Society (Paramount)
DIR: Edward H. Griffith
Madeleine Carroll, Shirley Ross

The Cat and the Canary (Paramount)
DIR: Elliott Nugent
Paulette Goddard, Bob Hope, Gale Sondergaard

Death of a Champion (Paramount)
DIR: Robert Florey
Virginia Dale, Lynne Overman

Disbarred (Paramount)
DIR: Robert Florey
Gail Patrick

Disputed Passage (Paramount)
DIR: Frank Borzage
Dorothy Lamour

Geronimo (Paramount)
DIR: Paul Sloane
Ellen Drew, Preston Foster

The Gracie Allen Murder Case (Paramount)
DIR: Alfred E. Green
Gracie Allen, Warren William

Grand Jury Secrets (Paramount)
DIR: James Hogan
John Howard, Gail Patrick

Edith Head's Hollywood

The Great Victor Herbert (Paramount)
DIR: Andrew L. Stone
Susanna Foster, Mary Martin

Heritage of the Desert (Paramount)
DIR: Lesley Selander
Evelyn Venable, Donald Woods

Honeymoon in Bali (Paramount)
DIR: Edward H. Griffith
Madeleine Carroll, Fred MacMurray

Hotel Imperial (Paramount)
DIR: Robert Florey
Ray Milland, Isa Miranda

Invitation to Happiness (Paramount)
DIR: Wesley Ruggles
Irene Dunne, Fred MacMurray

Island of Lost Men (Paramount)
DIR: Kurt Neumann
Anthony Quinn, Anna May Wong

I'm from Missouri (Paramount)
DIR: J. Theodore Reed
Bob Burns, Gladys George

King of Chinatown (Paramount)
DIR: Nick Grinde
Akim Tamiroff, Anna May Wong

The Lady's from Kentucky (Paramount)
DIR: Alexander Hall
Ellen Drew, George Raft

Law of the Pampas (Paramount)
DIR: Nate Watt
William Boyd, Ann Demetrio, Steffi Duna

The Llano Kid (Paramount)
DIR: Edward D. Venturini
Tito Guizar, Gale Sondergaard

The Magnificent Fraud (Paramount)
DIR: Robert Florey
Mary Boland, Patricia Morison, Lloyd Nolan

Man About Town (Paramount)
DIR: Mark Sandrich
Binnie Barnes, Jack Benny, Betty Grable, Dorothy Lamour

Man of Conquest (Republic)
w/Adele Palmer
DIR: George Nicholls, Jr.
Joan Fontaine, Gail Patrick

Midnight (Paramount)
w/Irene Sharaff
DIR: Mitchell Leisen
Mary Astor, John Barrymore, Claudette Colbert

Million Dollar Legs (Paramount)
DIR: Nick Grinde
Betty Grable, Donald O'Connor

Never Say Die (Paramount)
DIR: Elliott Nugent
Bob Hope, Martha Raye

The Night of Nights (Paramount)
DIR: Lewis Milestone
Olympe Bradna, Pat O'Brien

Night Work (Paramount)
DIR: George Archainbaud
Mary Boland, Charles Ruggles

$1,000 a Touchdown (Paramount)
DIR: James Hogan
Susan Hayward, Martha Raye

Our Leading Citizen (Paramount)
DIR: Alfred Santell
Bob Burns, Susan Hayward

Our Neighbors, the Carters (Paramount)
DIR: Ralph Murphy
Fay Bainter, Frank Craven

Paris Honeymoon (Paramount)
DIR: Frank Tuttle
Bing Crosby, Franciska Gaal, Shirley Ross

Persons in Hiding (Paramount)
DIR: Louis King
Patricia Morison, Lynne Overman

Range War (Paramount)
DIR: Lesley Selander
William Boyd, Betty Moran

The Renegade Trail (Paramount)
DIR: Lesley Selander
William Boyd, Charlotte Wynters

Rulers of the Sea (Paramount)
DIR: Frank Lloyd
Douglas Fairbanks, Jr., Margaret Lockwood

Silver on the Sage (Paramount)
DIR: Lesley Selander
William Boyd, Ruth Rogers

Some Like It Hot (Paramount)
DIR: George Archainbaud
Bob Hope, Shirley Ross

The Star Maker (Paramount)
DIR: Roy Del Ruth
Louise Campbell, Bing Crosby

St. Louis Blues (Paramount)
DIR: Raoul Walsh
William Boyd, Dorothy Lamour

Sudden Money (Paramount)
DIR: Nick Grinde
Marjorie Rambeau, Charles Ruggles

The Sunset Trail (Paramount)
DIR: Lesley Selander
William Boyd, Charlotte Wynters

Television Spy (Paramount)
DIR: Edward Dmytryk
Judith Barrett, William Henry

This Man Is News (Paramount)
DIR: David McDonald
Barry K. Barnes, Valerie Hobson

Undercover Doctor (Paramount)
DIR: Louis King
Janice Logan

Union Pacific (Paramount)
w/Natalie Visart
DIR: Cecil B. DeMille
Barbara Stanwyck, Joel McCrea

Unmarried (Paramount)
DIR: Kurt Neumann
Buck Jones, Helen Twelvetrees

What a Life (Paramount)
DIR: J. Theodore Reed
Jackie Cooper, Betty Field

Zaza (Paramount)
DIR: George Cukor
Claudette Colbert

1940 *Adventure in Diamonds* (Paramount)
DIR: George Fitzmaurice
George Brent, Isa Miranda

Arise, My Love (Paramount)
w/Irene
DIR: Mitchell Leisen
Walter Abel, Claudette Colbert, Ray Milland, Dennis O'Keefe

The Biscuit Eater (Paramount)
DIR: Stuart Heisler
Billy Lee, Helen Millard

Buck Benny Rides Again (Paramount)
DIR: Mark Sandrich
Jack Benny, Ellen Drew

Cherokee Strip (Paramount)
DIR: Lesley Selander
Richard Dix, Florence Rice

Christmas in July (Paramount)
DIR: Preston Sturges
Ellen Drew, Dick Powell

Comin' Round the Mountain (Paramount)
DIR: George Archainbaud
Bob Burns, Una Merkel

Dancing on a Dime (Paramount)
DIR: Joseph Stanley
Virginia Dale, Grace McDonald, Robert Paige

Doctor Cyclops (Paramount)
DIR: Ernest Schoedsack
Albert Dekker, Janice Logan

Emergency Squad (Paramount)
DIR: Edward Dmytryk
Louise Campbell, William Henry

The Farmer's Daughter (Paramount)
DIR: James Hogan
Martha Raye, Charles Ruggles

French Without Tears (Paramount)
w/Charles Frederick Worth
DIR: Anthony Asquith
Ellen Drew, Ray Milland

The Ghost Breakers (Paramount)
DIR: George Marshall
Paulette Goddard, Bob Hope

Golden Gloves (Paramount)
DIR: Edward Dmytryk
Jeanne Cagney, Richard Denning

The Great McGinty (Paramount)
DIR: Preston Sturges
Muriel Angelus, Brian Donlevy

Hidden Gold (Paramount)
DIR: Lesley Selander
William Boyd, Ruth Rogers

I Want a Divorce (Paramount)
DIR: Ralph Murphy
Joan Blondell, Dick Powell

Knights of the Range (Paramount)
DIR: Lesley Selander
Russell Hayden, Jean Parker

Light of Western Stars (Paramount)
DIR: Lesley Selander
Victor Jory

The Light That Failed (Paramount)
DIR: William A. Wellman
Muriel Angelus, Ronald Colman

Love Thy Neighbor (Paramount)
DIR: Mark Sandrich
Jack Benny, Mary Martin

Moon over Burma (Paramount)
DIR: Louis King
Dorothy Lamour

Mystery Sea Raider (Paramount)
DIR: Edward Dmytryk
Carole Landis, Henry Wilcoxon

A Night at Earl Carroll's (Paramount)
DIR: Kurt Neumann
Rose Hobart, Ken Murray

Northwest Mounted Police (Paramount)
w/Natalie Visart
DIR: Cecil B. DeMille
Madeleine Carroll, Gary Cooper

Opened by Mistake (Paramount)
DIR: George Archainbaud
Janice Logan, Robert Paige

A Parole Fixer (Paramount)
DIR: Robert Florey
Virginia Dale, Gertrude Michael

The Quarterback (Paramount)
DIR: Bruce Humberstone
Lillian Cornell, Virginia Dale

Queen of the Mob (Paramount)
DIR: James Hogan
Jeanne Cagney, Blanche Yurka

Rangers of Fortune (Paramount)
DIR: Sam Wood
Fred MacMurray, Patricia Morison

Remember the Night (Paramount)
DIR: Mitchell Leisen
Fred MacMurray, Barbara Stanwyck

Rhythm on the River (Paramount)
DIR: Victor Schertzinger
Bing Crosby, Mary Martin

Road to Singapore (Paramount)
DIR: Victor Schertzinger
Bing Crosby, Bob Hope, Dorothy Lamour

Safari (Paramount)
DIR: Edward H. Griffith
Madeleine Carroll, Douglas Fairbanks, Jr.

Santa Fe Marshal (Paramount)
DIR: Lesley Selander
William Boyd, Jane Clayton

Seventeen (Paramount)
DIR: Louis King
Jackie Cooper, Betty Field

The Showdown (Paramount)
DIR: Howard Bretherton
William Boyd, Jane Clayton

Stagecoach War (Paramount)
DIR: Lesley Selander
William Boyd, Julie Carter

Texas Rangers Ride Again (Paramount)
DIR: James Hogan
Ellen Drew, John Howard

Those Were the Days (Paramount)
DIR: J. Theodore Reed
Bonita Granville, William Holden

Three Men from Texas (Paramount)
DIR: Lesley Selander
William Boyd, Esther Estrella

Typhoon (Paramount)
DIR: Louis King
Dorothy Lamour, Robert Preston

Untamed (Paramount)
DIR: George Archainbaud
Ray Milland, Patricia Morison

Victory (Paramount)
DIR: John Cromwell
Betty Field, Fredric March

The Way of All Flesh (Paramount)
DIR: Louis King
Muriel Angelus, Gladys George, Akim Tamiroff

Women Without Names (Paramount)
DIR: Robert Florey
Ellen Drew, Robert Paige

World in Flames (Paramount)
Gregory Abbott, Tom Chalmers, Gilbert Martin

1941   *Aloma of the South Seas* (Paramount)
DIR: Alfred Santell
John Hall, Dorothy Lamour

Among the Living (Paramount)
DIR: Stuart Heisler
Frances Farmer, Susan Hayward

Bahama Passage (Paramount)
DIR: Edward H. Griffith
Mary Anderson, Madeleine Carroll, Flora Robson

Ball of Fire (RKO)
DIR: Howard Hawks
Gary Cooper, Barbara Stanwyck

Birth of the Blues (Paramount)
DIR: Victor Schertzinger
Bing Crosby, Mary Martin

Border Vigilantes (Paramount)
DIR: Derwin Abrahams
William Boyd, Frances Gifford

Buy Me That Town (Paramount)
DIR: Eugene Forde
Constance Moore, Lloyd Nolan

Caught in the Draft (Paramount)
DIR: David Butler
Bob Hope, Dorothy Lamour

Doomed Caravan (Paramount)
DIR: Lesley Selander
William Boyd, Minna Gombell

Flying Blind (Paramount)
DIR: Frank McDonald
Richard Arlen, Jean Parker

Forced Landing (Paramount)
DIR: Gordon Wiles
Richard Arlen, Eva Gabor

Glamour Boy (Paramount)
DIR: Ted Tetzlaff
Jackie Cooper, Susanna Foster

Henry Aldrich for President (Paramount)
DIR: Hugh Bennett
Mary Anderson, Jimmy Lydon, June Preisser

Here Comes Mr. Jordan (Columbia)
DIR: Alexander Hall
Rita Johnson, Evelyn Keyes, Robert Montgomery

Hold Back the Dawn (Paramount)
DIR: Mitchell Leisen
Charles Boyer, Paulette Goddard, Olivia de Havilland

I Wanted Wings (Paramount)
DIR: Mitchell Leisen
Veronica Lake, Constance Moore

In Old Colorado (Paramount)
DIR: Howard Bretherton
William Boyd, Margaret Hayes

Kiss the Boys Goodbye (Paramount)
DIR: Victor Schertzinger
Don Ameche, Mary Martin

The Lady Eve (Paramount)
DIR: Preston Sturges
Henry Fonda, Barbara Stanwyck

Las Vegas Nights (Paramount)
DIR: Ralph Murphy
Virginia Dale, Constance Moore

Life with Henry (Paramount)
DIR: J. Theodore Reed
Jackie Cooper, Leila Ernst

The Mad Doctor (Paramount)
DIR: Tim Whelan
Ellen Drew, Basil Rathbone

The Monster and the Girl (Paramount)
DIR: Stuart Heisler
Ellen Drew, Robert Paige

New York Town (Paramount)
DIR: Charles Vidor
Madeleine Carroll, Fred MacMurray, Mary Martin

The Night of January 16th (Paramount)
DIR: William Clemens
Ellen Drew, Robert Preston

Nothing But the Truth (Paramount)
DIR: Elliott Nugent
Paulette Goddard, Bob Hope

One Night in Lisbon (Paramount)
DIR: Edward H. Griffith
Madeleine Carroll, Fred MacMurray, Patricia Morison

The Parson of Panamint (Paramount)
DIR: William McGann
Ellen Drew, Charles Ruggles, Phillip Terry

Pirates on Horseback (Paramount)
DIR: Lesley Selander
William Boyd, Eleanor Stewart

Power Dive (Paramount)
DIR: James Hogan
Richard Arlen, Jean Parker

Reaching for the Sun (Paramount)
DIR: William A. Wellman
Ellen Drew, Joel McCrea

Road to Zanzibar (Paramount)
DIR: Victor Schertzinger
Bing Crosby, Bob Hope, Dorothy Lamour

Roundup (Paramount)
DIR: Lesley Selander
Richard Dix, Patricia Morison

Secret of the Wastelands (Paramount)
DIR: Derwin Abrahams
William Boyd, Barbara Britton

Shepherd of the Hills (Paramount)
DIR: Henry Hathaway
Betty Field, John Wayne

Skylark (Paramount)
w/Irene
DIR: Mark Sandrich
Claudette Colbert, Ray Milland

Sullivan's Travels (Paramount)
DIR: Preston Sturges
Veronica Lake, Joel McCrea

There's a Magic in the Music (Paramount)
DIR: Andrew L. Stone
Susanna Foster, Margaret Lindsay, Diana Lynn

Virginia (Paramount)
DIR: Edward H. Griffith
Madeleine Carroll, Fred MacMurray, Marie Wilson

West Point Widow (Paramount)
DIR: Robert Siodmak
Richard Carlson, Anne Shirley

Wide-Open Town (Paramount)
DIR: Lesley Selander
William Boyd, Evelyn Brent

World Premiere (Paramount)
DIR: Ted Tetzlaff
John Barrymore, Frances Farmer, Eugene Pallette

You Belong to Me (Columbia)
DIR: Wesley Ruggles
Henry Fonda, Barbara Stanwyck

You're the One (Paramount)
DIR: Ralph Murphy
Bonnie Baker, Orrin Tucker

1942 *Are Husbands Necessary?* (Paramount)
DIR: Norman Taurog
Betty Field, Ray Milland, Patricia Morison

Beyond the Blue Horizon (Paramount)
DIR: Alfred Santell
Richard Denning, Dorothy Lamour

The Fleet's In (Paramount)
DIR: Victor Schertzinger
William Holden, Betty Hutton, Dorothy Lamour

Forest Rangers (Paramount)
DIR: George Marshall
Paulette Goddard, Susan Hayward, Fred MacMurray

The Gay Sisters (Warner Brothers)
w/Milo Anderson
DIR: Irving Rapper
Nancy Coleman, Geraldine Fitzgerald, Barbara Stanwyck

The Glass Key (Paramount)
DIR: Stuart Heisler
Brian Donlevy, Bonita Granville, Alan Ladd, Veronica Lake

The Great Man's Lady (Paramount)
DIR: William A. Wellman
Joel McCrea, Barbara Stanwyck

Henry Aldrich, Editor (Paramount)
DIR: Hugh Bennett
Jimmy Lydon, Rita Quigley

Holiday Inn (Paramount)
DIR: Mark Sandrich
Bing Crosby, Virginia Dale, Marjorie Reynolds

I Married a Witch (United Artists)
DIR: René Clair
Susan Hayward, Veronica Lake

The Lady Has Plans (Paramount)
DIR: Sidney Lanfield
Paulette Goddard, Margaret Hayes

Lucky Jordan (Paramount)
DIR: Frank Tuttle
Alan Ladd, Helen Walker

The Major and the Minor (Paramount)
DIR: Billy Wilder
Diana Lynn, Ray Milland, Ginger Rogers

Mrs. Wiggs of the Cabbage Patch (Paramount)
DIR: Ralph Murphy
Fay Bainter, Hugh Herbert

My Favorite Blonde (Paramount)
DIR: Sidney Lanfield
Madeleine Carroll, Bob Hope

My Heart Belongs to Daddy (Paramount)
DIR: Robert Siodmak
Richard Carlson, Martha O'Driscoll

The Palm Beach Story (Paramount)
w/Irene
DIR: Preston Sturges
Mary Astor, Claudette Colbert

The Remarkable Andrew (Paramount)
DIR: Stuart Heisler
Ellen Drew, William Holden

Road to Morocco (Paramount)
DIR: David Butler
Bing Crosby, Bob Hope, Dorothy Lamour

Star-Spangled Rhythm (Paramount)
DIR: George Marshall
Bing Crosby, Bob Hope, Dorothy Lamour

This Gun for Hire (Paramount)
DIR: Frank Tuttle
Alan Ladd, Veronica Lake

Wake Island (Paramount)
DIR: John Farrow
Barbara Britton, Brian Donlevy

Young and Willing (United Artists)
DIR: Edward H. Griffith
Susan Hayward, William Holden, Martha O'Driscoll

1943   *China* (Paramount)
DIR: John Farrow
Alan Ladd, Loretta Young

The Crystal Ball (United Artists)
DIR: Elliott Nugent
Paulette Goddard, Ray Milland

Five Graves to Cairo (Paramount)
DIR: Billy Wilder
Anne Baxter, Erich von Stroheim, Franchot Tone

Flesh and Fantasy (Universal)
w/Vera West
DIR: Jules Duvivier
Barbara Stanwyck

For Whom the Bell Tolls (Paramount)
DIR: Sam Wood
Ingrid Bergman, Gary Cooper, Katina Paxinou

The Good Fellows (Paramount)
DIR: Jo Graham
James Brown, Helen Walker

Happy Go Lucky (Paramount)
DIR: Curtis Bernhardt
Betty Hutton, Mary Martin, Dick Powell

Henry Aldrich Gets Glamour (Paramount)
DIR: Hugh Bennett
Olive Blakeney, Jimmy Lydon

Henry Aldrich Haunts a House (Paramount)
DIR: Hugh Bennett
Olive Blakeney, Jimmy Lydon

Hostages (Paramount)
DIR: Frank Tuttle
William Bendix, Katina Paxinou, Luise Rainer

Lady Bodyguard (Paramount)
DIR: William Clemens
Eddie Albert, Anne Shirley

Lady of Burlesque (United Artists)
w/Natalie Visart
DIR: William A. Wellman
Barbara Stanwyck

Let's Face It (Paramount)
DIR: Sidney Lanfield
Eve Arden, Betty Hutton, Zasu Pitts

Night Plane from Chungking (Paramount)
DIR: Ralph Murphy
Ellen Drew, Robert Preston

No Time for Love (Paramount)
w/Irene
DIR: Mitchell Leisen
Ilka Chase, Claudette Colbert, June Havoc, Fred MacMurray

Riding High (Paramount)
DIR: George Marshall
Cass Daley, Dorothy Lamour, Dick Powell

Salute for Three (Paramount)
DIR: Ralph Murphy
MacDonald Carey, Betty Rhodes

Tender Comrade (RKO)
w/Renie
DIR: Edward Dmytryk
Ruth Hussey, Ginger Rogers

They Got Me Covered (RKO)
w/Adrian
DIR: David Butler
Bob Hope

True to Life (Paramount)
DIR: George Marshall
Mary Martin, Dick Powell, Franchot Tone

1944 *And Now Tomorrow* (Paramount)
DIR: Irving Pichel
Susan Hayward, Loretta Young

And the Angels Sing (Paramount)
DIR: Claude Binyon
Betty Hutton, Dorothy Lamour, Diana Lynn

Double Indemnity (Paramount)
DIR: Billy Wilder
Mona Freeman, Fred MacMurray, Barbara Stanwyck

Going My Way (Paramount)
DIR: Leo McCarey
Bing Crosby, Rise Stevens

The Great Moment (Paramount)
DIR: Preston Sturges
Betty Field, Joel McCrea

Hail the Conquering Hero (Paramount)
DIR: Preston Sturges
Eddie Bracken, Ella Raines

Henry Aldrich's Little Secret (Paramount)
DIR: Hugh Bennett
Jimmy Lydon, Joan Mortimer

Here Come the Waves (Paramount)
DIR: Mark Sandrich
Bing Crosby, Betty Hutton

The Hitler Gang (Paramount)
DIR: John Farrow
Robert Watson

The Hour Before the Dawn (Paramount)
DIR: Frank Tuttle
Binnie Barnes, Veronica Lake, Franchot Tone

I Love a Soldier (Paramount)
DIR: Mark Sandrich
Beulah Bondi, Paulette Goddard, Sonny Tufts

I'll Be Seeing You (David O. Selznick)
DIR: William Dieterle
Joseph Cotten, Ginger Rogers, Shirley Temple

Lady in the Dark (Paramount)
w/Raoul Pène du Bois, Madame Karinska, Kate Wilometz
DIR: Mitchell Leisen
Phyllis Brooks, Ginger Rogers

The Man in Half Moon Street (Paramount)
DIR: Ralph Murphy
Nils Aster, Helen Walker

Ministry of Fear (Paramount)
DIR: Fritz Lang
Ray Milland, Marjorie Reynolds

The Miracle of Morgan's Creek (Paramount)
DIR: Preston Sturges
Betty Hutton, Diana Lynn

National Barn Dance (Paramount)
DIR: Hugh Bennett
Jean Heather, Charles Quigley

Our Hearts Were Young and Gay (Paramount)
DIR: Lewis Allen
Diana Lynn, Gail Russell

Rainbow Island (Paramount)
DIR: Ralph Murphy
Dorothy Lamour

Standing Room Only (Paramount)
DIR: Sidney Lanfield
Paulette Goddard, Fred MacMurray

Till We Meet Again (Paramount)
DIR: Frank Borzage
Barbara Britton, Ray Milland

The Uninvited (Paramount)
DIR: Lewis Allen
Ruth Hussey, Ray Milland, Gail Russell, Cornelia Otis Skinner

You Can't Ration Love (Paramount)
DIR: Lester Fuller
Jenny Johnston, Betty Rhodes

1945 *The Affairs of Susan* (Paramount)
DIR: William Seiter
George Brent, Joan Fontaine

The Bells of St. Mary's (RKO)
DIR: Leo McCarey
Ingrid Bergman, Bing Crosby

Bring on the Girls (Paramount)
DIR: Sidney Lanfield
Veronica Lake

Christmas in Connecticut (Warner Brothers)
w/Milo Anderson
DIR: Peter Godfrey
Dennis Morgan, Barbara Stanwyck

Duffy's Tavern (Paramount)
w/Mary Kay Dodson
DIR: Hal Walker
Paulette Goddard, Betty Hutton

Hold That Blonde (Paramount)
DIR: George Marshall
Eddie Bracken, Veronica Lake

Incendiary Blonde (Paramount)
DIR: George Marshall
Arturo de Cordova, Betty Hutton

The Lost Weekend (Paramount)
DIR: Billy Wilder
Ray Milland, Jane Wyman

Love Letters (Paramount)
DIR: William Dieterle
Joseph Cotten, Jennifer Jones

Masquerade in Mexico (Paramount)
DIR: Mitchell Leisen
Arturo de Cordova, Dorothy Lamour

A Medal for Benny (Paramount)
DIR: Irving Pichel
Arturo de Cordova, Dorothy Lamour

Miss Susie Slagle's (Paramount)
w/Mary Kay Dodson
DIR: John Berry
Joan Caulfield, Lillian Gish, Veronica Lake

Murder He Says (Paramount)
DIR: George Marshall
Fred MacMurray, Marjorie Main

Out of This World (Paramount)
DIR: Hal Walker
Cass Daley, Veronica Lake, Diana Lynn

Road to Utopia (Paramount)
DIR: Hal Walker
Bing Crosby, Bob Hope, Dorothy Lamour

Salty O'Rourke (Paramount)
DIR: Raoul Walsh
Alan Ladd, Gail Russell

The Stork Club (Paramount)
DIR: Hal Walker
Barry Fitzgerald, Betty Hutton

You Came Along (Paramount)
DIR: John Farrow
Robert Cummings, Lizabeth Scott

1946 *The Blue Dahlia* (Paramount)
DIR: George Marshall
Alan Ladd, Veronica Lake

Blue Skies (Paramount)
w/Waldo Angelo
DIR: Stuart Heisler
Fred Astaire, Joan Caulfield, Bing Crosby, Olga San Juan

The Bride Wore Boots (Paramount)
DIR: Irving Pichel
Robert Cummings, Diana Lynn, Barbara Stanwyck

Monsieur Beaucaire (Paramount)
DIR: George Marshall
Joan Caulfield, Bob Hope

My Reputation (Warner Brothers)
w/Leah Rhodes
DIR: Curtis Bernhardt
George Brent, Barbara Stanwyck

Notorious (RKO)
DIR: Alfred Hitchcock
Ingrid Bergman, Cary Grant

Our Hearts Were Growing Up (Paramount)
DIR: William D. Russell
Gail Russell

The Perfect Marriage (Paramount)
DIR: Lewis Allen
David Niven, Loretta Young

The Strange Love of Martha Ivers (Paramount)
DIR: Lewis Milestone
Kirk Douglas, Lizabeth Scott, Barbara Stanwyck

To Each His Own (Paramount)
DIR: Mitchell Leisen
Mary Anderson, Olivia de Havilland

The Virginian (Paramount)
DIR: Stuart Gilmore
Barbara Britton, Joel McCrea

The Well-Groomed Bride (Paramount)
DIR: Sidney Lanfield
Olivia de Havilland, Ray Milland

1947 *Blaze of Noon* (Paramount)
DIR: John Farrow
Anne Baxter, William Holden

Calcutta (Paramount)
DIR: John Farrow
Alan Ladd, Gail Russell

California (Paramount)
w/Gile Steele
DIR: John Farrow
Ray Milland, Barbara Stanwyck

Cross My Heart (Paramount)
DIR: John Berry
Ruth Donnelly, Betty Hutton

Cry Wolf (Warner Brothers)
w/William Travilla
DIR: Peter Godfrey
Geraldine Brooks, Barbara Stanwyck

Dear Ruth (Paramount)
DIR: William D. Russell
Joan Caulfield, Mona Freeman, William Holden

Desert Fury (Paramount)
DIR: Lewis Allen
Mary Astor, Burt Lancaster, Lizabeth Scott

Easy Come, Easy Go (Paramount)
DIR: John Farrow
Diana Lynn, Sonny Tufts

I Walk Alone (Paramount)
DIR: Byron Haskin
Burt Lancaster, Lizabeth Scott

The Imperfect Lady (Paramount)
w/Gile Steele
DIR: Lewis Allen
Ray Milland, Teresa Wright

My Favorite Brunette (Paramount)
DIR: Elliott Nugent
Bob Hope, Dorothy Lamour

The Other Love (United Artists)
w/Herwood Keyes
DIR: André de Toth
Joan Loring, David Niven, Barbara Stanwyck

The Perils of Pauline (Paramount)
DIR: George Marshall
Betty Hutton

Ramrod (United Artists)
DIR: André de Toth
Veronica Lake, Joel McCrea, Arleen Whelan

Road to Rio (Paramount)
DIR: Norman Z. McLeod
Bing Crosby, Bob Hope, Dorothy Lamour

The Trouble with Women (Paramount)
DIR: Sidney Lanfield
Ray Milland, Teresa Wright

The Two Mrs. Carrolls (Warner Brothers)
w/Milo Anderson
DIR: Peter Godfrey
Humphrey Bogart, Alexis Smith, Barbara Stanwyck

Variety Girl (Paramount)
w/Dorothy O'Hara, Waldo Angelo
DIR: George Marshall
Bing Crosby, Mary Hatcher, Olga San Juan

Welcome Stranger (Paramount)
DIR: Elliott Nugent
Joan Caulfield, Bing Crosby

Where There's Life (Paramount)
DIR: Sidney Lanfield
Signe Hasso, Bob Hope

Wild Harvest (Paramount)
DIR: Tay Garnett
Alan Ladd, Dorothy Lamour, Robert Preston

1948   *The Accused* (Paramount)
DIR: William Dieterle
Robert Cummings, Loretta Young

Arch of Triumph (United Artists)
w/Herwood Keyes
DIR: Lewis Milestone
Ingrid Bergman, Charles Boyer

Beyond Glory (Paramount)
DIR: John Farrow
June Havoc, Donna Reed

The Big Clock (Paramount)
DIR: John Farrow
Ray Milland, Maureen O'Sullivan

Dream Girl (Paramount)
DIR: Mitchell Leisen
Virginia Field, Betty Hutton

*The Emperor Waltz** (Paramount)
w/Gile Steele
DIR: Billy Wilder
Bing Crosby, Joan Fontaine

Enchantment (MGM)
w/Mary Wills
DIR: Irving Reis
Leo G. Carroll, Evelyn Keyes, Jayne Meadows, David Niven

A Foreign Affair (Paramount)
DIR: Billy Wilder
Jean Arthur, Marlene Dietrich, John Lund

Isn't It Romantic? (Paramount)
DIR: Norman Z. McLeod
Mona Freeman, Mary Hatcher, Veronica Lake

June Bride (Warner Brothers)
w/Leah Rhodes
DIR: Bretaigne Windust
Bette Davis, Robert Montgomery

Miss Tatlock's Millions (Paramount)
DIR: Richard Haydn
Ilka Chase, Wanda Hendrix

My Own True Love (Paramount)
DIR: Campton Bennett
Phyllis Calvert, Wanda Hendrix

The Night Has a Thousand Eyes (Paramount)
DIR: John Farrow
Virginia Bruce, Edward G. Robinson, Gail Russell

Rachel and the Stranger (RKO)
DIR: Norman Foster
William Holden, Robert Mitchum, Loretta Young

Saigon (Paramount)
DIR: Leslie Fenton
Alan Ladd, Veronica Lake

The Sainted Sisters (Paramount)
DIR: William D. Russell
Joan Caulfield, Veronica Lake

The Sealed Verdict (Paramount)
DIR: Lewis Allen
Florence Marly, Ray Milland

So Evil My Love (Paramount)
w/Sophie Harris
DIR: Lewis Allen
Ray Milland, Ann Todd

Sorry, Wrong Number (Paramount)
DIR: Anatole Litvak
Burt Lancaster, Ann Richards, Barbara Stanwyck

Whispering Smith (Paramount)
w/Mary Kay Dodson
DIR: Leslie Fenton
Alan Ladd, Brenda Marshall

1949 *Beyond the Forest* (Warner Brothers)
DIR: King Vidor
Bette Davis, Dona Drake, Ruth Roman

The Great Gatsby (Paramount)
DIR: Elliott Nugent
Betty Field, Ruth Hussey, Alan Ladd, Shelley Winters

The Great Lover (Paramount)
DIR: Alexander Hall
Rhonda Fleming, Bob Hope

*The Heiress*** (Paramount)
w/Gile Steele
DIR: William Wyler
Montgomery Clift, Olivia de Havilland, Miriam Hopkins

Malaya (MGM)
w/Irene, Valles
DIR: Richard Thorpe
Valentina Cortese, Spencer Tracy

Manhandled (Paramount)
DIR: Lewis Foster
Dan Dailey, Sterling Hayden, Dorothy Lamour

My Foolish Heart (Samuel Goldwyn)
w/Mary Wills
DIR: Mark Robson
Dana Andrews, Susan Hayward

My Friend Irma (Paramount)
DIR: George Marshall
Martin and Lewis, Diana Lynn, Marie Wilson

Red, Hot, and Blue (Paramount)
DIR: John Farrow
June Havoc, Betty Hutton, Victor Mature

Rope of Sand (Paramount)
DIR: William Dieterle
Corinne Calvet, Burt Lancaster

*Samson and Delilah*** (Paramount)
w/Gile Steele, Dorothy Jeakins, Gwen Wakeling, Elois Jenssen
DIR: Cecil B. DeMille
Hedy Lamarr, Angela Lansbury, Victor Mature

Song of Surrender (Paramount)
DIR: Mitchell Leisen
Wanda Hendrix, Claude Rains

1950 *All About Eve*** (Twentieth Century-Fox)
w/Charles LeMaire
DIR: Joseph L. Mankiewicz
Anne Baxter, Bette Davis, Marilyn Monroe

Copper Canyon (Paramount)
w/Gile Steele
DIR: John Farrow
Hedy Lamarr, Ray Milland

The Dark City (Paramount)
DIR: William Dieterle
Charlton Heston, Viveca Lindfors, Lizabeth Scott

Fancy Pants (Paramount)
w/Gile Steele
DIR: George Marshall
Lucille Ball, Bob Hope

The File on Thelma Jordan (Paramount)
DIR: Robert Siodmak
Wendell Corey, Barbara Stanwyck

The Furies (Paramount)
DIR: Anthony Mann
Barbara Stanwyck

Let's Dance (Paramount)
DIR: Norman Z. McLeod
Fred Astaire, Betty Hutton

Mr. Music (Paramount)
DIR: Richard Haydn
Bing Crosby, Ruth Hussey, Nancy Olson

My Friend Irma Goes West (Paramount)
DIR: Hal Walker
Martin and Lewis, Diana Lynn, Marie Wilson

No Man of Her Own (Paramount)
DIR: Mitchell Leisen
Barbara Stanwyck, Phyllis Thaxter

Paid in Full (Paramount)
DIR: William Dieterle
Robert Cummings, Diana Lynn, Lizabeth Scott

Riding High (Paramount)
DIR: Frank Capra
Bing Crosby, Frances Gifford, Ruth Hussey

September Affair (Paramount)
DIR: William Dieterle
Joseph Cotten, Joan Fontaine

Sunset Boulevard (Paramount)
DIR: Billy Wilder
William Holden, Nancy Olson, Gloria Swanson

1951 *The Big Carnival* (Paramount)
DIR: Billy Wilder
Kirk Douglas, Jan Sterling

Branded (Paramount)
DIR: Rudolph Mate
Mona Freeman, Alan Ladd

Crosswinds (Paramount)
DIR: Lewis Foster
Rhonda Fleming, John Payne

Darling, How Could You? (Paramount)
DIR: Mitchell Leisen
Joan Fontaine, Mona Freeman

Dear Brat (Paramount)
DIR: William Seiter
Edward Arnold, Mona Freeman

Detective Story (Paramount)
DIR: William Wyler
Kirk Douglas, Lee Grant, Eleanor Parker

Here Comes the Groom (Paramount)
DIR: Frank Capra
Bing Crosby, Alexis Smith, Jane Wyman

Hong Kong (Paramount)
DIR: Lewis Foster
Rhonda Fleming, Ronald Reagan

The Last Outpost (Paramount)
DIR: Lewis Foster
Rhonda Fleming, Ronald Reagan

The Lemon Drop Kid (Paramount)
DIR: Sidney Lanfield
Bob Hope, Marilyn Maxwell

My Favorite Spy (Paramount)
DIR: Norman Z. McLeod
Bob Hope, Hedy Lamarr

Payment on Demand (RKO)
w/Walter Plunkett
DIR: Curtis Bernhardt
Bette Davis, Frances Dee

Peking Express (Paramount)
DIR: William Dieterle
Corinne Calvet, Joseph Cotten

*A Place in the Sun*** (Paramount)
DIR: George Stevens
Montgomery Clift, Elizabeth Taylor, Shelley Winters

Rhubarb (Paramount)
DIR: Arthur Lubin
Ray Milland, Jan Sterling

Silver City (Paramount)
DIR: Byron Haskin
Yvonne DeCarlo, Barry Fitzgerald

The Stooge (Paramount)
DIR: Norman Taurog
Polly Bergen, Martin and Lewis, Marion Marshall

Submarine Command (Paramount)
DIR: John Farrow
William Holden, Nancy Olson

That's My Boy (Paramount)
DIR: Hal Walker
Polly Bergen, Ruth Hussey, Martin and Lewis

When Worlds Collide (Paramount)
DIR: Rudolph Mate
Judith Ames, Richard Derr, Barbara Rush

1952   *Aaron Slick from Punkin Crick* (Paramount)
DIR: Claude Binyon
Adele Jergens, Dinah Shore, Alan Young

Anything Can Happen (Paramount)
DIR: George Seaton
Jose Ferrer, Kim Hunter

Caribbean (Paramount)
DIR: Edward Ludwig
Arlene Dahl, John Payne

*Carrie** (Paramount)
DIR: William Wyler
Miriam Hopkins, Jennifer Jones

Come Back, Little Sheba (Paramount)
DIR: Daniel Mann
Shirley Booth, Burt Lancaster, Terry Moore

Denver and Rio Grande (Paramount)
DIR: Byron Haskin
Laura Elliott, Zasu Pitts

*The Greatest Show on Earth** (Paramount)
w/Dorothy Jeakins, Miles White
DIR: Cecil B. DeMille
Charlton Heston, Betty Hutton, Dorothy Lamour

Hurricane Smith (Paramount)
DIR: Jerry Hopper
Yvonne DeCarlo, John Ireland

Jumping Jacks (Paramount)
DIR: Norman Taurog
Mona Freeman, Martin and Lewis, Marcy McGuire

Just for You (Paramount)
w/Yvonne Wood
DIR: Elliott Nugent
Ethel Barrymore, Bing Crosby, Jane Wyman

My Son John (Paramount)
DIR: Leo McCarey
Helen Hayes, Robert Walker

Red Mountain (Paramount)
DIR: William Dieterle
Alan Ladd, Lizabeth Scott

Road to Bali (Paramount)
DIR: Hal Walker
Bing Crosby, Bob Hope, Dorothy Lamour

Ruby Gentry (Twentieth Century-Fox)
DIR: King Vidor
Charlton Heston, Jennifer Jones

Sailor Beware (Paramount)
DIR: Hal Walker
Corinne Calvet, Martin and Lewis, Marion Marshall

The Savage (Paramount)
DIR: George Marshall
Charlton Heston, Susan Morrow, Joan Taylor

Somebody Loves Me (Paramount)
DIR: Irving Brecher
Betty Hutton, Ralph Meeker

Something to Live For (Paramount)
DIR: George Stevens
Joan Fontaine, Ray Milland, Teresa Wright

Son of Paleface (Paramount)
DIR: Frank Tashlin
Bob Hope, Jane Russell

This Is Dynamite (Paramount)
DIR: William Dieterle
William Holden, Alexis Smith

The Turning Point (Paramount)
DIR: William Dieterle
William Holden, Alexis Smith

1953 *Arrowhead* (Paramount)
DIR: Charles Warren
Judith Ames, Charlton Heston, Katy Jurado

The Caddy (Paramount)
DIR: Norman Taurog
Barbara Bates, Martin and Lewis, Donna Reed

Forever Female (Paramount)
DIR: Irving Rapper
Pat Crowley, Paul Douglas, William Holden, Ginger Rogers

Here Come the Girls (Paramount)
DIR: Claude Binyon
Rosemary Clooney, Arlene Dahl, Bob Hope

Houdini (Paramount)
DIR: George Marshall
Tony Curtis, Janet Leigh

Jamaica Run (Paramount)
DIR: Lewis Foster
Arlene Dahl, Laura Elliott, Ray Milland

Little Boy Lost (Paramount)
DIR: George Seaton
Bing Crosby, Colette Dereal, Nicole Maurey

Off Limits (Paramount)
DIR: George Marshall
Bob Hope, Marilyn Maxwell

Pleasure Island (Paramount)
DIR: Herbert F. Hugh
Audrey Dalton, Joan Elan, Elsa Lanchester

Pony Express (Paramount)
DIR: Jerry Hopper
Rhonda Fleming, Charlton Heston, Jan Sterling

*Roman Holiday*** (Paramount)
DIR: William Wyler
Audrey Hepburn, Gregory Peck

Sangaree (Paramount)
DIR: Edward Ludwig
Arlene Dahl, Fernando Lamas, Pat Medina

Scared Stiff (Paramount)
DIR: George Marshall
Martin and Lewis, Carmen Miranda, Lizabeth Scott

Shane (Paramount)
DIR: George Stevens
Alan Ladd

Stalag 17 (Paramount)
DIR: Billy Wilder
William Holden, Don Taylor

The Stars Are Singing (Paramount)
DIR: Norman Taurog
Anna Maria Alberghetti, Rosemary Clooney, Lauritz Melchior

Those Redheads from Seattle (Paramount)
DIR: Lewis Foster
Teresa Brewer, Rhonda Fleming, Agnes Moorehead

Thunder in the East (Paramount)
DIR: Charles Vidor
Corinne Calvet, Deborah Kerr, Alan Ladd

Tropic Zone (Paramount)
DIR: Lewis Foster
Rhonda Fleming, Ronald Reagan

The Vanquished (Paramount)
DIR: Edward Ludwig
John Payne, Jan Sterling

War of the Worlds (Paramount)
DIR: Byron Haskin
Gene Barry, Ann Robinson, Les Treymayne

1954   *About Mrs. Leslie* (Paramount)
DIR: Daniel Mann
Margie Millar, Robert Ryan

Alaska Seas (Paramount)
DIR: Jerry Hopper
Jan Sterling, Kent Taylor

The Bridges at Toko-ri (Paramount)
DIR: Mark Robson
William Holden, Grace Kelly

The Country Girl (Paramount)
DIR: George Seaton
Bing Crosby, William Holden, Grace Kelly

Elephant Walk (Paramount)
DIR: William Dieterle
Dana Andrews, Elizabeth Taylor

Jivaro (Paramount)
DIR: Edward Ludwig
Rhonda Fleming, Fernando Lamas

Knock on Wood (Paramount)
DIR: Norman Panama, Melvin Frank
Danny Kaye, Mai Zetterling

Living It Up (Paramount)
DIR: Norman Taurog
Janet Leigh, Martin and Lewis

Money from Home (Paramount)
DIR: George Marshall
Pat Crowley, Martin and Lewis, Margie Millar

Mr. Casanova (Paramount)
DIR: Norman Z. McLeod
Audrey Dalton, Joan Fontaine, Basil Rathbone

The Naked Jungle (Paramount)
DIR: Byron Haskin
Charlton Heston, Eleanor Parker

Rear Window (Paramount)
DIR: Alfred Hitchcock
Grace Kelly, Thelma Ritter, James Stewart

Red Garters (Paramount)
w/Yvonne Wood
DIR: George Marshall
Rosemary Clooney, Pat Crowley, Joanne Gilbert

Sabrina** (Paramount)
DIR: Billy Wilder
Humphrey Bogart, Audrey Hepburn, William Holden

Secret of the Incas (Paramount)
DIR: Jerry Hopper
Charlton Heston, Nicole Maurey

Three-Ring Circus (Paramount)
DIR: Joseph Pevney
Joanne Dru, Zsa Zsa Gabor, Martin and Lewis

White Christmas (Paramount)
DIR: Michael Curtiz
Rosemary Clooney, Bing Crosby, Danny Kaye, Vera-Ellen

1955 *Artists and Models* (Paramount)
DIR: Frank Tashlin
Anita Ekberg, Martin and Lewis, Shirley MacLaine, Dorothy Malone

Conquest of Space (Paramount)
DIR: Byron Haskin
Walter Brooke, Joan Shawlee

The Desperate Hours (Paramount)
DIR: William Wyler
Humphrey Bogart, Mary Murphy, Martha Scott

The Far Horizon (Paramount)
DIR: Rudolph Mate
Barbara Hale, Charlton Heston, Donna Reed

The Girl Rush (Paramount)
DIR: Robert Pirosh
Gloria DeHaven, Rosalind Russell

Hell's Island (Paramount)
DIR: Phil Karlson
Mary Murphy, John Payne

Lucy Gallant (Paramount)
DIR: Robert Parrish
Edith Head, Claire Trevor, Jane Wyman

*The Rose Tattoo** (Paramount)
DIR: Daniel Mann
Burt Lancaster, Anna Magnani

Run for Cover (Paramount
DIR: Nicholas Ray
James Cagney, Viveca Lindfors

The Seven Little Foys (Paramount)
DIR: Melville Shavelson
Angela Clark, Bob Hope, Milly Vitale

Strategic Air Command (Paramount)
DIR: Anthony Mann
June Allyson, James Stewart

*To Catch a Thief** (Paramount)
DIR: Alfred Hitchcock
Cary Grant, Grace Kelly

The Trouble with Harry (Paramount)
DIR: Alfred Hitchcock
John Forsythe, Edmund Gwenn, Shirley MacLaine, Mildred Natwick

You're Never Too Young (Paramount)
DIR: Norman Taurog
Nina Foch, Diana Lynn, Martin and Lewis

1956 *Anything Goes* (Paramount)
DIR: Robert Lewis
Bing Crosby, Mitzi Gaynor, Jeanmaire

The Birds and the Bees (Paramount)
DIR: Norman Taurog
Mitzi Gaynor, George Gobel

The Come-On (Allied Artists)
DIR: Russell Birdwell
Anne Baxter, Sterling Hayden

The Court Jester (Paramount)
w/Yvonne Wood
DIR: Norman Panama, Melvin Frank
Mitzi Gaynor, Glynis Johns, Danny Kaye

Hollywood or Bust (Paramount)
DIR: Frank Tashlin
Pat Crowley, Anita Ekberg, Martin and Lewis

The Leather Saint (Paramount)
DIR: Alvin Ganzer
John Derek, Jody Lawrence

The Man Who Knew Too Much (Paramount)
DIR: Alfred Hitchcock
Doris Day, James Stewart

The Mountain (Paramount)
DIR: Edward Dmytryk
Spencer Tracy, Claire Trevor

Pardners (Paramount)
DIR: Norman Taurog
Martin and Lewis, Agnes Moorehead, Lori Nelson

*The Proud and the Profane** (Paramount)
DIR: George Seaton
William Holden, Deborah Kerr, Thelma Ritter

The Rainmaker (Paramount)
DIR: Joseph Anthony
Katharine Hepburn, Burt Lancaster

The Scarlet Hour (Paramount)
DIR: Michael Curtiz
Maureen Hurley, Jody Lawrence, Carol Ohmart

The Search for Bridey Murphy (Paramount)
DIR: Noel Langley
Louis Hayward, Teresa Wright

*The Ten Commandments** (Paramount)
w/Dorothy Jeakins, Ralph Jester, Elois Jenssen, Arnold Frieberg
DIR: Cecil B. DeMille
Anne Baxter, Charlton Heston, Debra Paget

That Certain Feeling (Paramount)
DIR: Norman Panama, Melvin Frank
Pearl Bailey, Bob Hope, Eva Marie Saint

Three Violent People (Paramount)
DIR: Rudolph Mate
Anne Baxter, Charlton Heston

1957 *Beau James* (Paramount)
DIR: Melville Shavelson
Bob Hope, Vera Miles, Alexis Smith

The Buster Keaton Story (Paramount)
DIR: Sidney Sheldon
Ann Blyth, Rhonda Fleming

The Delicate Delinquent (Paramount)
DIR: Don McGuire
Martha Hyer, Jerry Lewis, Mary Webster

The Devil's Hairpin (Paramount)
DIR: Cornel Wilde
Jean Wallace, Cornel Wilde

Fear Strikes Out (Paramount)
DIR: Robert Mulligan
Norma Moore, Anthony Perkins

*Funny Face** (Paramount)
w/Hubert de Givenchy
DIR: Stanley Donen
Fred Astaire, Audrey Hepburn, Kay Thompson

Gunfight at the O.K. Corral (Paramount)
DIR: John Sturges
Kirk Douglas, Rhonda Fleming, Burt Lancaster, Jo Van Fleet

Hear Me Good (Paramount)
DIR: Don McGuire
Merry Anders, Jean Willes

The Joker Is Wild (Paramount)
DIR: Charles Vidor
Jeanne Crain, Mitzi Gaynor, Frank Sinatra

The Lonely Man (Paramount)
DIR: Henry Levin
Elaine Aiken, Jack Palance, Anthony Perkins

Loving You (Paramount)
DIR: Hal Kanter
Dolores Hart, Elvis Presley, Lizabeth Scott

The Sad Sack (Paramount)
DIR: George Marshall
Phyllis Kirk, Jerry Lewis, Liliane Montevecci

Short Cut to Hell (Paramount)
DIR: James Cagney
Robert Ivers, Georgann Johnson

The Tin Star (Paramount)
DIR: Anthony Mann
Henry Fonda, Betsy Palmer

Wild Is the Wind (Paramount)
DIR: George Cukor
Dolores Hart, Anna Magnani, Anthony Quinn

Witness for the Prosecution (United Artists)
DIR: Billy Wilder
Marlene Dietrich, Elsa Lanchester, Charles Laughton, Tyrone Power

1958   *As Young As We Are* (Paramount)
DIR: Bernard Gerard
Robert Harland, Pippa Scott

*The Buccaneer** (Paramount)
w/Ralph Jester, John Jensen
DIR: Anthony Quinn
Claire Bloom, Yul Brynner, Charlton Heston, Inger Stevens

The Geisha Boy (Paramount)
DIR: Frank Tashlin
Jerry Lewis, Marie McDonald

Hot Spell (Paramount)
DIR: Daniel Mann
Shirley Booth, Shirley MacLaine, Anthony Quinn

Houseboat (Paramount)
DIR: Melville Shavelson
Cary Grant, Martha Hyer, Sophia Loren

I Married a Monster from Outer Space (Paramount)
DIR: G. Fowler, Jr.
Gloria Talbot, Tom Tryon

King Creole (Paramount)
DIR: Michael Curtiz
Dolores Hart, Carolyn Jones, Elvis Presley

Maracaibo (Paramount)
DIR: Cornel Wilde
Abbe Lane, Jean Wallace, Cornel Wilde

The Matchmaker (Paramount)
DIR: Joseph Anthony
Shirley Booth, Shirley MacLaine, Anthony Perkins

Me and the Colonel (Columbia)
DIR: Peter Glenville
Curt Jurgens, Danny Kaye, Nicole Maurey

The Party Crashers (Paramount)
DIR: Bill Girard
Robert Driscoll, Connie Stevens

Rock-a-Bye Baby (Paramount)
DIR: Frank Tashlin
Jerry Lewis, Marilyn Maxwell, Connie Stevens

Separate Tables (United Artists)
w/Mary Grant
DIR: Delbert Mann
Rita Hayworth, Deborah Kerr, Burt Lancaster, David Niven

St. Louis Blues (Paramount)
DIR: Allen Reisner
Pearl Bailey, Nat King Cole, Eartha Kitt

Teacher's Pet (Paramount)
DIR: George Seaton
Doris Day, Clark Gable, Mamie Van Doren

Vertigo (Paramount)
DIR: Alfred Hitchcock
Barbara Bel Geddes, Kim Novak, James Stewart

1959   *Alias Jesse James* (Paramount)
DIR: Norman Z. McLeod
Rhonda Fleming, Bob Hope

The Black Orchid (Paramount)
DIR: Martin Ritt
Ina Balin, Sophia Loren, Anthony Quinn

But Not for Me (Paramount)
DIR: Walter Lang
Carroll Baker, Clark Gable, Lilli Palmer

*Career** (Paramount)
DIR: Joseph Anthony
Carolyn Jones, Shirley MacLaine

Don't Give Up the Ship (Paramount)
DIR: Norman Taurog
Jerry Lewis, Dina Merrill

*The Five Pennies** (Paramount)
DIR: Melville Shavelson
Barbara Bel Geddes, Danny Kaye

The Hangman (Paramount)
DIR: Michael Curtiz
Tina Louise, Robert Taylor

A Hole in the Head (United Artists)
DIR: Frank Capra
Rita Hayworth, Carolyn Jones, Frank Sinatra

The Jayhawkers (Paramount)
DIR: Melvin Frank
Jeff Chandler, Nicole Maurey

Last Train from Gun Hill (Paramount)
DIR: John Sturges
Kirk Douglas, Carolyn Jones, Anthony Quinn

That Kind of Woman (Paramount)
DIR: Sidney Lumet
Tab Hunter, Sophia Loren

Too Young for Love (Paramount)
DIR: Bill Girard
Majel Barrett, Phillipa Scott

218

The Trap (Paramount)
DIR: Norman Panama
Lee J. Cobb, Tina Louise, Richard Widmark

The Young Captives (Paramount)
DIR: Irvin Kershner
Steven Marlo, Luana Patten

1960 *The Bellboy* (Paramount)
DIR: Jerry Lewis
Alex Gerry, Jerry Lewis

A Breath of Scandal (Paramount)
DIR: Michael Curtiz
Sophia Loren

Cinderfella (Paramount)
DIR: Frank Tashlin
Anna Maria Alberghetti, Judith Anderson, Jerry Lewis

The Facts of Life** (United Artists)
w/Edward Stevenson
DIR: Melvin Frank
Lucille Ball, Bob Hope, Ruth Hussey

G.I. Blues (Paramount)
DIR: Norman Taurog
Elvis Presley, Juliet Prowse

Heller in Pink Tights (Paramount)
DIR: George Cukor
Sophia Loren, Margaret O'Brien, Anthony Quinn

It Started in Naples (Paramount)
DIR: Melville Shavelson
Clark Gable, Sophia Loren

Pepe* (Columbia)
DIR: George Sidney
Cantinflas, Shirley Jones

The Rat Race (Paramount)
DIR: Robert Mulligan
Tony Curtis, Debbie Reynolds

A Touch of Larceny (Paramount)
DIR: Guy Hamilton
James Mason, Vera Miles

A Visit to a Small Planet (Paramount)
DIR: Norman Taurog
Joan Blackman, Jerry Lewis

1961 *All in a Night's Work* (Paramount)
DIR: Joseph Anthony
Shirley MacLaine, Dean Martin

Blue Hawaii (Paramount)
DIR: Norman Taurog
Joan Blackman, Angela Lansbury, Elvis Presley

Breakfast at Tiffany's (Paramount)
w/Hubert de Givenchy, Pauline Trigere
DIR: Blake Edwards
Audrey Hepburn, Patricia Neal

The Errand Boy (Paramount)
DIR: Jerry Lewis
Felicia Atkins, Joan Engstrom, Jerry Lewis

The Ladies' Man (Paramount)
DIR: Jerry Lewis
Eddie Bracken, Jerry Lewis, Helen Traubel

Love in a Goldfish Bowl (Paramount)
DIR: Jack Sher
Fabian, Toby Michaels, Jan Sterling

Mantrap (Paramount)
DIR: Edmund O'Brien
Jeffrey Hunter, Stella Stevens

On the Double (Paramount)
DIR: Melville Shavelson
Danny Kaye, Dana Wynter

The Pleasure of His Company (Paramount)
DIR: George Seaton
Fred Astaire, Lilli Palmer, Debbie Reynolds

*Pocketful of Miracles** (United Artists)
w/Walter Plunkett
DIR: Frank Capra
Bette Davis, Glenn Ford, Hope Lange

Summer and Smoke (Paramount)
DIR: Peter Glenville
Rita Moreno, Geraldine Page, Pamela Tiffin

1962 *The Counterfeit Traitor* (Paramount)
DIR: George Seaton
William Holden, Lilli Palmer

Escape from Zahrain (Paramount)
DIR: Ronald Neame
Yul Brynner, Madlyn Rhue

A Girl Named Tamiko (Paramount)
DIR: John Sturges
Martha Hyer, France Nuyen

Girls! Girls! Girls! (Paramount)
DIR: Norman Taurog
Laurel Goodwin, Elvis Presley, Stella Stevens

Hatari (Paramount)
DIR: Howard Hawks
Red Buttons, Elsa Martinelli, John Wayne

It's Only Money (Paramount)
DIR: Frank Tashlin
Jerry Lewis, Joan O'Brien

*The Man Who Shot Liberty Valance** (Paramount)
DIR: John Ford
Vera Miles, James Stewart, John Wayne

*My Geisha** (Paramount)
DIR: Jack Cardiff
Shirley MacLaine, Yves Montand

The Pigeon That Took Rome (Paramount)
DIR: Melville Shavelson
Charlton Heston, Elsa Martinelli

Too Late Blues (Paramount)
DIR: John Cassavetes
Bobby Darin, Stella Stevens

Who's Got the Action? (Paramount)
DIR: Daniel Mann
Dean Martin, Nita Talbot, Lana Turner

1963   *The Birds* (Universal)
DIR: Alfred Hitchcock
Tippi Hedren, Suzanne Pleshette, Jessica Tandy

Come Blow Your Horn (Paramount)
DIR: Bud Yorkin
Barbara Rush, Frank Sinatra, Jill St. John

Critic's Choice (Warner Brothers)
DIR: Don Weis
Lucille Ball, Bob Hope, Jessie Royce Landis, Marilyn Maxwell

Donovan's Reef (Paramount)
DIR: John Ford
Elizabeth Allen, Dorothy Lamour, John Wayne

Fun in Acapulco (Paramount)
DIR: Richard Thorpe
Ursula Andress, Elsa Cardenas, Elvis Presley

Hud (Paramount)
DIR: Martin Ritt
Patricia Neal, Paul Newman

I Could Go on Singing (United Artists)
DIR: Ronald Neame
Dirk Bogarde, Judy Garland

*Love with the Proper Stranger** (Paramount)
DIR: Robert Mulligan
Steve McQueen, Natalie Wood

My Six Loves (Paramount)
DIR: Gower Champion
Eileen Heckart, Debbie Reynolds

*A New Kind of Love** (Paramount)
w/Yves Saint Laurent, Christian Dior, Lanvin-Castillo
DIR: Melville Shavelson
Paul Newman, Thelma Ritter, Joanne Woodward

The Nutty Professor (Paramount)
DIR: Jerry Lewis
Jerry Lewis, Stella Stevens

Papa's Delicate Condition (Paramount)
DIR: George Marshall
Jackie Gleason, Glynis Johns

Who's Been Sleeping in My Bed? (Paramount)
DIR: Daniel Mann
Carol Burnett, Elizabeth Montgomery, Jill St. John

Who's Minding the Store? (Paramount)
DIR: Frank Tashlin
Jerry Lewis, Agnes Moorehead, Jill St. John

*Wives and Lovers** (Paramount)
DIR: John Rich
Martha Hyer, Van Johnson, Janet Leigh, Shelley Winters

1964   *The Carpetbaggers* (Paramount)
DIR: Edward Dmytryk
Elizabeth Ashley, Carroll Baker, Martha Hyer, George Peppard

The Disorderly Orderly (Paramount)
DIR: Frank Tashlin
Glenda Farrell, Jerry Lewis, Susan Oliver

*A House Is Not a Home** (Embassy)
DIR: Russell Rouse
Robert Taylor, Shelley Winters

Lady in a Cage (Paramount)
DIR: Walter Grauman
Olivia de Havilland, Ann Sothern

Man's Favorite Sport (Paramount)
DIR: Howard Hawks
Rock Hudson, Maria Perschy, Paula Prentiss

Marnie (Universal)
DIR: Alfred Hitchcock
Diane Baker, Sean Connery, Tippi Hedren

The Patsy (Paramount)
DIR: Jerry Lewis
Ina Balin, Jerry Lewis

Roustabout (Paramount)
DIR: John Rich
Joan Freeman, Elvis Presley, Barbara Stanwyck

Sex and the Single Girl (Warner Brothers)
w/Norman Norell
DIR: Richard Quine
Lauren Bacall, Tony Curtis, Natalie Wood

Thirty-Six Hours (MGM)
DIR: George Seaton
James Garner, Eva Marie Saint

*What a Way to Go** (Twentieth Century-Fox)
w/Moss Mabry
DIR: J. Lee Thompson
Gene Kelly, Shirley MacLaine, Paul Newman, Dick Van Dyke

Where Love Has Gone (Paramount)
DIR: Edward Dmytryk
Bette Davis, Susan Hayward, Joey Heatherton

1965 *Boeing, Boeing* (Paramount)
DIR: John Rich
Tony Curtis, Suzanne Leigh, Jerry Lewis, Thelma Ritter

The Family Jewels (Paramount)
DIR: Jerry Lewis
Donna Butterworth, Jerry Lewis

The Great Race (Warner Brothers)
w/Donfeld
DIR: Blake Edwards
Tony Curtis, Jack Lemmon, Natalie Wood

The Hallelujah Trail (United Artists)
DIR: John Sturges
Burt Lancaster, Lee Remick

Harlow (Paramount)
w/Moss Mabry
DIR: Gordon Douglas
Carroll Baker, Angela Lansbury

*Inside Daisy Clover** (Warner Brothers)
w/Bill Thomas
DIR: Robert Mulligan
Robert Redford, Natalie Wood

John Goldfarb, Please Come Home (Twentieth Century-Fox)
w/Adele Balkan
DIR: J. Lee Thompson
Shirley MacLaine

Love Has Many Faces (Columbia)
DIR: Alexander Singer
Stefanie Powers, Ruth Roman, Lana Turner

Red Line 7000 (Paramount)
DIR: Howard Hawks
James Caan, Laura Devon

The Slender Thread* (Paramount)
DIR: Sidney Pollock
Anne Bancroft, Sidney Poitier

The Sons of Katie Elder (Paramount)
DIR: Henry Hathaway
Martha Hyer, Dean Martin, John Wayne

Sylvia (Paramount)
DIR: Gordon Douglas
Carroll Baker, George Maharis, Ann Sothern

Who Has Seen the Wind? (Universal)
DIR: George Sidney
Veronica Cartright, Maria Schell

The Yellow Rolls-Royce (MGM)
w/Lanvin-Castillo, Pierre Cardin
DIR: Anthony Asquith
Ingrid Bergman, Shirley MacLaine, Jeanne Moreau

1966 *Assault on a Queen* (Paramount)
DIR: Jack Donohue
Virna Lisi, Frank Sinatra

The Last of the Secret Agents (Paramount)
DIR: Norman Abbott
Marty Allen, Steve Rossi, Nancy Sinatra

Nevada Smith (Paramount)
DIR: Henry Hathaway
Steve McQueen, Suzanne Pleshette

Not with My Wife, You Don't! (Warner Brothers)
DIR: Norman Panama
Tony Curtis, Virna Lisi, George C. Scott

The Oscar* (Paramount)
DIR: Russell Rouse
Edith Head, Elke Sommer, Jill St. John

Paradise, Hawaiian Style (Paramount)
DIR: Michael Moore
Suzanne Leigh, Elvis Presley, Irene Tsu

Penelope (MGM)
DIR: Arthur Hiller
Ian Bannen, Natalie Wood

The Swinger (Paramount)
DIR: George Sidney
Ann-Margret, Anthony Franciosa, Yvonne Romaine

This Property Is Condemned (Paramount)
DIR: Sidney Pollock
Robert Redford, Natalie Wood

Torn Curtain (Universal)
DIR: Alfred Hitchcock
Julie Andrews, Paul Newman

Waco (Paramount)
DIR: R. G. Springsteen
Howard Keel, Jane Russell

1967 *Barefoot in the Park* (Paramount)
DIR: Gene Saks
Jane Fonda, Robert Redford

The Caper of the Golden Bulls (Embassy)
DIR: Russell Rouse
Stephen Boyd, Yvette Mimieux

Chuka (Paramount)
DIR: Gordon Douglas
Ernest Borgnine, Luciana Paluzzi

Easy Come, Easy Go (Paramount)
DIR: John Rich
Elsa Lanchester, Dodie Marshall, Elvis Presley

Hotel (Warner Brothers)
w/Howard Shoup
DIR: Richard Quine
Merle Oberon, Catherine Spaak, Rod Taylor

Warning Shot (Paramount)
DIR: Buzz Kulik
Lillian Gish, David Janssen, Eleanor Parker

1968 *In Enemy Country* (Universal)
DIR: Harry Keller
Anjanette Comer, Anthony Franciosa

Madigan (Universal)
DIR: Donald Siegel
Inger Stevens, Richard Widmark

The Pink Jungle (Universal)
DIR: Delbert Mann
James Garner, Eva Renzi

The Secret War of Harry Frigg (Universal)
DIR: Jack Smight
Sylva Koscina, Paul Newman

What's So Bad About Feeling Good? (Universal)
DIR: George Seaton
Mary Tyler Moore, George Peppard, Susan St. James

1969 *Butch Cassidy and the Sundance Kid* (Twentieth Century-Fox)
DIR: George Roy Hill
Paul Newman, Robert Redford, Katharine Ross

Downhill Racer (Paramount)
DIR: Michael Ritchie
Robert Redford, Camilla Sparv

Eye of the Cat (Universal)
DIR: David Lowell Rich
Gayle Hunnicutt, Eleanor Parker

The Hellfighters (Universal)
DIR: Andrew V. McLaglen
Vera Miles, Katharine Ross, John Wayne

House of Cards (Universal)
DIR: John Guillermin
George Peppard, Inger Stevens, Orson Welles

The Lost Man (Universal)
DIR: Robert Alan Aurthur
Sidney Poitier, Joanna Shimkus

*Sweet Charity** (Universal)
DIR: Bob Fosse
Shirley MacLaine, Chita Rivera

Tell Them Willie Boy Is Here (Universal)
DIR: Abraham Polonsky
Robert Redford, Katharine Ross

Topaz (Universal)
DIR: Alfred Hitchcock
John Forsythe, Michel Piccoli, Frederick Stafford

Winning (Universal)
DIR: James Goldstone
Paul Newman, Joanne Woodward

1970 *Airport** (Universal)
DIR: George Seaton
Helen Hayes, Burt Lancaster, Dean Martin, Jean Seberg

Colossus: The Forbin Project (Universal)
DIR: Joseph Sargent
Eric Braeden, Susan Clark

Myra Breckinridge (Twentieth Century-Fox)
w/Theodora Van Runkle
DIR: Michael Sarne
Raquel Welch, Mae West

Skullduggery (Universal)
DIR: Gordon Douglas
Susan Clark, Burt Reynolds

Story of a Woman (Universal)
DIR: Leonardi Bercovici
Bibi Andersson, Annie Girardot, Robert Stack

1971 *Red Sky at Morning* (Universal)
DIR: James Goldstone
Claire Bloom, Richard Crenna, Richard Thomas

Sometimes a Great Notion (Universal)
DIR: Paul Newman
Henry Fonda, Paul Newman, Lee Remick

1972 *Hammersmith Is Out* (Cinerama)
DIR: Peter Ustinov
Richard Burton, Elizabeth Taylor

Pete 'n' Tillie (Universal)
DIR: Martin Ritt
Carol Burnett, Walter Matthau

1973   *Ash Wednesday* (Paramount)
        DIR: Larry Peerce
        Henry Fonda, Elizabeth Taylor

        Divorce His, Divorce Hers (Harlech—TV Movie)
        DIR: Waris Hussein
        Richard Burton, Elizabeth Taylor

        A Doll's House (World Film)
        w/John Furness
        DIR: Joseph Losey
        Jane Fonda, Trevor Howard

        The Don Is Dead (Universal)
        DIR: Richard Fleischer
        Joanne Meredith, Anthony Quinn

        The Life and Times of Judge Roy Bean (National General)
        w/Yvonne Wood
        DIR: John Huston
        Jacqueline Bisset, Ava Gardner, Paul Newman

        The Showdown (Universal)
        DIR: George Seaton
        Susan Clark, Rock Hudson, Dean Martin

        *The Sting*** (Universal)
        DIR: George Roy Hill
        Paul Newman, Robert Redford, Robert Shaw

1974   *Airport '75* (Universal)
        DIR: Jack Smight
        Karen Black, Charlton Heston, Gloria Swanson

1975   *The Great Waldo Pepper* (Universal)
        DIR: George Roy Hill
        Margot Kidder, Robert Redford, Susan Sarandon

        *The Man Who Would Be King** (Columbia)
        DIR: John Huston
        Michael Caine, Sean Connery

        Rooster Cogburn (Universal)
        DIR: Stuart Miller
        Katharine Hepburn, John Wayne

1976 *The Bluebird* (Twentieth Century-Fox)
DIR: George Cukor
Jane Fonda, Ava Gardner, Elizabeth Taylor, Cicely Tyson

Family Plot (Universal)
DIR: Alfred Hitchcock
Karen Black, Bruce Dern

Gable and Lombard (Universal)
DIR: Sidney J. Furie
James Brolin, Jill Clayburgh

W. C. Fields and Me (Universal)
DIR: Arthur Hiller
Valerie Perrine, Bernadette Peters, Rod Steiger

1977 *Airport '77** (Universal)
DIR: Arthur Hiller
Olivia de Havilland, Jack Lemmon, Brenda Vaccaro

1978 *The Big Fix* (Universal)
DIR: Jeremy Paul Kagen
Susan Anspach, Richard Dreyfuss

Olly Olly Oxen Free (Universal)
DIR: Richard A. Colla
Katharine Hepburn

Sextette (Briggs and Sullivan)
DIR: Ken Hughes
George Hamilton, Ringo Starr, Mae West

1979 *The Last Married Couple in America* (Universal)
DIR: Gilbert Cates
Valerie Harper, George Segal, Natalie Wood

1982 *Dead Men Don't Wear Plaid* (Universal)
DIR: Carl Reiner
Steve Martin, Carl Reiner, Rachel Ward

INDEX